THE MIDDLE OF
MY TETHER

THE MIDDLE OF MY TETHER

Familiar Essays by

JOSEPH EPSTEIN

W · W · NORTON & COMPANY

NEW YORK · LONDON

The text of this book is composed in photocomposition Jason Alternate, with display type set in Weiss. Composition by the Haddon Craftsmen, Inc. Book design by Marjorie J. Flock.

First published as a Norton paperback 1987

Library of Congress Cataloging in Publication Data
Epstein, Joseph, 1937–
The middle of my tether.
I. Title.
AC8.E665   1983   081   83–8237

ISBN 0-393-30407-8

W. W. Norton & Company, Inc.,
500 Fifth Avenue, New York, N.Y. 10110
W. W. Norton & Company Ltd.,
37 Great Russell Street, London WC1B 3NU

1 2 3 4 5 6 7 8 9 0

For Edward Shils
My great teacher, my dear friend

Contents

THE MIDDLE OF
MY TETHER

In and Around Books

I AM ABOUT TO PUBLISH A BOOK. Nothing fancy, merely a book of essays. In a way, I wish it were a rather fancier book. What I mean by a fancier book is one loaded down with what, if the book business were the car business, might be called accessories: footnotes, appendixes, a foreword, a preface, an introduction, a prolegomenon, blurbs, a dust-jacket photograph, eight or nine pages of acknowledgments, a translator's note, both a topic and a name index, epigraphs in six or seven languages, a glossary of terms, an afterword by a foreign dignitary, and on the front flap a notice from the publisher that after Christmas this book is going to cost two bucks more than it does now. My own book in its entirety will not be as long as would the combined accessories I have just named, but then one can't have everything.

Still, rather like a poor man at a Rolls Royce agency, one can peer in at the dash, lift up the hood, kick the tires. So I, the poor man of my own simile, have come to look at the accessories in and around other people's books, and these have come to exert their own peculiar fascination. Reading through an author's acknowledgments, looking through his index can tell you a great deal about his book. His photograph on the dust-jacket can tell you something about the man himself:

whether he has had a hard or easy life, whether he is modest or vain, and so forth. This is, one might argue, judging a book by its cover (and its acknowledgments and index), a thing which from earliest education we are instructed not to do; but with so many books in the world, what else are we to do—read the entire work? Let them, I say, make better covers.

But apart from the utility of discovering whether or not one would wish to spend a few days of one's life with a certain book, other treasures are to be found among the accessories of books. If someone wanted to study the reasons for the current wave of feminism, he could do worse than read the acknowledgments of husband authors to their wives. Debts to wives, in these acknowledgments, are almost always "incalculable." "The debt I owe to my wife," runs a typical such acknowledgment (written in 1964), "is incalculable. For the better part of two years, she conducted research, typed manuscript, criticized drafts, ran down leads, corrected proofs, and somehow simultaneously cared for two small children and a home. Her sacrifice has improved every page of this book; the errors and shortcomings are mine." Ah, but yes, one can hear a feminine voice adding, and so was the pleasure all yours and so shall be the glory.

Now, though, the tables appear to be turning, and women who write books acknowledge their husbands' help, which usually turns out to be "indescribable." Thus the author of a recent study of Edith Wharton notes that her husband's "enthusiasm and loving support can never be described adequately. Perhaps the quality of his 'sacrifice' might best be measured by totaling the hours he has spent of a Saturday afternoon in the sticky darkness of a movie theater with Walt Disney and two boisterous little boys—so that I might write." If there is a moral in all this, it is that being married to a writer, male or female, involves a person, one way or another, in a great deal of Mickey Mouse.

But acknowledgments also have much to tell about how books are being made nowadays. Sometimes this process seems to resemble nothing so much as an assembly line, as the author goes down the line thanking squads of research teams, librarians, graduate students, government agencies, and private foundations. Some authors run on for five or six pages thanking people who have spoken with them or read portions of their manuscript, or offered helpful advice of one kind or another. Except to the chronically grudging, giving acknowledgment seems to be a highly pleasurable activity. Once begun, it is not easily brought to a close, for it is something akin to handing out gratuities with play money—one may as well be a big spender. "Thanks are owed, too, to my fifth wife, whose departure with my chauffeur for South America left me the quiet and composure necessary to finish this lengthy work. . . ."

I suspect that giving acknowledgments is much to be preferred to being acknowledged, where the pleasure is not always unequivocal. Being publicly acknowledged for one's "invaluable help" in producing what turns out to be a very shoddy book is at best a droopy flower in one's boutonniere. I have myself been acknowledged in some five or six books but never, if I may say so, adequately. Generally I either felt that my aid was vastly overestimated or, in some instances, found myself bridling slightly at having my name put in a longish list that included people I have no very high regard for. The closest I have come to what I consider adequate acknowledgment is in a book about writers and revolution, whose author notes: "I am indebted to Joseph Epstein for (among other things) directing me toward Alexander Herzen." I did so direct the author, but I will be damned if I know what those "other things" are. Requiring precision even in thanks—can there be a better definition of a true pedant?

Acknowledgments can also tell us a good deal about contemporary notions of privacy, vanity, and gratitude. On occasion a book's acknowledgments will reveal quite as much about an author as anything that appears in the pages which follow. In his acknowledgments in *The Pendulum Years,* the one book he has written, the excellent British journalist Bernard Levin makes it very clear that journalism is his true métier, and that to get this book out he very nearly needed to be dragged to the bindery: "To Tom Maschler, now Chairman of Jonathan Cape Ltd., and to Graham Watson of Curtis Brown Ltd., my Literary Agent, I owe a debt of a different kind: for their understanding patience with one who must repeatedly have tempted them to wash their hands of him." In that sentence one can make out the effluvia of many missed deadlines, unreturned phone calls, unanswered letters.

If Bernard Levin seems to have been brought to book filled with remorse, Sir Isaiah Berlin, in his author's preface to *Concepts and Categories* (the second of his four volumes of collected essays), comes to publication aswirl with demurrers. He claims —and there is no reason not to take him at his word—that he could not bring himself to reread the essays in his book; he thinks they are too much of their time and place, containing "little or nothing worth resuscitating thirty years later"; and he wonders if his editor's decision to publish the book at all "was not more generous than just." Acknowledgments, authors' prefaces, dedications are written after books are completed, and the tendency is for people to come to them in various states that follow intellectual fatigue, ranging from dubiety to exaltation. Yet Lillian Breslow Rubin, author of *Worlds of Pain,* obviously wasn't feeling any pain when she wrote her acknowledgments, for unconscious vanity not so much sneaks as strides in everywhere. A number of friends supplied "thoughtful criticisms [that] helped make this a better book." Another friend will "surely recognize her stimulating and thought-provoking contributions to the final product." Yet another friend is cited for having "enriched both my life and this book in ways too numerous to cite." As for Mrs. Rubin's husband, she "could say how much the book benefited from his participation," but "instead I would rather say that I, as a person, am better, stronger, richer, more open, and more honest for having him in my life." Better, richer, stronger, more open, more honest though she may be, Mrs. Rubin seems not to have noticed that she has used her acknowledgments to puff her own book and, through her husband, herself. Gratitude, it seems, is sometimes its own reward.

I am not sure when elaborate acknowledgments first came into being. My guess is that they are an innovation of our own century and are connected with the need to secure permission for extensive quotations from other works. But by now acknowledgments have become quite formulaic, and nowhere more so than in that phrase with which most of them end. After handing out thanks all round for help and advice, support and love, our author, brave fellow, remarks, "Any errors of fact or judgment are of course my own"—which is sometimes varied to read, "Of course these persons do not necessarily concur in my analysis and conclusions." This always leaves me a bit uneasy. What errors? Why do his friends not concur with him? Is our author not only careless but wrongheaded into the bargain? Jan Morris, in her revised edition of *Oxford*, handles this point in her acknowledgments as nicely as I have seen it done: "So many other people have helped me with the work in its original edition and in revisions, that I hope they will accept the book itself as a token of my gratitude, forgiving its faults and claiming its merits as their own."

Not least among the problems presented by acknowledgments is to decide how far down one ought to dip in the well of debts incurred when ladling out thanks. One can easily enough imagine acknowledging one's parents—if not precisely for help on the book in question, then certainly for one's intellectual development generally. But what about the man who made it all possible to begin with—one's mother's obstetrician, "without whose steady hands and grace under pressure this book might never have been written"? And while at it, "I should like also to thank the dentist of my early years, Dr. Joseph Chulock, whose program of sound dental hygiene made possible the dazzling smile I display on the back of this dust-jacket. My janitor, Tony Ardecelli, in the midst of a serious energy crisis, kept the heat coming into my apartment, making it possible for me to work on this book through the exceptionally severe winters of 1978 and 1979. My postman, Lester Goodman. . . ."

At the university where I teach, the story is told about a graduate student whose dissertation director was the very reverse of helpful. The minimal advice he gave the student was useless. Letters the student wrote to him went unanswered. Appeals for aid were unavailing. On all the administrative details for which the dissertation director should have been responsible he proved dependably unreliable. Despite all this, the graduate student managed to complete his dissertation; and having done so, the time came for him to write his acknowledgments. Not to mention his dissertation director—whom, by now, he thoroughly and rightly detested—would have been unseemly. Yet to give him any credit at all nearly made the student ill. He solved the problem thus: "This is the place to acknowledge my dissertation director, Professor Samuel Smith; only he and I know how much he contributed to this work."

Nicely done, that, yet why not take it a step further? Ought not an author to acknowledge, along with those who aided the progress of his work, those who impeded it? For most authors, this list of negative acknowledgments figures, I fear, to be rather longer than that of positive acknowledgments, and rather more impassioned as well. Here is the kind of thing that might result:

I wish to acknowledge the contribution of my editor, whose advice, usually delivered in bullying tones, consistently led me far astray, causing me constant discouragement. The title of this book, so dull and yet so vulgar, is his, foisted upon me against my will. The Guggenheim, Ford, and Rockefeller foundations, always ready to loose their purse strings for projects both idiotic in themselves and likely to have been repulsive to their founders, saw fit, each of them, to deny my urgent grant applications, thus forcing me to live, at hazard to my health, on my publisher's piddling advance. The Widener, Regenstein, and New York Public libraries were all rather more pettifogging than even bureaucratic temperaments would seem to require. But the obstacles that these institutions put in my way were as nothing compared to the direct acts of sabotage attempted by the heirs of the subject of this biography. They will not, I think, be altogether uninterested in my findings, not the least of which is that my subject died, as he lived, retaining a large cold spot in his heart for his family. My own dealings with this same family have placed me in a splendid position to understand his unflagging animus. To the Internal Revenue Service. . . .

But I see that I am rather better at this than I had thought, and so had better stop here.

On, then, to the back of the book; more specifically, to its index. An index can be a superior guide to the quality of a book, and usually has more to say about its content than the table of contents. The inadequacy of indexes is something for a certain kind of academic book reviewer to complain about, but, be it adequate or inadequate, I like to roam in the index of a serious book. There, in a single column of print, one meets up with people who may have lived at the same time but who cannot be imagined in the same room together. From a single column in the index of Frederick R. Karl's *Joseph Conrad: The*

Three Lives, one can make up a little party whose guests would include Edith Wharton and Beatrice Webb, Alfred North Whitehead and James Whistler, H. G. Wells and Woodrow Wilson. And—ah yes, I nearly forgot—President Wilson, may I present Oscar Wilde?

"All writers," Orwell remarked in his essay "Why I Write," "are vain, selfish, and lazy . . . ," and I for one can testify to the truth of the first of these qualities. Having over the years written superficially on a superfluity of subjects, I have discovered that I am not above, in looking over any book on a subject I have written about, sneaking a peek into the index to see if I have been quoted or if my name comes up. (Apparently I am not alone in this act of peeping egotism. William F. Buckley, Jr., tells of sending a copy of one of his collections of essays to Norman Mailer, but before doing so marking in the index next to Mailer's name the single word, "Hi.") I am currently attempting to shake off this habit, for I began to realize it might be rather dangerous when, one day, I found myself looking for my name in the index of a book written before I was born.

But to get to the bottom of things, what about footnotes, the accessory that is coming to be a misnomer, now that footnotes are less and less often printed at the foot of the page? Noel Coward claimed to detest footnotes, likening the eyes' trip from the text to the note to having to go downstairs to answer the doorbell while having sex. Put in such flat-out hedonistic terms, I suppose it is all a question of who is waiting downstairs when one arrives there. If the man writing the footnotes is Gibbon, the trip is likely to be worth making. For example, the famous sentence in Gibbon about the younger Gordian—"Twenty-two acknowledged concubines, and a library of sixty-two thousand volumes, attested the variety of his inclinations, and from the production which he left behind him, it appears that the former as well as the latter were designed for use rather than ostentation"—meets with the following footnote: "By each of his concubines, the younger Gordian left three or four children. His literary productions were by no means contemptible."

Today, under most publishing dispensations, one would have to go to the end of Gibbon's chapter, or indeed to the back of the book, to read that note; and by the time one got there, lo, the joke would be gone. What would an editor today make of the 165-page footnote, said to be the longest in the world, in the nineteenth-century work *The History of Northumberland?* Doubtless he would direct the author to chapter 12 of Horrelbrow's *Iceland* (1758), a chapter entitled "Concerning Owls in Iceland," which reads in toto: "There are no owls of any kind in the whole island." The printing of footnotes at the end of chapters or all the way in the back of the book is a publishing economy which higher printing costs have forced on most publishers of scholarly books. But as a result, an art, that of the pointed footnote, is on its way out.

Yet there are other publishing economies that make no sense at all, and can be infuriating. Consider the habit of some scholarly publishers—highly regarded ones, too—of advertising other works on the back dust-jacket of one's own book. "Books of Related Interest," these ads are generally designated. The effect of such an ad, it has always seemed to me, is rather like walking around town in a sandwich board marked "Read at Sam's." Something similar can occur on the front cover of a book, at least in its foreign or its paperback edition. I speak of the use of blurbs. Strewn across the front cover of a paperback edition of a book I published a few years back is the phrase "Personally insightful," which is what a *Newsweek* reviewer said of the book. At the time I was pleased enough to have had his praise, but I now wish he could have found a phrase I loathe less than I do "Personally insightful." Whenever I see that book I feel as a man must who has the name Betty tattooed on his arm though he is married to a woman named Sally.

If I had my choice of a puff for my book, I think I should like one written by an English writer named Henry Puffmore. I first noted Mr. Puffmore's name on the back of the reissued edition of Quentin Bell's little book on Ruskin. "In just over a hundred pages," writes Mr. Puffmore, "Ruskin had been presented and probed with such skill that one hardly knew whether to admire more the patient or the surgeon." A perfect puff by Puffmore—except that, technically, it is not quite a pure puff, in that it was extracted from a review Mr. Puffmore wrote in the English journal *The Bookseller*. A pure puff is one that does not originate in a review, but in the request from author or publisher to supply endorsements for the book of the kind that may be used either on the dust-jacket or in advertisements. In most instances, these puffs are less testaments to the quality of the book than to the friendship of puffer and author. This being the case, perhaps it would be best to have puffs from the biggest names—the Aga Kahn, the Prince of Wales, Greta Garbo—so that, even if the puffs have nothing true to say about the quality of one's book, at least the roster of one's friends will seem impressive.

To impress is of course the point of a book's dust-jacket. Serious books cannot avail themselves of the flash or luridness of dust-jacket art of the kind used by, say, the sort of Gothic novel that in the trade is known as "a bodice ripper." Puffs and blurbs are all they have, plus an occasional inflated author's biographical note. But these latter have become rather more dull than they once were. Novelists especially used to go in for flashy biographical notes, in the attempt, I suppose, to seem worldlier than thou. A not untypical biographical note might read that our novelist "has worked as a lumberjack, dishwasher, judo expert, encyclopedia salesman, janitor, cellist, and part-time circus roughy." Today such a note is more likely to read that our novelist is "a former Fulbright scholar and director of the Creative Writing Program at State University. He is a recipient of a Guggenheim Fellowship, a grant from the National Endowment for the Humanities, and an award from the American Academy and Institute of Arts and Letters." This change in the nature of notes on novelists reflects the chief change in the production of American novels: their increasing academicization.

The photographs of authors on the dust-jackets of books have changed, too, or so it seems to me. They are now by and large more professional than they once were—better, that is to say, but also less interesting. Many of the best known authors have in fact been photographed by the same photographer, Jill Krementz, who has made something of a specialty of photographing writers. For myself, I have come to like books that do not have photographs of their authors, preferring my imaginings of their looks to the reality. My imaginings, I should add, are almost always wrong, based as they usually are on an author's prose. (Thus I imagine, to cite a single example, that Tacitus was elegantly lean.) But if my own imaginings are often wrong, reality is even more often disappointing. Exceptions there may be—one is the splendid photograph of M. F. K. Fisher on the back of her little book on Marseille, *A Considerable Town,* in which Miss Fisher looks exactly as one who has read her imagines her to look: sturdy, handsome, and intelligent—but writers are for the most part better read than seen.

Better unseen, too, is the fairly new authorial tic of assigning a place-name and date to the preface or introduction to one's book. The most famous of these is that which James Joyce affixed to the last page of *Ulysses:* "Trieste-Zürich-Paris

1914–1921." I had thought Joyce was the first to do this, but not so. At the end of the introductory chapter of *The Genealogy of Morals*, Nietzsche affixed, "Sils-Maria, Upper Engadine, July 1887." The habit of doing this has caught on, so that today even the most arid tract in political science or agronomy is likely to have affixed to it "Evanston, Illinois," "Cambridge, Massachusetts," "Bombay-Rome-Muncie." It almost always leaves a small cloud, vaporous with pretension. Perhaps a good rule for authors might be to add place-names in one's book only if one is confident of being a writer of the Joyce or Nietzsche class; otherwise, abstain.

Although not a regular accessory, readers' underlinings and marginal comments found in books borrowed from libraries seem to me of especial interest. These marginal comments in his books are perhaps as close as a writer gets to a spontaneous response from his readers. Every writer would like to spin through a library copy of his book to find its margins decorated with such accolades as "How true!" "Beautifully formulated!" "Right on!" Alas, since people are more often animated by disagreement than by agreement, one is much more likely to find one's margins lacerated by such cuts as "Dubious!" "Wrong again!" "Sheer rubbish!" A bookseller told me of coming across, in one of the books of José Ortega y Gasset, the marginal comment, "C'mon Ortega!" Cyril Connolly has told of looking through one of Evelyn Waugh's copies of his (Connolly's) books and discovering on its margins a number of rough remarks in Waugh's hand which convinced him that Waugh held a furious grudge against him. But Connolly doubtless sensed this earlier from Waugh's acknowledgments to the British edition of *The Loved One*, which read: "My thanks are due to Lady Milbanke, who first set my feet on the path to Whispering Glades [his novelistic version of Los Angeles's Forest Lawn Cemetery]; to Mrs. Reginald Allen who corrected my *American;* to Mr. Cyril Connolly who corrected my *English.*"

As acknowledgments can be ambiguous, so too can dedications. Sydney Smith, for example, dedicated his first book, *Six Sermons,* to Lord Webb Seymour, in the following terms:

My Lord—I dedicate these few sermons to you, as a slight token of my great regard and respect, because I know no man who, in spite of the disadvantages of high birth, lives to more honorable and commendable purposes than yourself.

The most famous dedication in American literature is surely that of Thomas Wolfe to Maxwell Perkins, his editor at Charles Scribner's Sons, which appears in Wolfe's *Of Time and the River:*

To
Maxwell Evarts Perkins

A great editor and a brave and honest man, who stuck to the writer of this book through times of bitter hopelessness and doubt and would not let him give in to his own despair, a work to be known as "Of Time and the River" is dedicated with the hope that all of it may be in some way worthy of the loyal devotion and the patient care which a dauntless and unshaken friend has given to each part of it, and without which none of it could have been written.

Like nearly everything else about him, even Thomas Wolfe's dedication required editing; it was cut down from an original version that ran to three pages. But as interesting as the dedication is its aftermath: not long after it had been written, Wolfe left Scribner's and Maxwell Perkins in a heat of paranoid hatred.

Dedications run the gamut from the simple ("To my mother") to the sweet (Rebecca West's dedication of *The Strange Necessity:* "To Irita Van Doren Whom One Would Like to Be Like"), to the slightly mysterious (M. L. Rosenthal's dedication to *Poetry and the Common Life:* "For Sally Moor Gall, gratitude for clear thoughts, disturbing questions"), to the wiseacre (Dwight Macdonald's dedication to his splendid anthology *Parodies:* "To my dear sons Michael and Nicholas, without whose school bills this anthology would not have been made"), to the straight-out clownish (Bruce Jay Friedman's dedication to *The Lonely Guy's Book of Life:* "To BJF [Friedman himself], This one's for you, fella"). Among modern dedications I know none more touching than Arnaldo Momigliano's dedication to the third volume of his *Contributo:*

> *To Felice and Atillo Momigliano,*
> *Masters and friends beyond the grave;*
> *and to my daughter, Anna Laura,*
> *in whose eyes their light shines.*

Ships, buildings, monuments, bridges, and books receive dedications, but only books have a chance to exert an influence in the world. The chance is not necessarily great, to be sure, and even if one's book does exert an influence, who can say for certain that it will be for the good? Because of the problematic nature of the fate of a book in the world, perhaps an author ought also to include, along with the other accessories to his book, a Disclaimer. This Disclaimer ought to appear, as we say nowadays, up-front and probably in italic type. It ought not to be a place for false modesty but for a true statement of the authorial case.

"I wrote this book," a model for such a Disclaimer might read, "in the hope of making a persuasive argument, while giving pleasure to myself in forming my thoughts into sentences, paragraphs, and chapters. Whether I shall give anything even resembling an equivalent pleasure to my readers is highly doubtful, I realize, but an author retains his slender hopes. I wish my book were better than it is, but I fear that it is quite the best that I have had the skill and patience to make. If any justification for this book is needed, it is that the book seeks, in its stuttering way, to take a very small part in a conversation which has been going on for a very long while now. For myself, I hope to be able to read it ten years hence without shame or regret."

A Man of Letters

MY DEFINITION OF A PESSIMIST is a person who doesn't check his mail. Although with age my illusions about human nature become fewer, my belief that people learn from history slighter, my confidence in youth lesser, nonetheless my feelings about the mail—about *my* mail—remain what they have always been: feelings of complete, utter, and abject hopefulness. When it comes to the mail, I am a Fabian, a lifetime member of the Americans for Democratic Action, a Pollyanna perpetually aglow and atremble with optimism. I love mail, I adore mail, I cannot get enough mail. Saul Bellow, in his novel *Humboldt's Gift*, remarks on his hero's receiving "heavy mail," and that is a phrase which, as the boys and girls in literary criticism nowadays say, resonates with me.

The mail generally arrives in my neighborhood between 11:15 and 11:45 A.M. As will scarcely be surprising, this is one of the high points of my day. The postman, quite heedless of James M. Cain's novel, always rings once. At his ring I stop my work, either reading or writing, usually in mid-sentence. If I am speaking over the telephone when the postman rings, my attention flags. My mind is now on that apartment building mailbox marked "Epstein" and on the small table beneath the mailboxes on which are placed magazines and packages. I walk down the stairs simulating a mien of casualness, though my heart bounds. What is it, exactly, that I expect to find in the day's mail? Notice of a large inheritance? Extravagant praise for my character? Unexpected checks for ample sums? Offers of ambassadorships in countries of gentle climate and stable government? Interesting proposals? Fascinating opportunities? Yes, all these things—and, who knows, perhaps something better.

In reality—now there is one of the coldest phrases in the English language—what generally awaits is a bill from the electric company, another from a dentist, two magazine subscription offers, and a box containing a sample of a new hair spray. Yet where there is mail there is desire, and sometimes there are surprises. Most of these derive from my occupation as a writer. Writing for publication makes for strange pen pals. People feel that writers are, somehow, in the public domain, which in a sense they are, and they write to them freely. Any sort of serious letter in response to something he has written is likely to be gratifying to a writer; I know it is to me. I suspect that I get my share of such letters: letters of touching appreciation, of correction, of untrammeled anger. "With all wishes for all kinds of bad luck," one recent correspondent ended a letter of the latter kind, which was positively charming next to the letter of an anonymous admirer that began, "May God castrate you!"

Which brings me to George Santayana's wing chair. More than a decade ago I wrote an essay for the *New Republic* about George Santayana, a writer who seemed to me to represent the height of intellectual elegance. The essay appeared in print, and then, some four weeks later, a letter turned up from Austria, forwarded to me from the *New Republic*. I no longer have the letter, but, as I recall, it was written on linen of a quality out of which I should have liked to have a summer suit made. The letter itself opened with a paragraph of carefully measured praise for my essay—praise which spoke of my mental penetration and exquisite sensibility. (Certainly there was nothing here of substance that I would care to argue about.) My correspondent went on to inform me that he had been a student of Santayana's at Harvard, and had been left a number of his personal effects. Among these was the philosopher's favorite wing chair. Would I, so clearly an admirer of Santayana, be interested in having it?

I thought a good bit about that wing chair. I set it in different rooms in my home, considered the ethics of having it reupholstered, wondered if it carried any talismanic qualities. Had Santayana written *Dominations and Powers* sitting in that chair? Was it the same chair in which he sat, in the single room provided him by the Hospital of Blue Nuns outside Rome, while making his own abridgment of *The Life of Reason?* Merely to sit in such a chair could not but increase my powers of ratiocination, subtlety, serenity. Did I want that wing chair? Do graduate students wear jeans? Do South American politicians go in for sunglasses?

I wrote to my correspondent in Austria to thank him, first, for his kind words and, second, for his generous offer. I should, I wrote, want to pay the expense of shipping the chair to the United States. He returned my letter by saying that he would foot the shipping costs, which would come out of the eight hundred dollars that he wanted for the chair. Thus ended our correspondence. I could be quite wrong about this, but I imagine him waiting out a month of silence on my end, picking up the current week's *New Republic*, skimming an essay therein on, say, Mark Twain. Then he takes out a sheet of that splendid stationery and writes to its author, saying that, through his mother, who as a young girl had lived two doors down from Samuel and Olivia Clemens in Hartford, he had come into ownership of the favorite wing chair of Mark Twain. . . .

But, it occurs to me now, I may have imagined that Santayana's wing chair was offered to me only because of an
authorly twist of pride. Perhaps my correspondent's first paragraph of praise for my writing lulled me into thinking that the
remainder of his letter had to do with my reward—as if by
writing well about Santayana I really deserved to have his
chair. "I find I have enough of the author in me," the young
Horace Walpole wrote, "to be extremely susceptible to flattery." As any writer knows, or anyone who has spent much
time around writers, when it comes to flattery, compliments,
praise generally, Walpole's "extremely susceptible" is putting
the case very gently indeed. I have known many writers so
extremely susceptible that, by comparison, they make George
Jessel seem as modest as Saint Theresa of Lisieux.

The need for praise on the part of writers is probably
greater than that of other workers in the arts, if only because
writers never get the direct response to their work that composers, visual artists, and performing artists do. Perhaps this is
why so many novelists and poets have attempted to write for
the stage, where they can hear the laughter, see the tears,
palpably feel the tension that their work creates. Writers receive reviews, of course, but these are of books only and hence
few and far between; moreover, the reviews, for one reason or
another, are likely to be unsatisfactory. Thus, most writers,
especially if they do not live in New York, must take their
injections of praise, if they are to get any at all, epistolarily.

This need for praise—great, heaping banana-split dishes of
it—is not on the whole a thing calculated to remind one of the
dignity of mankind. Lest I seem to exempt myself from the
need, I had better quickly say that I am not exempt. I do have
standards in praise, though they are rickety. I like my praise
to be intelligent and, preferably, convincing, delivered by a

person who has a respect for precision in language and a strong sense of history. If these qualities are lacking, I'll take it any other way I can. Rarely have I found the praise tendered me to be fulsome, though I do recall one instance where I thought things were getting out of hand. An editor for whom I once did a good deal of writing was hitting a crescendo of praise rather too early in our relationship, I thought; soon he would be comparing my pitiful scribblings with Dante and Homer. (Robert Southey is supposed to have said to a contemporary whose name I cannot recall, "You will be remembered long after Homer is forgot—but not until.") I requested him to cease and desist, and, in lieu of further praise, I asked him to send me a letter, on company stationery, proclaiming me and my writing a force for change in Latin America. This he promptly did, and thenceforth we were able to conduct a seemly editorial relationship, free on his side from the need to lavish further praise.

Sometimes the sunshine of epistolary praise turns into drizzles of oddly angled criticism, or, if not quite criticism, then a reaction quite other than what one had hoped for. In this category of letter I shall not soon forget the response to a segment of a book I wrote which was reprinted in the *Reader's Digest.* The segment had to do with the then new phenomenon of how-to-do-it sex manuals, a phenomenon that I, as an ethical platitudinarian, attacked on grounds aesthetic, psychological, and moral. Some months later, a letter, sent on to me from the *Reader's Digest,* arrived from a faithful subscriber in the Philippines. It read:

I perused with extreme interest your fine article in current *Readers Digest,* in which you make strong censure on such tomes as *Everything You Ever Wanted to Know About Sex, The Joy of Sex, New Approaches to Sex in Marriage* by Dr. Eichenlaub, *Sensuous Woman* by J., and studies by Johnson and Masters. What you say is most intriguing. But, may I inquire, do you still possess these above-mentioned tomes? If so, would you send them on to me? I should be more than willing to provide the postage moneys for them. Please answer soonest.

Ah, me, another rainy day in the Republic of Letters.

But what should a perfect delivery of mail contain? This of course will differ from person to person, but for me it would include a letter from an old friend with whom I have been too long out of touch, a letter from someone I love, two letters in airmail envelopes from overseas, a letter containing some found money (an unexpected tax rebate, say, or a reprint fee), a good book that has been long awaited, a letter from someone previously unknown but obviously good-hearted and intelligent, and (finally) a letter informing me that an engagement I had foolishly committed myself to, and that has worried me ever since, has been indefinitely postponed.

What a perfectly dreary mail delivery would contain is easier to imagine. In it would be a letter from the IRS headed "Final Notice Before Seizure," a letter requesting a large loan from an acquaintance to whom all of one's own previous letters have come back stamped "Addressee Unknown," a letter thick with praise from someone certifiably despicable, and a telegram reading "Ignore last wire" when no previous wire has been received. It would also contain invitations that one does not want and that one would, if possible, be willing to expose oneself to certain short-lived yet quite painful tropical diseases to get out of. In "The Adventure of the Noble Bachelor," Conan Doyle has Sherlock Holmes remark to Watson, "Yes, my correspondence has certainly the charm of variety, and the humbler are usually the more interesting. This looks like one of those unwelcome social summons which call upon a man either to be bored or to lie."

I can also do nicely without letters of the tutelary kind

Edmund Wilson often used to send to friends. I have recently read two collections of Wilson's letters, *The Nabokov-Wilson Letters* and *Letters on Literature and Politics, 1912–1972*. They are splendid to read, full of literary history and sharp observation, but many of them cannot have been too pleasant to receive. I think here particularly of those letters in which Wilson lectured, upbraided, and generally hectored his contemporaries on their literary shortcomings, a thing he was never loath to do. Not a man long on tact, Edmund Wilson—as, for example, when he wrote to the young Scott Fitzgerald that some lines in a poem Fitzgerald had written "possess a depth and dignity of which I didn't think you capable." A bit near the knuckle, as the English say, but worse, and lengthier, examples are ready to hand. Receiving one of these stinging letters from Wilson must have made a person feel, whatever his age, like Lord Chesterfield's son, forced to take all that instruction and abuse—but without the prospect of one day coming into a title.

No, the better letters carry lighter loads. Madame de Sévigné and Horace Walpole, two of the great letter writers, almost insist upon their lightness. Walpole wrote to one Henry Seymour Conway at the close of a letter: "Well! I have here set you the example of writing nonsense when one has nothing to say, and shall take it ill if you don't keep up the correspondence on the same foot. Adieu!" And Madame de Sévigné, in a letter to the Comte de Bussy, writes: "I know not how you can like my letters; they are written in a style of carelessness, which I feel, without being able to remedy it." Of course, neither Madame de Sévigné nor Walpole is finally light. Both are truly charming and, being considerate, cannot help charming others. They are born letter writers. (Madame de Sévigné wrote nothing but letters.) They take short views, living day by day. They are cheerful without being deluded about life. Their wit, their common sense, their perspective, their generosity—all these qualities give their letters a cumulative weight.

Small splendors are the stock in trade of the great letter writers: anecdotes, observations, aperçus. A man named John Chute writes to Walpole about being put on a "temperate diet," which causes Walpole to rejoin with this little disquisition on the roast-beef eating habits of Englishmen:

Only imagine that I here every day see men, who are mountains of roast beef, and only seem just roughly hewn out into the outlines of human form, like the giant-rock at Pratolino. I shudder when I see them brandish their knives in act to carve, and look on them as savages that devour one another. I should not stare at all more than I do, if yonder Alderman at the lower end of the table was to stick his fork into his neighbor's jolly cheek, and cut a brave slice of brown and fat. Why I'll swear I see no difference between a country gentleman and a sirloin; whenever the first laughs, or the latter is cut, there run out just the same streams of gravy! Indeed, the sirloin does not ask quite so many questions.

The greatest letter writer among Americans, in my view, is easily Justice Holmes. He is one of the few writers who can lift me out of such brief depressions as my withering attention span will allow. Holmes is the one American model of the good life; activist and intellectual both, he was a man of wide interests and absolutely no superficiality. Of late I have been reading his correspondence with Sir Frederick Pollock, the English jurist. While stretches of these letters are taken up with matters legal, from which I am intellectually excluded, this does not in the least put me off. Instead I fall into the rhythm of Holmes's life: his vacations at Beverly Farms, the longer months when the Supreme Court is in session, his reports on his reading, his comments upon the life around him. His style is virile, and he himself is—though one scarcely ever hears the word any more —manly in the most attractive way.

Good letters do not usually submit to the discipline of topic sentences. Thus Walpole, in a letter to George Montagu, writes, "If all the adventures don't conclude as you expect in the beginning of a paragraph, you must not wonder. . . ." Justice Holmes's letters, too, often have this pleasing jumble, this *méli-mélo*. Within the compass of a single paragraph of a letter written in 1928, when he was eighty-eight, Holmes remarks on thesis interpretations of American history of the kind produced by Charles Beard and Vernon Parrington that "belittling arguments often have a force of their own, but you and I believe that high-mindedness is not impossible to man"; that he finds Anita Loos's *But Gentlemen Marry Brunettes* dreary because "sexual talk or innuendo is displeasing from a woman, I think. Perhaps because we know, though the older literary tradition is the other way, that they take less interest in the business than we do"; and ends on yet another of his fresh, comical, yet serious metaphors for death: "Most of the places here now to me are sockets from which the occupants that I knew have been extracted by the final dentist."

In one of their exchanges Holmes and Pollock name those they deem to be literature's great letter writers. Both agree on Horace Walpole. Pollock places Samuel Johnson ahead of Charles Lamb. Holmes mentions Byron; Pollock adds Edward FitzGerald and Walter Raleigh. Neither, though, brings up the name of Justice Holmes's contemporary, Henry James, whose letters were not then as accessible as they have since become. No one surpassed Henry James for writing beautiful letters of condolence. The death of a friend was always the occasion for a moving tribute, in which James provided a celebratory portrait—making, as Leon Edel remarks in his biography of James, "his condolences into a muted epistolary elegy." So fine are these letters, so properly measured and elegantly turned, they seem almost worth dying for.

Initially, of course, the English novel was epistolary in

form. Letters play an important part in much of Henry James's fiction, and one of his finest stories, "In the Cage," is about a woman who works in a post-and-telegraph office. James M. Cain's *The Postman Always Rings Twice* is only peripherally about the post; but Albert Halper, in *The Chute,* wrote a novel about workers in a Chicago mail-order house. In *Herzog* Saul Bellow deploys letters brilliantly, having his hero write to historical personages to great comic effect: *"Dear Herr Nietzsche—My dear Sir, May I ask a question from the floor?" "Dear Governor Stevenson, Just a word with you, friend."* Many a novel and short story has turned on a letter sent, or discovered, or torn up at the last moment.

Nowadays such epistolary intervention in fiction will not quite do. A question of suspension of disbelief is involved; too few readers would be willing to believe that the decisive letter was actually delivered. I make this judgment on the basis of complaints I hear about postal delivery, which, to put it softly, are manifold. Postal delivery is another of those areas of civilization that give the lie to theories of progress. Currently people of cosmopolitan correspondence claim that the chance of winning in a state lottery is far better than the chance that a letter sent to Italy will reach the person it is addressed to. England once had the finest of all postal systems; fifty years ago a correspondent could send out a letter in the morning and receive an answer by evening. Edward Shils tells a story of a letter from Hungary tersely addressed to him as "Professor Edward Shils, Sociologist, England" reaching him safely at the London School of Economics. This was under the old dispensation; under the new dispensation, English mails seem scarcely better than American. Ours are erratic at best: sometimes a letter will take but a single day to make its way from the Middle West to either coast, whereas another letter will take four days to get across town.

I suppose one must partly blame the drop in the quality of postal service on the rise of what is rightly called "junk mail." The postmen's sacks are weighed down annually with some 34 billion pieces of junk mail, or roughly a third of all letters mailed in the United States. Selling through the mails is a brisk business, and there are professional brokers who deal exclusively with compiling and renting mailing lists to various firms and causes. Thus a person who subscribes to one magazine is considered fair game for all. Send in ten dollars to help save the whale, and before the year is out one is certain to be pitched for funds to put an end to the gelding of goldfish. For decades now *The New Yorker* has run, at the bottom of its slender columns, examples of silly opening gambits used in junk mail —under the rubric "Letters We Never Finished Reading." But there have been true advances in this sort of bumf. A recent letter soliciting a magazine subscription showed up in my mailbox bearing the line "Should you be punished for being born with a high I.Q.?" on the outside of the envelope. A new rubric, clearly, is called for: "Letters We Never Started Reading."

Letters I usually do finish reading are those printed in the letters columns of intellectual magazines. Controversies over some point in scholarship or in politics have an interest that transcends the points that originally gave rise to them; the interest is in seeing intellectuals in extremis, always a gaudy spectacle. Literary widows rush in to protect their husbands against what they deem defamation; disgruntled authors lash back at reviewers; intellectual kibitzers stick in their two cents' worth. Much about the character of an intellectual magazine can be discovered from the letters it prints. If most of them are congratulatory, something is amiss. Disagreement is the true oxygen of these magazines, argument and mental fencing their real exercise, intellectual bloodletting their only physic. Of present-day polemicists, I think Professor H. R. Trevor-Roper easily the best, the man most adept at laying a polemical opponent wide open; Noam Chomsky, on the subjects of Southeast Asia and the Middle East, has proved himself far and away the most boring; and the *T.L.S.* the site of the most entertaining of these polemical picnics. The tradition of the polemical letter goes well back, of course. Here, for example, is Oscar Wilde in 1890 in *Truth* magazine, answering Whistler's accusation of plagiarism by simply blowing Whistler off the court:

I can hardly imagine that the public are in the very smallest degree interested in the shrill shrieks of "Plagiarism" that proceed from time to time out of the lips of silly vanity or incompetent mediocrity.

However, as Mr. James Whistler has had the impertinence to attack me with both venom and vulgarity in your columns, I hope you will allow me to state that the assertions contained in his letters are as deliberately untrue as they are deliberately offensive.

The definition of a disciple as one who has the courage of the opinions of his master is really too old even for Mr. Whistler to be allowed to claim it, and as for borrowing Mr. Whistler's ideas about art, the only thoroughly original ideas I have ever heard him express have had reference to his own superiority as a painter over painters greater than himself.

It is a trouble for any gentleman to have to notice the lucubrations of so ill-bred and ignorant a person as Mr. Whistler, but your publication of his insolent letter leaves me no option in the matter.

I have extracted this little lyric of artful nastiness from a book entitled *Dear Sir, Drop Dead! Hate Mail Through the Ages,* edited by Donald Carroll (Collier Books). If there are 34 billion pieces of junk mail sent annually, another billion pieces of hate mail may well be aloft during the same period. A great deal of such mail is sent to people who appear on television regularly; politicians get a goodly share; athletes, authors, and others on public view come in for their epistolary abuse. Mr. Carroll remarks that the hate letter is "probably the most popular and enduring genre of folk literature in the world," adding that "it is the only literary form that has always had more practitioners than readers"—this last referring to the fact that most people who receive it throw their hate mail away unread. Although my scribblings have brought me only driblets of hate mail, such specimens of it as I have received I have read sedulously and saved. One day I plan to return each piece of hate mail in my possession to its owner, along with a note that reads:

Sir: Out of the distant and rather dim possibility that my correspondence will one day be made public, I now return your vicious little letter to you. Odious though you may be, I see no reason why your grandchildren should have to be presented with such clear and irrefutable evidence of their forebear's ill-temper and imbecility.

This, though, is rather heavy-handed next to the crisp volley that an impudent letter provoked from Voltaire: "I am seated in the smallest room in the house. I have your letter before me. Soon it will be behind me." H. L. Mencken, a professional controversialist, apparently received enough angry mail to warrant his printing up a postcard that read, "Dear Sir or Madam, You may or may not be right," which can only have left his antagonists purple with frustration.

Angry letters and sweet, Mencken used to answer all mail sent to him on the same day he received it. This is a noble ideal, to which the closest I can come is a weak sigh of aspiration. Alas, one serious drawback about letters is that, in order to get them, one must send some out. When it comes to the mail, I feel it is better to receive than to give. I suspect I am not alone in this view. Paul Horgan, in *Approaches to Writing*, suggests, "a test of characters in fiction: can you imagine how they would write letters?" This may be a good test for characters

in fiction, but I know too many people who could not pass it
in life.

I have never counted but I think I must write roughly eight
hundred letters a year. The great majority of them have to do
with business; many are little more than notes requesting this
or responding to that. Almost all these letters are written in fits
and starts, eight or ten at a sitting. Energy for writing letters
seems, in my case, to arrive in spurts. I have on a few occasions
had secretarial help, but I seem unable to dictate a letter to my
own satisfaction, being one of those people who can only think
with a pen in hand or a typewriter before them. I often wish
it were otherwise. Along with Mencken's promptitude, I wish
I could command the oil magnate Calouste Gulbenkian's
method of writing letters, as described by Kenneth Clark in the
first volume of his memoirs, *Another Part of the Wood:*

"Not an office man, Mr. Clark"; and sure enough he [Gulbenkian]
had no office. In summer he did his work in the park of St. Cloud.
His secretaries were seated at folding card tables situated in the
boscage at intervals of about half a mile. He would trot up and down
between them, with two detectives, heavily invisible, padding along
in the adjoining path. I sometimes accompanied him in these walks,
and his mind moved with such precision that by the time we reached
the next card table he was ready to dictate a detailed technical letter.

Not, to be sure, that the Gulbenkian method could ever
hope to produce beautiful letters in the style of Walpole or
Madame de Sévigné, et alia. It may well be that true literary
letters will soon be—if they are not already—a thing of the
past. To write chatty letters filled with news, descriptions,
observations, and anecdotes is an activity for which people no
longer seem to have the leisure or the energy—or, perhaps
more accurately, the habit. The telephone habit has partly
replaced it. Writers, editors, publishers must conduct fully as

much, or more, of their business over local and long-distance telephone as by letter. As a result, the literary record of the future figures to be more fragmentary than that of the past. Splendid volumes of collected letters by writers born twenty-five years from now are not easily imagined.

Yet I should not want to write off letters as an antiquated or dead form. Letters remain invaluable for carefully formulated thought, for good humor, for expressions of earnest sympathy. Sentiments that human shyness will not always allow one to convey in conversation—sentiments of gratitude, of apology, of love—can often be more easily conveyed in a letter. Having important or amusing or detailed information in writing, to reflect upon, to reconsider, to reread in tranquillity, remains a fine thing. Who has not carried a gratifying letter around with him for days after he has received it—to read it again at free moments and feel once more something of the pleasure it gave on first reading? Amidst the junk mail and the hate mail and the crank mail, splendid letters continue to be written. The prospect of receiving such letters still causes me to respond eagerly to the postman's ring. So write, as they used to say during the Depression, if you find work.

The Ephemeral Verities

A FEW MONTHS BACK, as is most distinctly not my wont, I had lunch with an editor of *Playboy* magazine. I should like to be able to report that this man was a cunning erotician, that we dined in an elegant restaurant atop an expensive bordello where we were served by eunuchs, and that talk at nearby tables was of white slavery. Not quite so. As it turned out, my luncheon companion was much engrossed in the prospect of purchasing a condominium, and we ate in a restaurant whose custom seemed chiefly to come from that corporate class known, I believe, as middle management. Worse still, all that each of us ordered for lunch was a salad. Not my idea of playboys dining out, I must say.

I had come to this lunch because the editor had sent me a note saying he had read some of my scribblings and would like to discuss the possibility of my writing something for *Playboy*. I recall having heard, roughly a decade ago, that the magazine paid $3,000 for an article. Had it, I wondered, kept pace with inflation—as I, a domestic Keynesian with a talent for deficit financing, had not? In short, as the hunter said about the quail, I was game. I even had an answer for anyone who might reproach me by saying, "You mean you write for *Playboy?*" "You mean," I was prepared to shoot back, "you read it?"

But, as will appear in my annual report to stockholders, nothing came of this lunch. I neglected even to find out if *Playboy* had raised its payments to authors. What I did find out in talking to this editor was that I am not an ideal *Playboy* contributor, though he was too kind to say so. As we spoke about what I might write for the magazine, he mentioned that *Playboy* was planning a series of articles predicting trends in the 1980s. I allowed that, from the standpoint of a writer, I found the future boring, the present pleasant, and the past best of all. But as we talked further, it became clear to me that what he really wanted, what every editor of a contemporary mass magazine for the college-educated middle classes wants, is not a body of useful or curious information, or the spectacle of an idiosyncratic and perhaps interesting mind at work, but a piece of writing that will spot a trend, put a new phrase into the language, erect a new truth that will endure until the next issue of the magazine appears. What is wanted, if I may say so, is a shiny new cliché.

A new cliché? Isn't this a contradiction? As a near-contributor to *Playboy* I don't see why I should have to define my terms—especially at these prices—so, if it is all the same to you, I think I'll adopt the definition set forth by someone who has thought about clichés longer than I have. In *On Clichés*, a Dutch sociologist named Anton C. Zijderveld defines a cliché thus:

A cliché is a traditional form of human expression (in words, thoughts, emotions, gestures, acts) which—due to repetitive use in social life—has lost its original, often ingenious heuristic power. Although it thus fails positively to contribute meaning to social interactions and communication, it does function socially, since it manages to stimulate behavior (cognition, emotion, volition, action), while it avoids reflection on meanings.

This is a definition that doesn't, you might say, throw the baby out with the bathwater; it leaves no stone unturned while offering several blessings in disguise, and in the final analysis provides an acid test. You might say all this, that is, if you have an ear dead to the grossest of clichés. But two elements in Professor Zijderveld's definition are especially worth notice. The first is its capaciousness, which lies in its recognition that the clichéic can extend well beyond the merely linguistic. There are, after all, cliché acts, cliché thoughts, cliché books, possibly cliché lives. The second is that Professor Zijderveld's definition comprehends that clichés can stimulate behavior even while discouraging thought.

Still, new clichés? One tends to think of clichés as made stale by use and overuse. Yet, in a letter to Harriet Monroe, Wallace Stevens remarks, "There is, of course, a cliché of the moment as well as a cliché of the past." In *Human, All-Too-Human,* Nietzsche speaks of those who are fifteen minutes ahead of their time—persons of whom he did not think at all well. And I (if I may insert myself into such high-flown company) think there are things that ought to be called Ephemeral Verities, which are clichés of the moment and up to the moment, but without the staying power of ordinary clichés. To adapt the old cliché about Chinese restaurants, the trouble with Ephemeral Verities is that, an hour after you have mouthed them, you are empty-headed again.

There is nothing new about clichés as such. As an appendix to *Bouvard and Pécuchet,* Flaubert included a "Dictionnaire des idées reçues," later enlarged, in my translated copy, into *A Dictionary of Platitudes, Being a Compendium of Conversational Clichés, Blind Beliefs, Fashionable Misconceptions, and Fixed Ideas.* Flaubert intended his *Dictionary* to contain "everything that it is necessary to repeat in society in order to pass for a

well-mannered and agreeable person." Befitting a book devoted to the cultivation of the commonplace, the *Dictionary*
has long stretches that are tedious, though every now and again
a small nugget flashes. The proper cliché to mouth about Ca-
tholicism, for example, is "Has had a very beneficial influence
on the arts"; the advice on the subject of Metaphysics is "To
laugh at it is proof of a superior mind"; and, as for Memory,
"Complain about your own, and even boast about having none.
But roar when told you have no judgment."

I myself do not despise all clichés. Some of them usefully
relieve life of its complications. The fully examined life, I have
come to think, may not be worth living. Into each life a lot of
cliché must fall. It may be a sign of maturity to accept this,
smile, and pass on. Of the young Lytton Strachey, Max Beerbohm wrote that his prose had not a jot of preciosity. "He
makes no attempt to dazzle," Beerbohm writes. "He is not even
afraid of clichés." One of the finest obituaries I have ever read,
that of the extraordinary Baroness Moura Budberg, which
appeared in *The Times* (of London), ended flat dab and altogether correctly on a cliché: "There is an old American saying
that fits her well: 'After they made that one, they broke the
mould.' "

One can only begin to lay claim to knowing a foreign
language, it has been said, when one can spot clichés in it. H.
W. Fowler, in his article on the cliché in *Modern English Usage,*
remarks, "What is new is not necessarily better than what is
old; the original felicity that made a phrase a cliché may not
be beyond recapture." Well to remember, too, that clichés
often become in time the inevitable burial ground of even the
most strikingly original phrase or thought or gesture; perhaps
the more striking the more inevitably will it end as a cliché.
"And the witty gentleman," says Fowler, in his article on
hackneyed phrases, "who equipped coincidence with her long

arm has doubtless suffered even in this life at seeing that arm so mercilessly overworked."

Some activities are quite unthinkable unembellished by clichés, and clichés can sometimes gently slide into tradition. For the sports fan, clichés are nearly as important to spectatorial pleasure as are statistics; the best contemporary writer on the subject of baseball, Roger Angell, is especially adept at carefully deploying clichés throughout his compositions. Certain events call for the clichéic: who wants veal limone for Thanksgiving dinner? Clichés can help us get through awkward situations; they keep things superficial where skimming the surface may be the wisest course. In *On Clichés* Professor Zijderveld notes: "In fact, if one were to collect clichés, like stamps or jokes, one would find a rich field of exploration in obituaries, in letters of condolence, and in funeral orations. It seems as if variations are deemed uncouth, or almost magically harmful and hazardous. Indeed, by leaving the set of clichés in such precarious situations one may easily hurt feelings inadvertently." Each of us, in short, has to be ready to call upon the Polonius that is part of us all.

But a little cliché goes a long way. The way things stand now, though, under the dispensation of the Ephemeral Verities, a great many clichés are asked to go a short way. We are today, I believe, being bombarded, indeed blitzed, by clichés. Professor Zijderveld maintains that modern society is especially susceptible to clichés—"clichégenic," he calls it, in a word that gets to look less hideous once one gets used to it— for the reason that, where meaning has in so many places been undermined, men and women swim about in choppy waters, desperately reaching out for something to keep themselves afloat. "Clichés," Professor Zijderveld writes, give "artificial clarity, stability, and certainty." While he is not in favor of this, nor of the clichéic as a mode of thought, he does think it is better than nothing. I am inclined to believe it is about the same as nothing.

Clichés are sometimes thought of as wisdom gone stale. But just as often they represent the devastation that time can wreak on serious ideas. Take the phrase "Protestant ethic," surely one of the leading clichés of our time. Nowadays it pops up everywhere, with a range of meanings that vary from the description of a person intent on success to a tag for the compulsion to work unrelentingly. The origin of this contemporary cliché is, of course, Max Weber's magnificent essay, "The Protestant Ethic and the Spirit of Capitalism," which I first read some twenty years ago as an undergraduate in a condition I can only describe as one of intellectual heat—so swept up was I by its learning, its subtlety, its power. Having read the essay, I now wince slightly when I hear, say, Jimmy Carter described as a product of the Protestant ethic. But then perhaps he is, in the sense that, say, Dick Cavett is a real Renaissance man.

Max Weber's phrase took some seventy-five years to lapse into cliché status, but usually the process by which thought turns to cliché is much more rapid. Indeed certain notions or phrases seem to come into the world as full-blown clichés. Joseph Kraft's "Middle America," Henry Fairlie's "establishment," Spiro Agnew's speech writer's "silent majority," and, on a somewhat higher level, Erik Erikson's "identity crisis"— these seem clichés almost out of the gate. What makes them so, I think, is that each of these alluring phrases is nonetheless finely inexact, fuzzy enough to be put to multiple uses, and exquisitely suited to what Santayana called "the habit of abbreviated thinking." Consider: "The silent majority, freshly emergent as Middle America, no longer feels an identity crisis vis-à-vis the establishment." There is something gratifying about striking off such a sentence—even though it is, of course, nonsense.

The rise of the Ephemeral Verities has been nicely attuned to, if not abetted by, the rise in the numbers of people who have attended college since World War II. Current undergraduate education seems splendidly set up for the transmission of clichés. Many college courses today are very with-it, are taught by teachers whose eyes are blurry from spotting trends, and use books that are themselves largely composed of clichés: *Future Shock, The Best and the Brightest, Passages.* Students themselves are very keen at discerning the cliché possibilities in their education, and a few years ago (I do not know if the phrase is still current) used to speak of the clichéic distillation of complex thought as "cepts"—cepts being short for concepts. "Oedipus complex," "categorical imperative," Emerson's "Oversoul," "marginal utility," Nietzsche's "Superman," "alienation"— such are cepts. Some days, listening to these cepts pinging off classroom walls, it seems as if the chief effect of the spread of education has been to allow more people to live, not more thoughtfully, but by somewhat more complicated clichés.

If undergraduate education often spreads the fertilizer for the implantation of clichés, the great harvest is yielded in newspapers, in news magazines, and on television. The media are the largest users of clichés, and they require, like certain large-scale discount houses (since they discount ideas), a fast turnover. There is all that space to fill, all that time to kill, and what better way to do it than with clichés: about people, about politics, about social problems. Having myself once committed a book on a social problem, the lugubrious one of divorce, I used often to be invited to write for women's magazines about different aspects of this dreary topic—or to go on obscure radio and television talk shows to parade my rather tired opinions. It was my big chance to set myself up as a false expert, a cliché merchant, the Divorce Man, a figure akin to the anti-ERA lady and the touring transsexual. I demurred.

I recall one such invitation that came long after my book on the subject had been safely "pulped" (publishers go in for strong verbs). I was invited by a small downtown FM station to take part in a discussion with a divorce lawyer and an aggrieved divorcée. Since this conversation was scheduled for midnight, I gathered it was staged for the delectation of insomniacs, folks coming off the night shift, and driving drunks. No fee was offered, and I should mention that one does not travel downtown at midnight in my city without a U.S. Cavalry escort.

"Now let me get this straight," I said to the enthusiastic man who ran the show. "You want me to appear at 12 A.M. to talk with a very angry woman and a lawyer with a reputation for being a sharper—and to do this for the sheer pleasure of talking about a hideously sad subject."

"Yep."

"Well, sir, my answer is an unalterable and implacable no. What possible point can there be to my coming down there at midnight, at risk to my life and without pay, except to add to the contemporary noise?"

A moment's silence on his side, and then, "Hey, how would you like to come on the show to discuss that?"

"To discuss what?"

"Why, the contemporary noise!"

Indefatigable!

If the contemporary noise has not yet made it as popular cliché, two items that are especially cliché-prone continue to be those of decades and of generations. "Yours is a lost generation," Gertrude Stein is supposed to have remarked to Ernest Hemingway (I have always suspected she said a *louche génération*), and ever since no generation has been allowed to pass without a label: the Depression generation, the silent genera-

tion, the Woodstock generation, et cetera. But even more per-
sistent is the penchant for clichés about decades. Here is a
recent offering from the pages of the *New Republic:*

It is becoming increasingly clear with the approaching end of the
aimless 1970s, a decade so reminiscent of the 1950s and 1920s, that
American politics is in for another of its periodic sea changes: ready
or not, a more energetic public life looms before us in the 1980s.

I myself am not ready; I am not even ready for the analogy
between the 1970s and the 1920s, having only recently become
accustomed to that between the 1960s and the 1920s. But these
clichés change quickly, which is what makes them, as verities,
only ephemeral. Attend now, though, to that old cliché-
meister the Reverend Norman Vincent Mailer, in an interview
in *Publishers Weekly:* "The '70s have been too much for me.
They appalled me the way the '50s appalled me." As one good
cliché deserves another, Mailer caps his with an empty chias-
mus: "I used to hate America for what it was doing to all of
us. Now I hate all of us for what we're doing to America."

The cliché seal was set on the 1970s, long before its completion, by Tom Wolfe, who called it the "Me Decade." The
1970s, in Mr. Wolfe's reading, was a decade given over to the
self—to self-improvement programs, religious and therapeutic,
to self-exhibition, and to self-absorption generally. When Tom
Wolfe sent the Me Decade up the flagpole, nearly everyone,
it seems, saluted. These boys, to adopt another advertising
cliché, certainly know how to pick up the ball and run with
it. Suddenly, everywhere one turned, the 1970s were all Me and
narcissistic and dreadfully spineless. A young writer named
Mark Crispin Miller remarked that those years have been "hospitable to narcissism." Michael Harrington, a fellow keen for
political activism, referred to "the passive 1970s." Christopher
Lasch published a collection of essays entitled *The Culture of*

Narcissism, which turned out to be a best-seller. And then, at midyear of 1979, Jann Wenner, the publisher of *Rolling Stone* and hence presumably a careful reader of the zeitgeist, announced that "The Me Decade is over."

But before the decade congeals into the plaster of paris of cliché, I think that a few things ought to be said on behalf of the 1970s—not least among them that they weren't the 1960s. Properly speaking, of course, the 1960s were not the '60s either, or at least exclusively; insofar as they stand for a period of political tumult and intellectual incivility, they continued on well into the early 1970s. What is more, in what decade without a major war or economic catastrophe have people *not* been self-absorbed? The labeling of decades often tells less about the decades than about strangely skewed views of history. A period such as the 1960s, when our nation was very nearly ripped apart by riot and ill feeling all around, is now known as one of social idealism. Another decade, such as the middle and late 1950s under President Eisenhower, and after Korea and Senator Joseph McCarthy—a time when people could carry on their work—is known as passive and conformist and boring. The fact is, I don't see me in the Me Decade. If people insist on a label for the 1970s, however, I would settle for calling it the You Decade.

Not that all this talk of decades is entirely wrong. Many people who came of age in the 1920s, when Prohibition was in force, seem never to have lost their excitement about alcohol. Many people who were young in the 1930s have never quite been able, owing to the Depression, to shake their anxiety about money. And many people who came of age in the 1960s are likely to have a wide acquaintance with drugs. I am not sure, though, that one can safely say much more than these loose and banal things about any ten-year period. Yet people seem to crave more. Labels for decades help them pack up the complications of history and even of their own lives, and put these away in the empty valise of clichés. Once packed up, thinking can cease. Here is the real utility of clichés: they explain the world, usually crudely and sometimes quite falsely. But for many people a false explanation is better than no explanation at all.

So great is the need for explanations that certain thinkers gain ascendancy over others because, intricate and elaborate though their thought might originally have been, it presents a rich mine from which clichés can be easily extracted. Marxism is a prime example, with its two whopping clichés: the eternal class struggle and economic determinism. Freudianism is another example. Perhaps as few people have read Freud as have read Marx, yet everyone is in on the id, ego, superego, the determinism of early infancy, the importance of the sexual life, and the rest of it. Existentialism has been yet another fountain of clichés, so much so that the very word "existential" has itself become a cliché—one of the true wooden nickels of intellectual discourse. Professor Zijderveld remarks of such intellectual clichés that they "are like mantras providing modern man with a semi-magical sense of security and stability . . . in which permanent reflection can come to rest."

The fact that all these items, from the class struggle to the Oedipus complex, have become clichés does not necessarily disqualify them as truth-bearing. Ideas, like statistics, cannot be held responsible for the people who use them. Yet some ideas do allow easier access, and coarser usage, than others. Finer-grained writers—Montaigne, Pascal, Santayana—are not so easily summarized. Their thought cannot be grasped by the reins of a leading idea or two; rather like poets, they can scarcely be paraphrased. Marx and Freud are writers of great power in any case, but surely a large part of their popularity is owing to their supreme nomenclatural skill. They could name things with cogency, and this cogency is decisive for the adaptation of ideas to use as clichés. "Just another example of thinking that if you name something you've explained it," says the protagonist of Kingsley Amis's novel *Jake's Thing*. "Like . . . like permissive society."

The permissive society, the consumer society, post-industrial society, the meritocratic society, the culture of narcissism, the culture of poverty, the adversary culture, the organization man, the lonely crowd, the Spock generation—there seems to be no end to these clichés, these Ephemeral Verities. Nor to ephemeral veritists, those philosophers who sail in on a phrase —Norman O. Brown ("polymorphous perverse"), Marshall McLuhan ("the medium is the message"), Herbert Marcuse ("repressive toleration")—and sail out again. Perhaps some day they will be used as names in an intellectual trivia game, like Monopoly—let's call it Doctorate. Pick a question card: "Who in the late 1960s said that in an insane society the most truly sane person was the schizophrenic?" Answer: the English psychiatrist R. D. Laing. If you answered incorrectly, return to another year as a teaching assistant at Eastern Illinois University. If you answered correctly, take credit for two master's degree courses, and apply to Columbia.

Marcuse and McLuhan, Brown and Laing, these are very great geysers of pishposh, as Mencken used to call such temporary sages, and very high-blowing ones at that. Their writings are scarcely accessible to the common reader, and even the uncommon reader needs a fairly broad streak of masochism and the mental equivalent of hip boots to trudge through their works. But if these ephemeral veritists are an acquired taste, like that for eating cactus, who is working the larger crowds —what in Las Vegas are called the "big rooms"?

One night not long ago when I was watching the local television news, a suburban high school teachers' strike was reported. Various teachers were asked how the strike would affect them personally. One of the respondents was a man with hairdo and mustache reminiscent of Kurt Vonnegut. "I was forty last month," he said into the microphone thrust under his mustache, "and this summer my wife and I separated, and now there's this strike. One more thing and I'll be going through a mid-life crisis." It took me a moment to realize what he was saying: here was a reader of, and apparently a true believer in, *Passages.*

Passages is a book about adult development by the journalist Gail Sheehy. Among ephemeral veritists, Miss Sheehy works the lower end of the vineyard. The air is not so rarefied down there, but the yield is much greater; *Passages* has been, as its mass paperback edition announces, "#1 from Coast to Coast." I have read only a hundred or so of its more than five hundred pages, but that is enough to recognize that, of its kind, the book is a work of genius—a structure built almost entirely of other people's clichés, though chiefly using materials from those two great brickyards of contemporary cliché, psychology and sociology. Miss Sheehy artfully uses jargon, supplies endless case-study interviews, exudes an air of scientism, and paints over the whole with a rich coat of hopefulness. "If I've been convinced by one idea in the course of collecting all the life stories that inform this book, it is this: Times of crisis, of disruption or constructive change, are not only predictable but desirable. They mean "growth." Hmmm. Do try to remember that the next time you undergo bankruptcy, divorce, a coronary, or the death of someone you love: it means growth.

But all this is old news. Miss Sheehy has now moved on to fresh verities. *Esquire* not long ago ran a segment from her latest book; the segment is entitled "Introducing the Postponing Generation, the Truth About Today's Young Men." Ah, "the Postponing Generation"—who can fail to find the deft touch of the cliché artist in that, a woman with a sure sense of *le cliché juste?* One can be reasonably certain that there is plenty more where that came from.

Professor Zijderveld makes the interesting observation that intellectual clichés do not demand any serious moral responsibility. One adopts them for a while, wearing them rather like a sweater. When something warmer or more attractive comes along, one switches to that. A continual shedding and changing of clichés, like sweaters, goes on and doubtless will continue to do so. One can attempt to beat back these clichés, but in the end the task can never be successfully completed, for it too closely resembles cleaning out the Augean stables without removing the horses.

Besides, the process has been going on for a very long while. Dostoevski, in the early pages of *The Diary of Writer,* remarks, "In our day, thoughtfulness is next to impossible: it is too expensive a luxury. True enough, ready ideas are being bought. They are being sold everywhere, even gratis, but gratuitously, in the long run, they prove more expensive, and people begin to forbode this fact." Nearly seventy years later, Wallace Stevens, in more than one of his letters, notes that he is reading too much and, as a result, thinking too little. One might once have thought of reading as indistinguishable from thinking, but no longer. With so many clichés buzzing about in books and in the atmosphere generally, it is sometimes like trying to think with one's head in a beehive.

Meanwhile, should another *Playboy* or other slick magazine editor invite me to lunch, I will not again make the mistake of arriving unprepared. I have an idea for an article that will, I think, fill the bill. Its working title is "The New Incest."

Interested editors may contact my agent, Georges Borchardt, Inc., New York, New York. I have also begun work on an article that will explain what happened in the 1990s. Editors should know that for either of these articles the highest possible rates will be barely acceptable.

You Take Manhattan

OVER THE YEARS I have on several occasions been mistaken for a New Yorker. I am never quite sure how to take this. If the person who makes the mistake is himself a New Yorker, I generally take it as a compliment. It means, I have come to conclude, that he recognizes in me a certain suavity, the sophistication and quality of a cosmopolitan, none of which I have ever deigned to deny. But if the person who takes me for a New Yorker is not himself a New Yorker, I get a trifle nervous. What have I done, I wonder, to merit this accusation? Have I seemed too aggressive? Have I gone, somehow, too far? Have I, unbeknownst to myself, acquired an accent? New York and New Yorkers are subjects about which no one is neutral. "All right," John Dos Passos once remarked, in an entirely different context, "we are two nations." And so indeed we remain today, two nations, New York and the rest of the country.

I had better say right off that I like New York and New Yorkers. I have family living in New York. As a younger man, I lived there myself for some three years. I go to New York on business two or three times a year. I have in recent years even gone to New York for pleasure: to shop, to look in at the Frick Collection, to breakfast in the Edwardian Room of the

Plaza. The city's energy never ceases to excite me. The faces of New Yorkers are more impressive than those of people in other cities—more lively, more expressive, more flushed with expectation. Even among people who talk to themselves—of whom New York surely has greater numbers than any other city—New Yorkers seem to have more interesting conversations. ("He fools with me," I heard a man walking up 48th Street mutter to himself on my last trip there. "I'll cut his heart out.") In no other city do people seem so got up, so frankly sexual—and I do not refer here alone to the *gayim*, as a friend of mine refers to the resurgent homosexual community—so ready to go. In no other city are there so many shoe stores. It may be the last city in which a man can wear an ascot with a straight face.

New York is a world city, the only one in the United States. Saul Bellow has called it a European city, but of no known country. Over the years it has been fortunate in receiving ever fresh infusions of foreigners, having long ago been the first port of call from Europe, and no small part of its pleasures has been the cacophony of foreign accents and styles on exhibition there. British publishers, White Russian grandes dames, French agents, Israeli folksingers, Arabs with large digital wristwatches, Japanese without cameras—all are likely to be encountered in the same elevator in a New York hotel. On one corner in New York I have had my custom invited to a massage parlor and on the next corner I have been handed a small pamphlet invoking me to keep kosher, while in the middle of the block a five-piece steel band is playing African songs. New York, as befits a world city, is a polyglottony.

When I say New York, I of course mean Manhattan, the island thirteen miles long and two-and-a-half miles across at its widest point (which is 86th Street). Technically, New York's boroughs are part of New York, but spiritually they are not at

all the same. Brooklyn might as well be part of Chicago, the
Bronx part of Detroit, Queens of St. Louis. Manhattan, for
both better and worse, is different. Norman Podhoretz, in the
opening chapter of his book *Making It*, puts it well when he
writes, "One of the longest journeys in the world is the journey
from Brooklyn to Manhattan—or at least from certain neigh-
borhoods in Brooklyn to certain parts of Manhattan." Manhattan for many people, especially the young and ambitious, is
goal and consummation. "To Moscow! To Moscow! To Moscow!" cries Irina at the close of act 2 of Chekhov's *The Three
Sisters*. Manhattan is America's Moscow, the city of allure,
possibility, promise.

To Manhattan! To Manhattan! To Manhattan! This advice
I imbibed as a young man. If one wanted to make it, then
Manhattan was indisputably the place. Succeed in Manhattan,
where the competition was fiercest, and one could succeed
anywhere. I believed this then, and believe it still. I first trav-
eled to Manhattan alone for a few days of theater-going during
the spring holidays of my junior year at college. In unseason-
ably warm weather I sat in a wool suit of olive drab on two
consecutive nights, watching, back to back, Eugene O'Neill's
Long Day's Journey into Night and *The Iceman Cometh*—not
exactly a surefire recipe for glee. But the city itself swept me
up and away. I was not the first pilgrim to feel like this. There
is, in fact, almost a tradition of excitation at the prospect of
going to New York. Here, in 1915, is Theodore Dreiser, in his
autobiographical novel *The "Genius,"* describing feelings
about New York that were not so different from my own or
those of thousands of other young men and women at their
first encounter with the city:

He went about this early relationship to the city in the right spirit.
For a little while he did not try to think what he would do, but struck

out and walked here, there and everywhere, this very first day down Broadway to the City Hall and up Broadway from 14th to 42nd Street the same night. Soon he knew all Third Avenue and the Bowery, the wonders of Fifth Avenue and Riverside Drive, the beauties of the East River, the Battery, Central Park and the lower East Side. He sought out quickly the wonders of metropolitan life—its crowds at dinner and theatre time in Broadway, its tremendous throngs morning and afternoon in the shopping district. . . . He had marveled at wealth and luxury in Chicago, but here it took his breath away. It was obviously so much more fixed, so definite and comprehensible. Here one felt instinctively the far reaches which separate the ordinary man from the scion of wealth. It curled him up like a frozen leaf, dulled his very soul, and gave him a clear sense of his position in the social scale. He had come here with a pretty high estimate of himself, but daily, as he looked, he felt himself crumbling. What was he? What was art? What did the city care? It was much more interested in other things, in dressing, eating, visiting, riding abroad. The lower part of the island was filled with cold commercialism which frightened him. In the upper half, which concerned only women and show—a voluptuous sybaritism—caused him envy. He had but two hundred dollars with which to fight his way, and this was the world he must conquer.

No Dreiserian hero, I did not want to conquer but only to belong, to be part of the scene. So at the end of my college days, I packed up my olive drab suit and other clothes, brought along all the novels of Joseph Conrad and, with six hundred dollars in funds, moved to New York. I did not move to Manhattan but instead took a large furnished room in Brooklyn Heights, on Willow Street, not far down from the house in which W. H. Auden, Benjamin Britten, Carson McCullers, and Truman Capote had once lived; Norman Mailer was living in Brooklyn Heights at that time. Willow Street was quiet and even rather elegant, providing that combination of privacy and loneliness in which New York specializes. The river was only a few blocks away. Alongside it one could sit on a bench and gaze upon the man-made alp that is Manhattan.

Directly on my arrival, I sat down and wrote to the editors of *The New Yorker, Esquire,* and *Harper's,* putting them on notice that I was in town and available to improve their respective journals. While awaiting their replies, I daily boarded the subway to Manhattan and walked its streets, glittering and grubby alike. I discovered an employment agency given over exclusively to finding jobs in editorial enterprises. I roamed the bookstores of Fourth Avenue. I haunted the streets of the Village. I ate occasional dinners at a restaurant called Paddy's Clam House, sitting at long tables among strangers amid the clatter of the shells and skeletons of crustaceans. I ventured out to Queens to visit one set of cousins, and out to Coney Island to visit another. *The New Yorker, Esquire,* and *Harper's* were clearly having a difficult time finding exactly the right place for me. Meanwhile I registered at the editorial employment agency.

"The girls here are wonderful this summer," he announced when I phoned him. He had been a law student at the university I had gone to, and I had been attracted to him by that manic energy that I had come to think of as peculiarly New Yorkish. (Fifty years before, writing of New York in *The American Scene,* Henry James referred to "the vehemence of local life.") His opening remark was characteristic. He invited me for dinner that night at his parents' apartment on East 88th Street. When I appeared at the door, he greeted me by informing me that he had flunked out of law school and so things were a trifle tense at home at the moment. I had not been in the apartment ten minutes before he and his younger brother had a punch-up over a borrowed shirt. When his mother came in to break it up, he said: "All right, but no more threats of suicide, Mother. Your threats are growing tiresome. Either do it, for God's sake, or shut up about it." At table he directed his attention to me, largely ignoring his family. When he didn't respond to something his father said, his father—a very successful lawyer, noted for dealing in theatrical and musical copyrights—added in a loud voice: "You really ought to listen to me, Robert. I might have something valuable to say. I, at least, was able to get through law school." To which he rejoined, "I, at least, haven't been drunk since noon." His father's response to this was to throw the contents of his drink across the table at his son, most of which landed on me. I recall delicately extracting an ice cube from my mashed potatoes. Things were a trifle tense, no question about it. Yet, although extreme, this scene, too, seemed to me a part of New York— the down side of the manic energy.

Not having heard from any of the magazines I wanted to work for, I began to interview for jobs on magazines I had no interest even in reading. One warm morning I arrived to interview for a job as an editorial assistant on a trade journal that had to do with dental supplies, and found some fifteen people ahead of me, most of them quite a bit older than I. This was the camel that broke the straw's back. That afternoon I looked up the name Edmund Wilson in the Manhattan telephone directory, intending to ask him for advice about conducting a literary career. Whether this was the same Edmund Wilson whose works I had read and so much admired I never discovered, for an older woman with a very formidable voice answered the phone, and I, atremble, hung up. Nor did I discover whether *The New Yorker*, *Esquire*, or *Harper's* ever answered my letters. My money was running low and, rather than invest in another month's rent, I left for home, discouraged but making an italicized mental note to return.

Some four years later I did return, with a pregnant wife and an infant son and a low-paying job on a political magazine. My first disappointment was that there was not enough money to live in Manhattan except under conditions of beastliness, which, with a family, I was loath to do. So we installed ourselves in an apartment in Queens, which meant a half-hour subway ride to and from work. (". . . The religion of humanity is utterly unacceptable," noted Walter Lippmann, "to those who have to ride in the subways during rush hour.") Still, I did not mind. I didn't even much mind eating the foul Nedick's breakfast I began swallowing daily: a glass of orange drink, weak coffee, a donut (29¢). I learned to fold and read my *New York Times* on the subway amid an extremely clamorous humankind. Before long, I became a connoisseur of standard New York bumptious behavior: the scowl one receives when giving a clerk a ten-dollar bill; having a cab stolen out from under one in the rain; the general brusqueness of manner which makes all too real the joke about the Hoosier who, after two days in New York, asks a native of the city, "Excuse me, sir, could you tell me where the Empire State Building is, or would you prefer that I go screw myself?"

Such are the habits, customs, mores of New Yorkers that they really require a Malinowski, a first-class ethnographer, to record them properly. Take food. No one eats more quickly than do New Yorkers. Or with more variety. There may be better cities for food—Paris currently, Saigon before communism—but none in North America. This comes in part out of the sheer demandingness of New Yorkers, but in part, too, out of their insistence in treating the dreariest luncheonette as if it were their mothers' altogether hospitable kitchens. I have never heard people order food as I have in New York. "Sam, fix me a sardine on rye, with a very thin slice of onion, and a light rinse of lemon, pickle on the side." Nor in any other city have I heard customers order food in the argot of a fry cook.

"Sam, BLT down, hold the mayo, burgers a pair, c.b. on an onion, draw one white, shoot three, boots." (Translation: a bacon-lettuce-tomato sandwich on toast, no mayonnaise; two hamburgers; a corned-beef sandwich on an onion roll; coffee with milk, three cokes—all to take out.)

Antics of this kind come about because of the hyper-hastened pace of New York life. This pace, seeking always to cut away all that is extraneous in human relations, also results in a directness that can shock non-New Yorkers. A non-New Yorker, visiting one's apartment, might say, "My, what a nice place," then inquire about the number of rooms it has, ask if it gets good light, remark on the fireplace, question the lease arrangements. A New Yorker, on the other hand, is much more likely to say, "Nice place. What d'you pay?" Very up-front is one description of this behavior; extreme rudeness is another description of it. But, as with a car rounding a corner and splashing water on you, it is probably best not to take it personally.

Yet if New Yorkers are likely to ask for personal information, they also volunteer it more readily than one is ordinarily accustomed to. "How are you?" can be a dangerous question to ask a New Yorker: "How are you?" "I just ended a whirlwind affair." "How are you?" "My eighteen-year-old daughter is living with a man of fifty-seven." "How are you?" "I just changed shrinks." "How are you?" "My wife last week lost a job paying forty-two thousand dollars a year. How would you be?" There isn't, but there ought to be, a word for such unwonted (unwanted?) forthcomingness; perhaps it might be "candorous." Again, extremely personal though they are, such remarks are probably best not taken personally.

There are eight million stories in the naked city, as an old television show used to announce, and, before coming to New York to work, I had heard very few of them. I worked on 15th

Street, off Union Square, in a building that housed a number of union agents and the old Rand School Library. Hasidic Jews and elderly Mensheviks pottered in and out of the building. In the library, men spent lifetimes getting up the material for books no one wanted to read. I met a jazz critic, a teacher of literature courses at the School of General Education at Columbia University, who referred to his job as "working the lounge at Columbia." More than half the people I came across were at work on a novel, or painted, or sang, or danced. A pants salesman in our apartment building gave up his line to take acting lessons. Accountants were sure to have been Trotskyists in their youth. The city sagged under the weight of aspiration. Yet all this aspiration gave New York an appealing aspect of hope and dreaminess.

The other side of this aspiration—a side that often puts off strangers—is the sheer appalling knowingness of New Yorkers. Delicatessen countermen offer stock-market tips. Cabdrivers are flush with opinions on everything. (Agnes Repplier tells how, many years ago, she once entered a New York cab and announced, "I want to go to Brooklyn." "You mean," the driver corrected her, "you have to.") Even the New York bums seem a bit sharper than their confreres in other cities. I was once stopped on Waverly Place by a youngish panhandler who asked if he could have *all* my change. Thrown off balance by the originality of his request, I forked over a dollar and twenty cents. But for simple knowingness, for being simultaneously with it, inside it, and yet above it all, I shall never forget a man who one day sat in the chair alongside mine in a New York barbershop. When the barber asked him if he was going to that Sunday's pro football game, he said he hated crowds, and besides they piped the game into his club. Stock market looked bad, the barber said. He had got out last month, the man replied. Supposed to have snowstorms next week, the barber said. He couldn't care less, the man replied; he was off to Florida on Monday. If you told this man that his eyeballs had just dropped out, doubtless he would have responded, no sweat, he had another pair in the car. Clearly, here was a man who, even in hell, would have an air-conditioned room reserved.

In no other city does life seem such a perpetual balancing of debits and credits, of evils and virtues, as it does in New York. No other city seems so charming yet so crude, so civilized yet so uncouth. I recall once going out with two friends to bring back Chinese food from a restaurant on upper Broadway. With the food in hand, we were stopped by a young Puerto Rican drugged to the hairline who wanted the wristwatch worn by one of my friends. We were able to joke him out of it, but the prospect was fraught with danger. Such, paradigmatically, is New York: the prospect of the delight of first-class Chinese food, the danger of having a knife pulled on you while getting it home.

"East Side, West Side, all around the town," goes one of the lines from the song "The Sidewalks of New York," but much of the quality of one's days in Manhattan depends on which side of town one is in. I have a friend who, living in a spacious apartment on the West Side, had to use an elevator on whose interior door was scratched the invitation for an anatomically impossible sex act. Each morning, setting out for work, he faced this invitation; each evening, returning from work, it would be awaiting him on his ride up. The effect of this, day after day, cannot have been to induce serenity.

Not that serenity has ever been a New York ideal. Glamour has been the ideal, the chic life, stylish and joyous. But while the glamour of New York can be very real, it is at best half the story. In the magazine *New York* one can see this ideal turned into a full-fledged myth. *New York*, read week in, week out, conveys the notion of what fun the city is, what unalloyed pleasures it offers: so much to do and see, so much to buy and try. What it leaves unsaid is that, to bring off the life promised in its pages, an income of roughly $80,000 a year (after taxes) is required, and probably $150,000 if you are married and have children. I have, for example, yet to meet anyone living in Manhattan whose children go to public schools. I recently met a man in his late forties with children from a first marriage still in school and an infant daughter from a second marriage, who reported to me that he figures to be paying private school fees continuously for more than forty years. William Dean Howells called New York "a city where money counts for more and goes for less than in any other city in the world." "We'll turn Manhattan into an isle of joy," the old Rodgers and Hart song has it. Not quite.

Part of the problem that I had with Woody Allen's film *Manhattan* was its strict emphasis on the "isle of joy" side of New York life, even while attempting to show that modern life is unstable and empty—what I think of as the movie's Bergdorf-Goodman existentialism. The mise-en-scène for the movie is all duplex apartments and Elaine's, pizzas and ice-cream cones in Central Park. There is one scene in the movie where Woody Allen and Diane Keaton spend an entire night on a park bench, awaiting the sunrise over the East River. Watching this scene, all I could think was, "Oh, my God, they're sure to be mugged"—as in life they doubtless would have been. W. H. Auden, who referred to himself as a New Yorker and never an American, would not leave his apartment on St. Mark's Place without carrying a five-dollar bill, lest a mugger, angry at finding him without money, beat him up all the worse.

Although New York is preeminently the city of anxiety, as Auden himself felt, where much indifference and misery lurk under and indeed above the surface, it can also sometimes seem the very center of the universe. A single New York sight, a meeting, an incident can make all that is twitchy, neurotic, febrile about the city disappear on the instant. I recall walking along Fifth Avenue one day on my lunch hour, my head filled with standard New York thoughts—scheming to find a better job, looking for a larger apartment, wondering where I might scare up more freelance work—when across my path stepped, lo, Cary Grant. He seemed a figure made of the finest leather, porcelain, and silver. Dazzling. Wonderful. Splendiferous. "I love it here," I said to myself. "I never want to leave."

For reasons too complicated and boring to go into, I did leave New York, though I thought I should one day become, as a number of my friends have, a naturalized New Yorker. This phenomenon of naturalized citizenship in a city is also exclusive, in America at least, to New York. True, people move out to California and become, in some rough sense, Californians. A much smaller number, who are usually associated with Harvard or MIT, fall in love with Cambridge; but not in the same intense way, it seems to me, that people become New Yorkers. Life outside New York is quite simply unthinkable to them, and in time they themselves become unthinkable outside New York. No amount of aggravation can flush them out of the purlieus of Manhattan; no prospects elsewhere, no matter how lush, will bring them to leave. If forced to it, they will give up the work they do, their marriages, their children rather than abandon New York.

When this love of New York takes a chauvinistic turn, which it frequently does with New Yorkers both born and naturalized, it tends to get under the skin of non-New Yorkers. Being in any other city, to true New Yorkers, is considered merely camping out, and they often too openly show it. A cosmopolitan is someone who is at home anywhere in the world. Most New Yorkers do not fit this definition, being only really at home in New York. The common charge against them is that in their point of view they are New York provincial. In one of his most brilliant drawings, Saul Steinberg has caught this attitude precisely. I refer to his famous drawing—it originally appeared as a *New Yorker* cover—in which New York, from Ninth Avenue to the Hudson River, takes up all the foreground, with the world west of the Hudson given far less space than Ninth and Tenth Avenues. As I have said, New York sometimes seems as if it were the center of the universe, but to the New York provincial it *is* the center of the universe.

Even in its best days, New York has not been a narcotic that everyone could get high on. It has had its detractors, firm and fierce and famous. One of these was H. L. Mencken, who, in his essay "On Living in Baltimore," praised Baltimore by way of flogging New York. Mencken himself lived in the same house in Baltimore, the house he was born in, for nearly his entire life, and his chief complaint against New York was the transience of arrangements there. "What makes New York so dreadful, I believe," he wrote, "is mainly the fact that the vast majority of its people have been forced to rid themselves of one of the oldest and most powerful of human instincts—the instinct to make a permanent home." The average New Yorker, Mencken thought, was a vagabond. "He takes on the shallowness and unpleasantness of any other homeless man." True enough, it is difficult to imagine a New Yorker of the current day living in the same place for his entire life, let alone two generations of a family doing so. Years before Mencken, Henry James remarked that New York's buildings, even its skyscrapers, were "notes in the concert of the expensively provisional into which your supreme sense of New York resolves itself." In New York, transience has always been permanent.

This state of permanent transience gives New York its jagged quality, its jumpy rhythms. Robert Benchley, in a comic piece entitled "So You're Going to New York," advises tourists to study points of interest, then adds, "Most of these will either have been torn down or closed." That was written in 1929, and things have only worsened since. To the regular tearing down and rebuilding of patches of the city has been added every sort of strike: of newspapers, garbage collectors, transit workers. Then in recent years, the city for a time went, as the boys on Wall Street say, belly-up—kaput, tap city, bankrupt. Yet New Yorkers play through. Life in New York is assumed to be not business but chaos as usual.

The chaos of New York has had odd literary consequences. Although no other American city has had more writers among its denizens, there is not now, nor has there ever been, a novelist of New York in the way that Dickens was the novelist of London or Balzac the novelist of Paris. Different novelists have carved out different parts of New York, from Edith Wharton to Isaac Bashevis Singer, but none has ever taken on the city whole. Even Henry James, self-described as "the restless analyst," felt that New York was altogether too changeable, too volatile, to stand still long enough for literary analysis. In *The American Scene* James writes: "On New York soil . . . one is almost impudently cheated by any part of the show that pretends to prolong its actuality or to rest on its present basis. Since every part, however blazingly new, fails to affect us as doing more than hold the ground for something else, some conceit of the bigger dividend, that is still to come, so we may bind up the aesthetic wound, I think, quite as promptly as we feel it open."

A less refined view—my own, actually—holds that New York is a damnably difficult place for getting the chair up to the desk, always the first step in literary composition. Walt

Whitman once called New York "a good market for the harvest but a bad place for farming." For myself, I never wrote less than when I lived in New York. Most writers I know who live there tend to do their work on extended compositions—novels, memoirs, biographies, histories—outside New York: in summer spas in the Hamptons or on Martha's Vineyard, or at Yaddo or the MacDowell and other writers' colonies. New York offers too many distractions for sustained work; too much else is going on; things are too agitated. Even now, at the conclusion of my two- or three-day business trips to New York, I unfailingly return with a stiff case of what the French call *le surmenage intellectuel*, or brain fag, mental exhaustion.

New York must be the most talky city on earth, and I wonder if this talkativeness isn't related to New York's being so Jewish a city. William Cobbett objected to London because it had so many Jews, Quakers, and readers of the *Edinburgh Review*. New York has few Quakers and no readers of the *Edinburgh Review*, but Jews in plenty. Second only to Tel Aviv, I seem to have read somewhere, New York has more Jews than any other city in the world. In *The 42nd Parallel*, the first novel in his *U.S.A.* trilogy, John Dos Passos has Janey Williams, his sad little stenographer, remark upon her arrival in New York, "but everyone looked Jewish." This is not a bad observation, for in time everyone in New York does come to look Jewish, including most non-Jews. After a while the horses pulling cabs in Central Park look Jewish; even the eggs benedict come to look Jewish. Say what you like about the Jews—though not around me, please, since I am myself Jewish—but they are rarely dull. Get two Jews together, an old proverb has it, and you are certain to discover three factions and four arguments.

However much Jews lend to the spirit of contemporary New York, even Jewish vivacity and powers of endurance can be defeated by the city. On my last trip to New York, I drove in from La Guardia with a cabdriver named Alexander Zemonovitch, a Soviet Jew who has been living in New York for the past four years. In his middle twenties, bright and linguistically talented, he lives with a wife and young son in Brooklyn. He had left the Soviet Union on his own at eighteen, stopping en route in Italy for three years, and while he was very glad to be out of the Soviet Union, much of his conversation was about how difficult life in New York could be—this from a man who had grown up in a country whose leaders habitually treat its populace as if it were a conquered people. Still, one knows what he means. New York is a tough city to crack. Alexander Zemonovitch viewed himself as cut out for better things than driving a cab; yet, with a family and the expensiveness of New York, he was, for the time being, locked in. Day-to-day life in New York is a struggle.

I see New York only as a visitor, and usually an expense-account one at that, but there are times when the costliness of the city takes my breath away. A room for two at a good, though not top, hotel runs between $84 and $130. I recently met a friend at the Palm Court in the Plaza, where we had a pot of tea and two pieces of cheese cake; the bill, before tip, was $12.80. Why, I wondered, $12.80? Why not $37.15? Or $72.40? Trips to New York forced me, an economic puritan, to acquire an American Express card, for in visiting New York I could never be certain how much money I would need; and nowadays, to ring a change on the American Express commercial, I'd sooner leave home without me. But this costliness is part of the vigorish that New York extracts from visitors and natives alike. The priciness of the place is part of the dues that come with living in a world city, and what is of interest is the number of people who are willing to pay them.

"I should think," wrote Justice Holmes to Lewis Einstein,

when the latter was thinking of settling in New York at the end of his diplomatic career, "New York would be disagreeable unless one were rich or beginning a career." As one who is neither rich nor beginning a career, I tend to agree with Holmes's remark, and increasingly over the years I have begun to find New York's splendors outweighed by its horrors. Not that I am able to hold this view consistently. Sometimes New York seems nothing less than the treasure house in which all our culture's prizes are stored. Sometimes it seems nothing less than decline and fall made flesh, and I find, walking the city's streets, that I am unable to make a first-and-ten without passing a woman weeping, a man stirring around in garbage, or some other episode of human sadness and dilapidation. As a friend of mine, a naturalized New Yorker in my position—neither rich nor beginning a career—has put it: "You either develop the calluses needed for this city when you're young or it's quite an impossible place to live in." I thought I had developed the necessary calluses, but apparently I had not. I now no longer think that I can live in New York.

Yet I wonder if it is New York or I that has changed. Jan Morris, writing in *Rolling Stone*, reports that people believe New York reached its zenith between the Depression and the end of World War II. But literary evidence suggests otherwise. Thus, Edith Wharton, writing in 1906, notes that the New York of her youth, in the 1870s and 1880s, was a very special place, but it is finished now. Theodore Dreiser, writing in the early 1920s, notes that New York, when he arrived there in 1906, was a very colorful place, but it is all quite drab now. F. Scott Fitzgerald, writing in 1932, comments that New York, when he came to live there in the early 1920s, was a glamorous place, but it is so no longer. Saul Bellow, who remembers the New York of his young manhood as a city of intellectual excitement, says of it today, "It depresses me—there's such a sense of malignancy and despair." Fitzgerald, in his essay "My Lost City," described coming upon the young Edmund Wilson out for his afternoon walk in Manhattan as embodying Fitzgerald's idea of the "Metropolitan spirit." But in his last letter to Vladimir Nabokov, in 1971, Edmund Wilson writes, "We are eager to leave New York, which is now absolute hell. I don't know whether I can bring myself ever to come here again."

New York, as I think the above makes plain, is, if not quite a metaphor for youth, then best seen through youthful eyes. I am still far from achieving Edmund Wilson's utter disdain for the place, but already New York is coming to seem too tumultuous, too obstacle-laden, simply too much. I no longer harbor fantasies of returning to the city rich and famous—a small ticker-tape parade in my honor, standing applause as I walk into Sardi's, no argument or dirty look when I pay a cabdriver with a twenty. Does this mean that my own youth, belatedly and yet finally, is now over? I do not much cotton to the notion that the needle of my thoughts about New York is now stuck on that dreariest of clichés about the city—that it is a nice place to visit but, thank you very much, I shouldn't care to live there. "The man who is tired of London," said Dr. Johnson, "is tired of life." The same, I suspect, is true of New York. That worries me. So when I say, as I do now, "You take Manhattan," I can only say it equivocally, with regret, considerable self-doubt, and no real pleasure in the rejection.

About Face

"AT FIFTY," wrote Orwell, "everyone has the face he deserves." I believe this and repeat it with confidence, being myself forty-six and hopeful that for me there is still time. I hope, that is, that within the next four years I shall be able to develop a noble brow, a strong chin, a deep and penetrating gaze, a nose that doesn't disappoint. This may take some doing, for I have been told by different people at different times that I resemble the following odd cast of characters: the actors Sal Mineo, Russ Tamblyn, and Ken Berry, the scholar Walter Kaufmann, the assassin Lee Harvey Oswald, and a now-deceased Yorkshire terrier named Max. Despite this, and even though no one has ever noted a resemblance in me to Alexander the Great or Lord Byron, I tend to think of myself, as I expect most men do, as a nice-enough looking chap. Beyond that I am not prepared to go, for I have long appreciated the fact that the limits of self-knowledge begin at one's own kisser. To have stared at the damned thing so long and yet still not to know what it reveals is a true tribute to the difficulties of self-analysis. So while I tend to believe, with Orwell, that everyone has the face he deserves, I gaze into the mirror and cannot tell whether justice has been done.

The notion that the face is a text to be read for clues to

human character is one with a long history. It goes back at least as far as Aristotle, among whose works is that entitled *History of Animals and A Treatise on Physiognomy*. Almost all work in physiognomy, the putative science dealing with the connection between facial features and psychological characteristics, has been disqualified, and the *Encyclopædia Britannica*, in a brief article on the subject, notes: "Since many efforts to specify such relationships [between facial features and personal character] have been discredited, the term physiognomy commonly connotes pseudoscience or charlatanry (see Fortunetelling; Palmistry)." Which makes very good sense, except that I cannot bring myself altogether to believe it. On the subject of physiognomy, I find myself in the condition of a man I once heard about who, at the end of a career of thirty-odd years working for the Anti-Defamation League, remarked that, after fighting all that time against every racial and religious stereotype, he had come to believe that perhaps there was more to these stereotypes than he had thought when he had started on the job. Rather like that man, I fear that, while I believe physiognomy to have been largely discredited, there may be more to it than an intelligent person is supposed to allow.

But let me take a paragraph to hedge, qualify, and tone down what I have just written. I do not, for example, believe that a large head implies great intelligence, or even that a high forehead implies ample intellectual capacity, though apparently Shakespeare, himself well-endowed in this respect, did. Nor do I believe that a strong jaw inevitably translates into a character of great determination. I do believe, with the poet, that the eyes are the windows of the soul; yet I do not go so far as to say that Elizabeth Taylor, who has the most beautiful public eyes of our day, therefore has the most beautiful soul. I do not believe bad teeth or bad skin symbolic of a grave flaw in character. The handsomest man of our day is Harry Belafonte, but I am not prepared to say that, being the handsomest, he is also the best man. No, if anything, my perceptions here tend to run contrariwise: I wonder why so many people I know who have been dealt features neither elegant nor intrinsically interesting are often, in my view, quite beautiful. Or why many others with quite regular, even pretty features seem to have faces quite without interest: take a good look at your local television anchorman or anchorwoman. The mystery of personality is written in the human face—this I do believe. But, as with all truly intricate mysteries, this one must be read subtly, patiently, penetratingly.

Allow me to bring forth a text and a truly penetrating reader. I recently found an extraordinary exercise of this kind in the letters of St.-John Perse, the Nobel Prize-winning poet whose real name was Alexis Leger. Leger was asked by Jacques Rivière what he, Leger, thought of André Gide based solely on some photographs of Gide that Rivière had sent him. Leger writes:

The image, so far as I am able to call it up in my memory, was finally that of a type of man who is basically "serious," incurably serious, much more serious than he would like to appear. I also think that there are, behind that intent kind of face (nose, temples, mouth, and chin) a more painstaking recourse to duplicity, more tentative probings and ruses, more solicitations, in short, than were ever attributed to the impatient Ulysses. The man with the calabashes whom you presented to me in one of the photographs—didn't he look a little as if he were putting something over on himself? Besides, it's quite possible that this sort of man starts out by lying in the same way that one may be imploring—in order to enrich oneself and be tempted on every side, so as to end up liberating oneself, by which I mean, remaining free. But I also think there is something else about Gide, if the photographs didn't betray him, a very methodical urge to charm, a kind of real "coquettishness"—mere subservience and politeness, maybe, in order to keep a safer distance. (I'd prefer it to be only that!) There is usually in the faces of these fruit-tasters a whole elaborate cultivating of instability, dissatisfaction, and irreducible loneliness. And in the Gide you showed me, there was something more, especially in the jaws and hands, which in my eyes is—quite paradoxically—the highest and rarest quality, the mark of a thoroughbred, in an artist as in all other men—an enormous "good sense."—Stubbornness, too, most unexpected beneath so much flexibility.—And sadness, too, to be expected, beneath this art of yielding. Finally, this live human being will find out what it means to be abandoned along the way by all those who settle down; and perhaps he will nevertheless lead two generations of men toward their goals. But if what you wanted to know from me is this, I would trust in, but have little taste for, Gide's friendship—because I firmly believe that a man of this sort intoxicates himself with friendship more than he actually attaches himself to a friend.

From all that I have read of and about Gide, this brilliantly perceptive passage is on target; in fact, it is rather better than entire books devoted to Gide. How did Leger do it? Only, I suspect, by the same method that T. S. Eliot said one becomes a good critic: by being very intelligent.

Although I have never come anywhere near reading a face so well as Alexis Leger read André Gide's, I have always had an intense interest in faces and from as early as I can remember have watched them the way bird-watchers do birds. One of the pleasures that living in a large city provides is the delight of viewing a large human aviary. Can there be any doubt that the human face, even though it is of a very long run, is still the best game in town? Consider: we are all playing with essentially the same cards—eyes, a nose, a chin, a mouth, cheeks, eyebrows, hair, ears, a forehead—dealt out on the cloth of skin over the front of our skulls. But how inexhaustibly interestingly these cards have been dealt. Noses retroussé or Gogolian, lips sensuous or forbidding, eyebrows wispy or bushy, cheeks puffy or gaunt, chins prognathous or nonexistent, eyes though available in a limited number of colors nonetheless of limitless expressive possibilities—what variety, what modalities within the variety, what variegation within the modalities!

The given in the human face is, of course, heredity. Yet I wonder if heredity—providing skin and eye and hair color, bone structure, et cetera—really furnishes anything more than the broad canvas on which the more delicate and interesting strokes are painted by time and personal fate. What usually makes a face interesting—a priggish nose, quizzical eyebrows, sarcastic lips, lines and wrinkles oddly placed—is there as a result not of heredity but of experience. What time does to a face is most fascinating of all, and I sometimes think that no face, unless it be one of rare beauty or especial hideousness, is of great interest—rather like wine that hasn't had time to age properly—much before thirty.

How difficult to predict what time will do to a face! One of the things that makes prediction so difficult is that, on occasion, the passage of a face from youth to age is, or seems, so very predictable. Before me are the two Pléiade volumes devoted to the work of Paul Valéry (1871–1945). On the cover of the first is a photograph of the young Valéry, dressed in Proustian style, mustachioed, wearing a wide cravat, dark hair combed across his forehead. On the cover of the second, taken I should guess some thirty-five years later, Valéry's dark hair has turned gray and grown sparser; the cravat has been turned in for a polka-dotted bow tie; the mustache, though less carefully trimmed and now gray, is still intact. The progression from the youthful to the elder face is unmistakably of a piece: the face of the older Paul Valéry records the journey from passion to wisdom, from the poet to the Academician.

But consider another poet, W. H. Auden, on whose face time seems to have played every trick it knows, including changing the very shape of his face. The face of the young Auden was elongated, the ears stuck out prominently; it is a somewhat rural, yokel-like face, unmarked and, at least in photographs, not very interesting. The face of the older Auden is almost too interesting; it is scarcely a face at all but more like a mug of the kind produced by the Royal Doulton Company, a boon to descriptive writers, a face all topography, whose surface might be likened to a map of the moon or of the New Jersey interstate highway system or of the underground lines of Commonwealth Edison. The face of the older Auden resembles nothing so much as a face turned inside out, registering a hash mark for every anxiety and dissipation the poet had ever undergone. The boy cannot be discovered in the face of the man.

Perhaps it is impossible to predict the way a face will age. Most people of a physiognomic bent tend to work backward, which is to say from hindsight. Thus, to cite an example, Richard Perceval Graves, the recent biographer of A. E. Housman, writes of Housman's father: "Photographs of Edward [Housman] reinforce the impression of a man who has inherited some of his father's intelligence, but more of his determination than of his judgment. The mouth and jaw are firm, even obstinate, but the eyes are weak and uncertain." But this reading is entirely ex post facto; Mr. Graves already knows that A. E. Housman's father, though in some ways determined, even obstinate, was a man of poor judgment, uncertainty, and weakness. What he first found in the man's life he afterward discovered in his face. It is the way most of us work.

Yet read faces we must, for however unreliable a method it may be, none other exists for taking at least a rough measure of others. The face, the seat of four of the five human senses, is also the meter of the emotions. The art of the actor is based on this fact. Feelings veiled in fleshy shadows, secret enmities that must not be misread, insincerities that the voice and even the mouth may be able to disguise but not the eyes—all these are to be found in the face. Goodwill and admiration, possibly even love, are writ in the disposition of facial features, and these, too, must be correctly gauged. The significance of a tic could be decisive to one's fate.

Control of facial features is the first requisite for going out into polite—and, even more important, impolite—society. "False face must hide what the false heart doth know," wrote Shakespeare. Yet many are the occasions when false face must also hide what true heart knows, lest needless offense be given. To be too poker-faced won't do either, unless one happens to be a poker player. Some jobs—that of headwaiter, judge, pros- titute—call for a certain fixity of face. That of diplomatist is another. Recall Proust's M. de Norpois, of whom the novelist writes: He "would preserve a facial immobility as if you had been addressing some ancient and unhearing bust in a mu- seum. Until suddenly, falling upon you like an auctioneer's hammer, or a Delphic oracle, the Ambassador's voice, as he replied to you, would be all the more impressive, in that noth- ing in his face had allowed you to guess what sort of impression you had made on him, or what opinion he was about to ex- press."

Proust is a writer greatly fascinated by faces, and his pages are filled with the subtlest observations upon the human face. He thought "the nose is generally the organ in which stupidity is most readily displayed." In *Swann's Way*, he writes: "Later on, when in the course of my life, I have had occasion to meet with, in convents for instance, literally saintly examples of practical charity, they have generally had the brisk, decided, undisturbed, and slightly brutal air of a busy surgeon, the face in which one can discern no commiseration, no tenderness at the sight of suffering humanity, and no fear of hurting it, the face devoid of gentleness or sympathy, the sublime face of true goodness." Yet Proust never really describes a face in anything like full detail. Of M. Swann he tells us only of his "arched nose and green eyes, under a high forehead fringed with fair, almost red hair, dressed in the Bressant style." For Proust it is the face in action that is of the greatest interest—the face as an index for a feeling mind.

But not for all other novelists. Here is George Eliot describing the faces of the Gascoigne family in *Daniel Deronda:*

It was a noticeable group that these three creatures made, each of them with a face of the same structural type—the straight brow, the nose suddenly straightened from an intention of being aquiline, the short upper lip, the short but strong and well-hung chin: there was even the same tone of complexion and set of the eye. The grey-haired father was at once massive and keen-looking; there was a perpendicular line in his brow which when he spoke with any force of interest deepened; and the habit of ruling gave him an air of reserved authoritativeness.

Now if you can make out what the Gascoignes look like, you are a better reader than I. The straight brow, the short upper lip, the perpendicular line in the brow, the well-hung chin— although George Eliot has given me all the parts, I cannot assemble a convincingly vivid face out of them. She herself must have known this, for later in the same novel, George Eliot wrote: "Attempts at description are stupid: who can all at once describe a human being? even when he is presented to us we only begin that knowledge of his appearance which must be completed by innumerable impressions under differing circumstances. We recognize the alphabet; we are not sure of the language."

The great writers knew that the human face cannot be got

down on the page. Although Homer, Shakespeare, and Marlowe all wrote about Helen of Troy, none of the three actually attempted to describe her. Elizabeth Bennet, the heroine of Jane Austen's *Pride and Prejudice,* goes similarly undescribed, leaving every intelligent woman to believe that Elizabeth probably resembles her. Henry James, who did describe his heroines, always did so by way of indirection, limning in delicious touches, suggesting rather than fully describing, as in the following portrait of the Princess Casamassima:

She was fair, shining, slender, with an effortless majesty. Her beauty had an air of perfection; it astonished and lifted one up; the sight of it seemed a privilege, a reward. . . . Her dark eyes, blue or grey, something that was not brown, were as kind as they were splendid, and there was an extraordinary light nobleness in the way she held her head. . . . Purity of line and form, of cheek and chin and lip and brow, a colour that seemed to live and glow, a radiance of grace and eminence and success—these things were seated in triumph in the face of the Princess, and her visitor, as he held himself in his chair, trembling with the revelation, questioned if she were really of the same substance with the humanity he had hitherto known.

Yet outward beauty for Henry James is never quite to be trusted. In the novels of Henry James, as Desmond MacCarthy once neatly formulated it, only the good are beautiful, and there are no shortcuts to being good. Perhaps James had learned this lesson early, for one remembers his own meeting, at the age of twenty-six and described in a letter to his father, with George Eliot:

To begin with she is magnificently ugly—deliciously hideous. She has a low forehead, a dull grey eye, a vast pendulous nose, a huge mouth, full of uneven teeth and a chin and jaw-bone *qui n'en finnissent pas.* . . . Now in this vast ugliness resides a most powerful beauty which, in a very few minutes, steals forth and charms the mind, so that you end as I ended, in falling in love with her. Yes behold me literally in love with this great horse-faced blue-stocking. I don't know in what the charm lies, but it is thoroughly potent.

James's description of George Eliot recalls Stravinsky's remark about Nijinsky's "beautiful but certainly not handsome face." Beautiful but not handsome—one might apply this same formulation to the face of Samuel Johnson or of David Hume or of Leo Tolstoy, who had a potato nose roughly of the kind that the unknown sculptor gave to the actor Karl Malden. Now Karl Malden does not seem to me to qualify as having a face beautiful but not handsome, yet among actors Humphrey Bogart and Edward G. Robinson do. So does Fred Astaire, even though he has a disproportionately large forehead, ears that stick out, and an odd chin. Coming at things the other way, Robert Redford strikes me as very handsome but not at all beautiful. The most interesting faces, in my view, are the by no means conventionally handsome ones from which beauty nonetheless shines forth. Stan Laurel and Buster Keaton were beautiful; Milton Berle and Johnny Carson are not.

To be conventionally handsome or pretty, on the other hand, seems to me to carry certain penalties. Life seems almost too easy for the patently good-looking—as if, having one of life's most charming gifts, beauty, to begin with, why should they struggle like the rest of us for those rewards that come only by dint of effort. I once heard two eminent scholars comment about a young scholar that he might be too good-looking ever to do any serious work. When a beautiful woman writes—the young Mary McCarthy, say, or the young Susan Sontag—one feels rather as Dr. Johnson did about the dog walking on his hind legs: the wonder is that they do it at all. To be too good-looking is sometimes to incur the dislike, if not the hatred, of the ordinary-looking. The actors John Barrymore, Errol Flynn, and Rock Hudson fall, for most men,

into the category of the offensively good-looking. (Whether a
similar category exists for women I do not know, though I
suspect it must.) I have also known men who have broken off
with women because they were too beautiful, and to be out in
public with them, where they were the cynosure of all other
men's eyes, made these men greatly uneasy.

Beneath the gorgeous exteriors of too good-looking men
and women one expects a corresponding gorgeousness of soul.
Thus the too good-looking have far to fall, unlike the truly
homely, in whom beautiful actions are generally greeted as
such a pleasant surprise. Most of us expect to discover a correla-
tion between face and soul, and indeed between body and face.
How many times have I heard it said of a very fat woman, "But
she has such a pretty face," as if every fat woman ought to have
a misshapen face to go with her misshapen body. Fat women
have pretty faces almost as invariably as old men are wonderfully spry and kings kindly. It is one of the thousands of small
clichés we live by.

Another question is why some faces are photogenic and
others are not. It may be that good bones render one more
photogenic, but good bones do not necessarily make for a good
face. Photographs, like statistics, often lie. Except in the hands
of a photographer who is himself an artist, the camera generally
misses what is most interesting in the human face. The reason
is that faces are almost always most striking in animation. Or
an element or aspect is missed by the camera lens. F. Scott
Fitzgerald, for example, is generally spoken of as being strikingly handsome; from his photographs, though, he has never
seemed so to me. I gather that the color of his hair, eyes, and
skin must have contributed greatly to his good looks; and it is
color that is missing from the photographs we have of him.
Some people, on the other hand, seem almost too pliantly
camera-ready. Truman Capote, for instance, has for me the

look of someone who has been photographed much too often, the equivalent of a woman who has slept with too many men.

Does that last sentence strike you as goofy? Does it ring sexist, mystical, a mite mad? In his novel *Mr. Sammler's Planet*, Saul Bellow has a woman character whom he describes as showing, through her eyes, evidence of having slept with too many different men. Do such things show in the eyes? John Brophy, in his fine book, *The Human Face Reconsidered*, writes of the eyes, "Although the eyes can thus make vivid communications, their power of expression is restricted: they can plead but not argue; they can state but not analyze; they can declare effects but are helpless to explain causes." Still, to plead, state, or declare effects is to do a very great deal. The eyes are generally conceded to be the most expressive part of the face, though some say that the mouth can be equally expressive. But in this matter I go with the Polish proverb that runs, "Watch closely the eyes of him who bows the lowest."

I know I need to look at, if not deeply into, the eyes of someone with whom I am talking. I find myself slightly resentful—perhaps irritated comes closer to it—at having to talk to someone wearing sunglasses. Worst of all are those mirrored-lens sunglasses that, when you look into them, throw back two slightly distorted pictures of yourself, rather like old-time funhouse mirrors. I like eyes not only to be up front, where God put them, but out front, where I can see them.

What goes for eyes goes for other facial features. The ears are said to be the least expressive parts of the face—some talented people can twitch theirs while the ears of others redden when they lie or are under stress—but, in men at any rate, I prefer not to shoot conversationally till I see the lobes of their ears, a thing not always possible under the dispensation of recent masculine hairdos. Charles de Gaulle had big ears; John O'Hara had ears that stuck out from his head; and so do my own, though I do not own up to this fact easily. None of us, I suspect, easily owns up to his own irregularities. I was recently to be met at an airport by someone I had never met before. When I asked him what he looked like, so that I might recognize him upon arrival, he said he was blond, had a mustache, and would be wearing a blue suit. All of which turned out to be quite true, except that he neglected to mention that he also weighed around three hundred pounds.

In the matter of face, what the beholder has become accustomed to is crucial. On people who wear them regularly, eyeglasses come to seem as normal a part of their faces as their eyebrows, and it is often a bit of a surprise to see such people remove their glasses, giving them, momentarily, the look of someone who has freshly emerged from a lengthy underwater swim. Makeup for women, as another example, is now so standard an accessory that no one questions it. Except for brief intervals—the Victorian and Edwardian ages were two such intervals, according to James Laver, the historian of clothes and fashion—women have from biblical times "painted their faces," as was said of Jezebel. Yet no woman who uses makeup today would be judged Jezebelian, and most women, and their men, would agree with the poet Jacques Reval who, in his poem "Macquillage," wrote:

> Leave Nature's crudity to those
> Who'll take it, willy-nilly,
> I study to perfume the rose,
> I *like* to gild the lily.
> And you, my Love, as I have said—
> And I've no cause to doubt it—
> Can safely add a touch of red,
> Who are so sweet without it.

From cosmetics it is a long but all-too-natural jump to cosmetic surgery, as plastic surgery is now called. "God hath given you one face and you make yourselves another," wrote Shakespeare in *Hamlet*, in what might apply nicely as the cosmetic surgeon's motto. Although cosmetic surgery has done wondrous things in repairing facial damage incurred in fires or other accidents, increasingly a great deal of it is done to improve the work of the unknown sculptor. If one's features can be viewed as cards dealt to one in a poker game, the advent of cosmetic surgery has turned the game into draw poker. One can, with the aid of money to pay the surgeon, throw away two or three disagreeable cards—a comical nose, a weak chin, sunken cheeks—for new ones. Or one can draw new cards— a face lift, removal of bags from under the eyes—to cheat time. Under the aegis of cosmetic surgery, every man (or woman) can become his own Dorian (or Dora) Gray.

The arrangement of hair can do much to change the appearance of a face. Some hairdos soften a woman's face, others make it appear more severe. Baldness in certain men can be a positive feature, rendering them even better-looking than they might be with hair. Men have in their facial arsenal the additional weapons of mustaches and beards. I have friends who have worn beards for so long now that I have to strain to remember what they looked like clean-shaven. Some years ago, and while on holiday, I myself attempted to grow a mustache; I believe I had a cavalry effect in mind, but after two weeks I rather more resembled one of those nondescript *federales* in *The Treasure of the Sierra Madre*. Some masculine faces are what I think of as beard-optional. Aleksandr Solzhenitsyn, who is quite unthinkable without his defiant beard, is not among them. One of the most devastating put-downs I have ever been witness to occurred in the office of a man who, far from suffering fools gladly, did not suffer them at all. A co-worker was foolish enough to ask this man if he noticed anything different about him. The man looked up, briefly and contemptuously, to mutter that he didn't. His co-worker said that what was different was that he had shaved off his mustache. The man, this time without bothering even to look up, said, "I didn't know you had one."

In my neighborhood there walks a man who—through a war injury? a fire? an industrial accident?—has had the left side of his face blown away. Where features once were, a drape of flesh has been drawn. He is small, tidy, wears a cap, and through his walk and general demeanor gives an impression of thoughtfulness. The effect upon first seeing him is jolting. Life must be hard for him, and one wonders if he has ever grown inured to watching strangers recoil upon initial sight of him. But why is one jolted, why does one recoil? As much as from anything, I think it has to do with one's inability to read his face. One cannot sense his mood or know what he is (even roughly) thinking—and the result is disconcerting in the extreme.

Reading Faces by Leopold Bellak, M.D., and Samm Sinclair Baker not only maintains that the project of reading faces is a sensible one but offers a method for doing so. This method is called the Zone System, and the way it works is to divide the human face vertically down the center and horizontally under the eyes. It operates on the correct assumption that the face is asymmetrical. It speculates on the possibility that the division of the brain into left and right functions may have effects on the left and right sides of the face. One cannot say of this book, as Gibbon said of some *Lives* by Jerome, that "the only defect in these pleasing compositions is the want of truth and common sense." But as a self-help book it is, I think, helpful only in a very limited way. For example, by dividing a face horizontally one can sometimes determine that, though its mouth is smiling, its eyes are cold and scrutinizing. It is also interesting to note that, divided vertically, one side of a person's face can

seem cheery, while the other seems wary. One might go from
there to say that a face so divided may bespeak a person riven
in some fundamental way.

But whenever *Reading Faces* goes much beyond this it
becomes slightly suspect. Sensibly enough, its authors write,
"What one reads in the face are *potentialities*, from which
further inferences can be drawn—from conversation, observation, and experience with the person over a period of time."
The problem is, though, that most of the faces submitted for
study are those of well-known people from politics, sports, and
show business, and the analyses offered of their faces by the
authors are more than a touch commonplace. In some cases,
they show a political bias in favor of old-style New Deal
Democrats. Of Eleanor Roosevelt they write, "It is a most
unusual face about which one can only say good things." Having been brought up in a home in which Franklin and Eleanor
Roosevelt were well regarded, I tend to go along with this
reading. But where our authors find such traits in Mrs. Roosevelt's face as intelligence, compassion, and optimism, an old-
line Taft Republican could as easily find naiveté, smugness,
and self-righteousness.

One serious question about faces is whether one can find
beautiful or even agreeable-looking someone whom one de-
spises. Moral judgments, as Santayana noted, take precedence
over aesthetic ones, or at least do so for most of us. So when
confronted with a person one detests, perhaps the best one can
say is that he or she is very good-looking—yet one is likely to
add, "at least to the superficial observer." What makes this
observer superficial, of course, is that he is not privy to the real
lowdown about the despicable character in question. Yet how
much easier it is to read backward, through hindsight, from
behavior to evidence of behavior in the face. As John Brophy
reminds us, during Hitler's rise and early years in power, no

one detected the insanity we now see so clearly in his face. The aged, puffy, baby face of Winston Churchill, a cigar clamped in its mouth, might appear, to someone who has no knowledge of what Churchill accomplished, as a perfect subject for an anti-smoking poster.

Reading Faces being a self-improvement book, its authors suggest that one's own face might repay study in the coin of self-improvement. "The map of your face *can* be changed," they write, "resolving conflicts and strengthening feelings of self-esteem. This improvement will be reflected quickly or gradually in your facial expression." Specifically, they urge that one do all in one's power to make oneself seem a brighter, cheerier person—to put, in other words, a bit of gee-whiz in your phiz. Here they have hit home with this particular reader. I have been told innumerable times that I looked depressed, usually on occasions when I felt nothing of the kind. Is it necessary to say that the effect of being told this is itself quite depressing? Even more depressing is that I have never found a useful retort, though I have considered the following: "Depressed, me? On the contrary, I was thinking about sex." Or: "Yes, I have been feeling rather depressed of late. What has been getting me down is the Sino-Soviet dispute. Do you have time to talk with me about it?"

The genius of the unknown sculptor is to have created what sometimes seems a rather limited number of human facial types yet, within this limited number of types, an infinite variety. With only rare exceptions, almost every face one sees one has seen before, if not in life, then in the work of the great painters. Walking the streets one sees here a pair of kindly Holbeinesque lips; there the porcelain cheeks of a Botticelli; elsewhere the rubicund coloring of one of Bruegel's peasants; and sometimes a face taken over from Rembrandt entire. If flesh and bone be the material of the face, time supplies its varnish. And what extraordinary things time does, leaving this face unmarked, that one looking as if it were a salmon mousse left out in the rain. To read the effects of time on a face requires, as the New Critics used to call it, close reading. "For in order to understand how beautiful an elderly lady can once have been," Proust wrote, "one must not only study but interpret every line of her face."

Nothing so improves the appearance as a high opinion of oneself. Let this stand as the first in a paragraph riddled with risky generalizations. Love of one's work tends to make one's face interesting. Artists have animated faces, and performing musicians the most animated of all. Suffering, too, confers interest on a face, but only suffering that, if not necessarily understood, has been thought about at length. Uninterested people have uninteresting faces. In ways blatant or subtle, personality sets its seal on every face. Some people have historical seals set on their faces as well; thus some men and women walk the streets today with Romanesque, Elizabethan, or Victorian faces. Intelligence is more readily gauged in a face than is stupidity. As a final generalization, let me say that the more precisely one thinks of the relation of face to character, and the more carefully one attempts to formulate the connection between the two, the madder the entire business begins to seem.

Yet what choice have we but to continue reading faces as best we can, bringing to the job all that we have in the way of intuition, experience, intelligence? We read most subtly of course those people we know most closely: our friends, our known enemies, our families. In the faces of such people we can recognize shifting moods, hurt and pride, all the delicate shades of feeling. But of that person we supposedly know most intimately, ourself, the project remains hopeless. Study photographs of ourselves though we may, stare at ourselves in mirrors though we do, our self-scrutiny generally comes to naught. If you don't believe me, stop a moment and attempt to describe yourself to someone who has never seen you. The best I can do is the following: "I look a bit like Lee Harvey Oswald and I also rather resemble my dog, though I seem more depressed. You can't miss me."

Onomastics, You and Me
Is Quits

SHOW ME a man or woman entirely happy with his or her name and I'll show you a somehow defective human being. Our name is another of those decisive items in life that we have not been called in to decide upon, another card dealt us while we were away from the table, along with the quality of our intelligence, our physique, the geographical and social location of our birth. However suitable it may appear to others, one's own name almost always seems rather a poor fit to oneself. But there it is, like a shoe that either pinches or flops loosely over the heel, and such as it is we are compelled to wear it through life. Names not our own generally seem more appropriate to us. For myself, had I been given a choice in my own name, I think I might have been content with Julian Havilan, or Jean-Louis Beaumarchais, though in earlier years the name Blackie Thurston had a certain ineffable allure for me.

Heraclitus says that character is destiny, but I wonder if, when accounting for destiny, one's name ought not to be thrown into the hopper as well. Until a few years ago there was, on the roster of the Chicago Bears, a wide receiver named

Golden Richards. Now Golden Richards sounds less like a name than a Homeric or Arthurian epithet. Is Mr. Richards happy with his name, shimmering thing that it is? Has that name determined much in his life—for example, his becoming a football player and in one of the more glamorous positions at that? The name Golden Richards is unthinkable in the middle of the line, at the position, say, of nose guard. The name seems to have been modeled to go with the phrase "touchdown by," as in "Touchdown by Golden Richards." Yet even this altitudinous name has potential problems. As Mr. Richards's career begins to fade, as he becomes less adept at what he does, will not sportswriters begin to talk about "Golden's tarnished record" or "Golden's hands of brass"? Every name, it seems, carries the seeds of its bearer's possible humiliation.

Be it in a given name or surname, a middle name or suffix to a name, somewhere in every name there lurks trouble for its owner. Either one's name is unpronounceable or inherently comic, pretentious or too plain, rhymes with or is reminiscent of something ignoble—one way or another cognominal impedimenta await nearly everyone. Even simple but uncommon names can cause problems. Four-letter names seem to be especially troublesome. I have known two men with the surnames, respectively, of Fike and Delp, and I have watched them wince as, inevitably, Fike (intended to rhyme with Mike) is pronounced Fick, and Delp, just as inevitably, was spelled by others as Delph or Delt. In the Army, in basic training, I served with a most unstuffy fellow named Daniel Thomas III. You can perhaps imagine what jollity the sergeants found in the poor fellow's regal suffix. "Hey, you, Third, get your [fill in your own blank] over to the orderly room!"

In the United States the comedy of names has been exacerbated by the fact that—apart from those people who emigrated from England, Scotland, Ireland, or Wales—so many immigrants found it convenient if not necessary to alter their names upon settling in their new country. H. L. Mencken has written charmingly and nearly exhaustively on this subject in his chapters on "Proper Names" in *The American Language* and in *Supplement Two* to *The American Language,* and much of what I know about the history of the subject I have learned—not to say lifted—from him. The names that first underwent change in America were those that were either unpronounceable or unspellable. Longish Slavic and Arabic names fell immediately. Many German names disappeared by way of translation: Schwartz to Black, for example, or Pfund to Pound. Greek names were dealt with by the clippers; Mencken cites the name Pappapolychronopoulos, which in America became Chronos. Still other names were altered by transliteration: Reuss becoming Royce, de l'Hotel becoming Doolittle. Now that ethnic feeling is running high in the United States, these name changes may in retrospect seem a betrayal of native heritage. Yet it can have been no comforting thing to have one's name perpetually bollixed up on the lips of one's newfound countrymen. My sympathies here are with the former Mr. Pappapolychronopoulos.

The most common American surnames offer few surprises. Among them are Smith and Johnson, Brown and Williams, Miller and Jones, trailed by Davis and Anderson, Wilson and Taylor, with Thomas and Moore, White and Martin not far behind. From this list it would appear that the United States remains chiefly a country of Protestants, most of English descent. The appearance, however, is wrong. Many of the Smiths were once Schmidts, the Johnsons Johannsons, the Moores Mohrs, the Millers Müllers, Davises Davidovitches. When we formulate demographic generalizations about the ethnic composition of America on the basis of certain common names, it is useful to remember that the Baltimore Orioles not long ago had an outfielder named Pat Kelly who is a Negro. Pershing, Hoover, Custer, Westinghouse, Rockefeller, to cite the names of five famous Americans, are none of them names that their forebears brought to this country; each was at some point altered as an accommodation to the less than supple Yankee larynx. "A self-made man," wrote Judge Learned Hand (and what a finely appropriate name his is!) "may prefer a self-made name."

But the greatest American name-changers have been the Jews—and for manifold reasons. In many European countries it was not until the late eighteenth and early nineteenth centuries that Jews were compelled to adopt surnames. Frequently the names officials gave them were deliberately outlandish, and Russian Jews often attempted to bribe those officials to avoid being stuck with ridiculous or even obscene names. The changing of Jewish names went on in the old world as well as in the new; perhaps the most famous old-world instance in this century being that of Leon Trotsky, née Bronstein. In the new world there is many a story about Jewish immigrants having names slapped upon them by impatient officials at Ellis Island. But generalizations here are difficult. Although many Jews seem more ready to change their names the further they get from the religious faith of their fathers, this is not everywhere so. In Israel, where anti-Semitism can scarcely be an issue, many Jews have shed names acquired in the Diaspora and taken on post-exilic or Israeli names, usually Hebrew in origin.

As so often in life, so with names: the grass is generally just as brown on the other side. Many a person with a plain surname would seem to prefer a gaudier handle. Primitive doctrine held that a man's or woman's name was intended to express his or her personality, and this doctrine, primitive though its origins may be, still retains some of its hold. I have rarely met a Smith or Jones who did not feel that his or her name was a bit too plain, too common—too drained, if not of distinction, then of the distinctiveness sufficient to express his or her by no means plain or common or indistinct personality. Whether they would be ready to trade in that Smith or Jones for a Scheittauer or an Abjørnsen is another question. Hollywood has long subscribed to the theory that names express personality. The actress Dyan Cannon (née something else) has the name she now bears because a Hollywood producer thought her looks required a name that was "explosive." Who is to say that, in their commercial instincts at least, the fantasy moguls of the West Coast were wrong? Would you go to see a movie starring Archie Leach and Issur Demsky, with Betty Perske in the female lead, a Gelbfisch Production? (Translation: a movie starring Cary Grant, Kirk Douglas, and Lauren Bacall, a Goldwyn Production.)

In this matter of names, apart from nomenclatural surgery or legal name changing, there appears to be nothing for it except to choose your parents with the greatest care—which is to say, there is nothing for it. Parents pass on surnames to their children, yet they confer first names—or, as they used to be called, Christian or baptismal or font names. I am at one with the father of Tristram Shandy in thinking that this is a serious matter, "that there was a strange kind of magic bias, which good or bad names, as he called them, irresistibly impressed upon our characters and conduct." I have always wondered, for example, why certain parents played the cruel trick on their children of matching up their names fore and aft, sending them into the world as Robert Roberts, or Thomas Thomas, or Johnny Johnson, or Edward Edwards? Possibly the only thing worse than a name of such silly symmetry is to have a first and last name that rhyme: Joan Cohen, say, or Art Hart. There is also the danger of names with internal rhymes.

In this respect the French literary critic Jacques Derrida is fortunate in not having been named either Gerald or Jerome; if he had, he might have been known to family and friends as Jerry Derrida.

Such names leave their bearers very much at the mercy of Profane Wits, a sect that never dies out. Profane Wits show up early in life; they take their basic training on gradeschool playgrounds, and God protect the fancifully named child from them, though, it must be said, He usually doesn't. I went to grade school with a boy named Cyril Jabowicz, whose chances for a quiet school career were demolished the first day he walked into kindergarten. He was roly-poly, wore glasses that perpetually slid down his nose even as his knicker stockings slid down his chubby calves; the only thing on him that seemed to stay up were his cowlicks, of which he had a fine crop. He was, in short, a mess—a real Cyril Jabowicz. This was a boy who needed a cognominal break. He needed to be Jim or Steve Jabowicz to have any kind of chance in life. But no such luck.

A Connolly or a Ritchard could get away with, even make elegant, a name such as Cyril, but a Jabowicz—never! Yet it is interesting how a particular bearer can bring dignity to an otherwise not particularly dignified name. What a debt the Freds of this world owe to the one whose last name was Astaire! Or take Oscar. In past decades it was borne by the pianist and show-business wit Oscar Levant—but only that, borne, like so many of the late Mr. Levant's tics, twitches, and other afflictions. Its diminutive, Ozzie, placed before the surname Nelson, as in that of the late bandleader, is no better than trivial. Before the name Hammerstein, Oscar becomes passable; before that of Handlin, a historian of solid accomplishment, it grows dignified. But in the name Oscar Robertson, a basketball player of seemingly limitless cool, skill, and physical grace—the Big O, as the sportswriters took to calling him—

Oscar becomes as elegant as its bearer, in fact almost princely. Yet not all names are subject to such transformation. Not Abraham Lincoln himself could have brought seriousness to the name Lum. Debbie, for women, seems to me similarly frozen; not even Rita Hayworth—Debbie Hayworth?—could have made it other than cloyingly cute.

Given names, of course, owe nearly everything to fashion, and what is of special interest in this connection is how long certain common names have stayed in use. E. G. Withycombe, in her very useful *Oxford Dictionary of English Christian Names*, remarks that "in the late 12th century and early 13th century there were probably more Christian names in use than at any subsequent period until the 20th century." Along with the old English names still in use, "there was the rich Norman stock with a sprinkling of Breton, in addition to the newly adopted saints' names which were drawn from Hebrew, Greek, Latin, and other tongues." But as the thirteenth century advanced, the number of names shrank, so that by the fourteenth century Henry, John, Richard, Robert, and William accounted for 64 percent of all masculine names. Biblical names came into fashion in the seventeenth century, Miss Withycombe reports, as part of the Puritan reaction against Catholic saints' names. But by the close of the eighteenth century the three commonest masculine names in England were William, John, and Thomas, and the three commonest feminine names were Elizabeth, Mary, and Anne.

For fairly obvious reasons, America followed England in the bestowal of given names. The most popular masculine names in America have been John, William, James, Charles, George, Thomas, Henry, Robert, Joseph, and Edward, while the most popular feminine names have been Anne, Dorothy, Elizabeth, Helen, Jane, Katherine, Margaret, and Mary. But it was very much in the cards that Americans would bring to their selection of first names an eclecticism that would have more than occasional comic effects. When ingenuity joins up with ignorance, pretension with a touch of poor taste, there are certain to be plenty of laughs all round.

H. L. Mencken simply couldn't get enough of comical American names, and in *Supplement Two* to *The American Language* he provided a list of more than twelve pages of nutty feminine names, from Adenesia through Jessoise through ReDonda and ending with Zzelle. From fancy spellings—Feby, Gladdis, Rhey, Qay—to monstrous inventions—Flouzelle, Vomera, Uretha, Margileth, Kewpie—Mencken prized every breach of tradition and decorum. But lest we think all goofy names are the province of the poor and uneducated, he adduced the names of Irita Van Doren, the reviewer for the old New York *Herald-Tribune,* and Tallulah Bankhead, and threw in for full measure a little list from the New York *Social Register* that included Ambolena, Dinette, Isophene, and Velvalee. It makes all too real that snippet of dialogue in Evelyn Waugh's *A Handful of Dust,* in which two women, thinking of how to interest the husband of one of them in another woman, have the following conversation:

"There's always old Sybil."
"Darling, he's known her all his life."
"Or Souki de Foucauld-Esterhazy."
"He isn't his best with Americans."

How do parents decide upon names for their children? "Ah, my son," says an American Indian in an old joke, "in our tribe a child is named for the first thing his father sees after being told of the infant's birth. I was fishing in the brook when I learned of your sister's birth, so I named her Laughing Brook. When informed of your older brother's birth, I was hunting, and a bear dashed across my path; hence your brother is now named Running Bear. Does this help you to understand how you came by your own name, Copulating Dogs?"

As names go, Copulating Dogs may be no bargain, but at least there is a certain logic in its mode of selection. Can the same be said for the major league infielder with the no-nonsense name of Mike Tyson who named his two sons Tory and Courtney? Or for the parents of the twin sisters who were University of Texas cheerleaders named Deirdre and Dawn Dodson? Or for the parents of the child—known to a friend of mine—who have named him Irony, and whose schooldays do not figure to be smooth.

A penchant for elegant names seems predominant at present. Novelists can be an aid in such choices, though there is nothing new about this. Goldsmith's Vicar, in *The Vicar of Wakefield*, complains that his wife, "who during her pregnancy had been reading romances," named their children after characters in novels. In our time I suspect that the influence of F. Scott Fitzgerald on the bestowal of names has been considerable. Above all, the name Scott among young men still under thirty has grown exceedingly common. Boys' names beginning with J that are tony and also hint at strength appear in the ascendant at the moment: Justin and Jason, Joshua and Jonathan. Among girls, Jessica and Jennifer are riding high, but then, J-less, so are Tracy and Stacy.

Nothing wrong with these names, of course, except that nowadays they are frequently harnessed to surnames with which they simply do not fit. Scott Schwartz is an example of a name I cannot hear without smiling. But this only proves that many people have neither a good ear nor any sense that one's name is at least a two-piece ensemble in which the pieces need to be worn together. Samantha O'Toole, Justin Lipschitz, Shannon Warshovski—these glistening first names joined with earthy ethnic names suggest something like the snug and elegant fit of a tiara worn over a baseball cap.

Some surnames present a problem of fit that is nearly insuperable: Klutz for one, Fink for another, Grubnik for a third. Finding a first name to go with any of them is no easy job. No less easy, I suppose, than those first names that are nearly impossible to mate up with last names. Obadiah, Uriah, and Zekedia are among such names; so, in an only slightly less exotic way, are Veronica, Hepzibah, and Hildegarde. Elmer and Clyde, which today seem rural names, are no picnic either. (In the National League in the 1940s there was a catcher named Clyde Kluttz—a man who, nomenclaturally, appears to have had the worst of both worlds.) If the choice of names appears of no moment, recall the question asked by Tristram Shandy's father: "Your Billy, Sir—would you, for the world, have called him Judas?" Which is itself a reminder that history can wreak hell on a name. After Hitler, Adolph, really a quite beautiful name, must be put in the cognominal freezer for at least a century and possibly much longer. In a less dramatic way, some years ago the comedian Jerry Lewis developed a character, the pure type of the nebbish, to whom he gave the name Melvin; for a long spell afterward no boy in America whose name was Melvin—and who could not pack a powerful punch —breathed easily. In the same wise, James Thurber's story "The Secret Life of Walter Mitty" softened up the name Walter, giving it, in the United States at least, a patina of milk toast.

Contrariwise, a big first name can do a good deal for a man. The name Alistair not only greatly enhances the rather plain name Cooke but, in a country as anglophile in its cultural interests as America is, such a name is an ornament nearly as valuable as an Oxbridge accent. As someone who thinks Alistair Cooke's reputation a hugely inflated one, I find it immeasurably helpful to let the air out of him, in my own mind if nowhere else, by thinking of him as Al Cooke.

Like endangered species, some first names seem to be dying out: Harry, Julius, and Max for men; Sylvia, Gladys, Fanny for women. In some seven years of teaching I do not recall having had a student named George or Alice. Other names apparently carry a time line; most men named Irving seem to have been born in the 1920s. The once-prevalent three-barreled names—Nicholas Murray Butler, Edwin Arlington Robinson, George Fielding Eliot, Raymond Gram Swing—are of an older vintage. In the late twenties through the early forties Jewish parents in the United States took to giving their sons English surnames for first names, names that have always seemed to me more appropriate for hotels: Seymour, Norman, Sheldon; Sherwin and Irwin; Arnold, Howard, and Myron. (A wit of my acquaintance suggested that such two-syllable names were excellent for calling a boy from the back porch: "Mor-ton!" "Har-vey!" "Mon-roe!") Southerners seem still to go in for two short given names back to back: Don Bob, Billy Ray, Johnny Jack. They also go in for diminutive versions of names, as witness Mrs. Carter's never referring to her husband as anything but "Jimmy." What, one wonders, is the outer age limit for a diminutive name? Can one still call a woman in her seventies "Judy"? Donald seems to be another of those names with a built-in youthful element, and to be a Mickey past fifty is unseemly, to say the least.

Most people, when naming their children, tend to select a name that has pleasant associations in their own experience. They frequently choose a name borne by solid or beautiful or winning people they have known or heard about. I never met a David I didn't like, at least during the first twenty-five or so years of my life. Yet I have never met a Seymour who didn't seem rather troublesome. But some names are altogether too common to apply the test of personal association to. Such names as Jack, Dick, and Tom, Tristram Shandy's father called "neutral names, affirming of them, without satire, That there had been as many knaves and fools, at least as wise and good men, since the world began, who had indifferently borne them. . . ." If the debit side of too common a name—Robert or Joseph, Mary or Barbara—is its undistinctiveness, the credit side is that it neither tells too much about one nor prejudices other people in one's disfavor straight off.

Better, surely, a quiet, even quite common name than one that perpetually confuses a person with someone else. Although my own fame as a writer is certainly slight, I once met a man, roughly twenty years older than I, whose name was the same as mine and who told me that on more than one occasion something I had written had been attributed to him. A good-humored fellow, he allowed that it was all right with him if I continued to write, but asked if I would mind muting my opinions a bit. Coming at things the other way, I not long ago discovered, in the obituary pages, that I also shared my name with a man well known as a bookmaker in the 1920s and 1930s. He turns out to have been a bookish bookie, of all things, and was described in the headline over his obituary as "Gentleman Bookie."

But greater, more maddening confusions abound. I know that on more than one occasion I have had to explain that John Wain, the excellent English writer, is not John Wayne, the cowboy impersonator. How often must Mr. Wain have had to suffer bad jokes about the similarity between his own name and —if you will pardon the familiarity—the Duke's! I note that a man at the Hoover Institution on War, Revolution and Peace is named W. Glen Campbell, the same name, less the first initial, of a particularly vacuous country-western singer. Tom Wolfe, the contemporary journalist, must have chosen to use his first name in the familiar form in order to distinguish himself from the novelist Thomas Wolfe. Willie Morris, I suspect, used the diminutive to distinguish himself not only from William Morris, the nineteenth-century writer and designer, but from the William Morris who gave his name to the famous talent agency.

Tom and Willie seem fit enough for Messrs. Wolfe and Morris, yet some people's names are unthinkable in the diminutive. Chuck de Gaulle, Maury Bowra, Wally Stevens—all are clearly impossible. Yet Eliot was called Tom by his friends; Russell was Bertie; and Churchill, Winnie. While many people do not mind having their names reduced to the familiar or diminutive, others are repelled by it. An acquaintance of mine, a fairly formal fellow, does not mind his name James being reduced to Jim but felt things had gotten out of hand when a real estate salesman he had met five minutes before addressed him as Jimbo. His wife, who was seated behind him at the time, reported that until that moment she had never realized the hairs on the back of her husband's neck had the ability to stand straight up.

Jimbo comes near to shading off from a diminutive to a nickname. A nickname is usually a form of verbal caricature, and behind most nicknames is the spirit of fun—though fun, be it said, that can sometimes turn a touch vicious. In *The Lore and Language of School Children,* Iona and Peter Opie remind one that perhaps the majority of childhood nicknames refer to physical irregularities, and their own categories of nicknames are divided off into those reserved for Fatties, Skinnies, Little 'Uns, Redheads, and the Funny Faced. Are nicknames among school children less frequent than they once were? My guess is that they are—a guess based on the weak fact that I seldom hear children in my own neighborhood call one another by anything other than their first names. But even if I am correct in this, I do not know whether it means that children have become kinder or just less imaginative.

In my own youth, nicknames did not set in in a big way until high school. Here is a short list of some of the more exotic; nearly all of them are by no means self-explanatory, but all have a touch of street poetry:

> Dickie "The Owl" Levinson
> Fred "Remus" Richmond
> Daniel "The Mikado" Brodsky
> Lloyd "The Lump" Stein
> Loren "Boss Tweed" Singer
> Leslie "Magwa" Handler
> Richard "Rags" Rosen
> Robert "Jose Nosé" Cole
> Harvey "Cess" Poole

Our crowd was, I have since come to believe, exceptionally fertile verbally, but I also believe that more energy went into nicknames then than now. Sports was a fecund field, and sportswriters awarded athletes such wondrous sobriquets as The Big Train, The Manassa Mauler, The Georgia Peach, Bullet-Bill, and Three-finger Mordecai Brown. The Granges' son Harold had a nickname and sobriquet both, being Red Grange, the Galloping Ghost. In baseball there was no shortage of Caseys, Babes, Dizzys, and Leftys, but, so far as I know, only one Yogi. Gangsters wore nicknames like hundred-dollar shirts, and no bigtime gangster seemed complete without one. This started in the 1920s but has carried over into the modern era, where we have had Murray "The Camel" Humphrey, Sam "Teets" Battaglia, and Tony "Big Tuna" Acardo. Al Capone's nickname was Scarface, though it was highly recommended never to call him that when meeting him.

Certain once-standard boys' nicknames seem to have departed the scene—Butch, Spike, Bud, Buzzy—and to have done so unmourned. The nickname Whitey must now be quite dead, a casualty of racial tensions. Red is still current, clinging to life even after outliving its accuracy when a man's red hair has turned white. Zoological nicknames hang on. Bear Bryant seemed apposite for the University of Alabama football coach, but Bunny has never seemed apposite for that most uncuddly of literary men, Edmund Wilson. Perhaps the best zoological nickname I have ever heard was in college, when I heard one young man refer to another as Pro. "Why Pro?" I asked. "It's short for Protozoan," I was told. "But why Protozoan?" "Because he is an organism of extremely simple organization."

Some nicknames derive from middle names. Even slightly irregular middle names, once revealed, can be a potential source of taunting by the Profane Wits of the playground. Let it be discovered that between his first and last name a boy is harboring a middle name such as Reginald, or Eustace (rhymes with Useless), or Percy, or Ezekiel, and his days generally become less easeful. According to George Philip Krapp, in his *The English Language in America*, "throughout the 17th and 18th centuries it was extremely rare for a person to bear more than one given name," and hence middle names were largely unknown. "But," Professor Krapp continues, "in the early 19th century in America, grandiosity was in the air." In many instances, especially among southerners, one kept one's mother's maiden name as a middle name, particularly if there were pretensions to aristocracy on the maternal side. The increasing bestowal of middle names also allowed one to spread around the largesse acquired in naming a child, for now he or she could be named after two persons instead of one. As for the people on whom middle names were bestowed, it gave them more nomenclatural material—"nomenclay"?—to work with in shaping names for themselves. They could thus use the three-barreled name, or two names parted by a middle initial, or a first initial followed by the middle and last name, or two initials in place of any given names, or drop the first name if it did not please them and use only their middle name.

As far as I am aware, only Americans seem to use a middle initial, as in Thomas L. Menzenberger. The English do not go in for it, and neither do the French. No major writer has ever used a middle initial, and merely to insert one betwixt the names of a few such writers is to make a bit of a mockery of the practice: William G. Shakespeare, or Dante P. Alighieri, or Marcel C. Proust. The best middle initials are the exotic ones. The Q. in the name James Q. Wilson is a fine touch, distinguishing, by separating, two otherwise very plain names. So too is the X. in Francis X. Bushman, an actor none of whose silent movies I remember ever having seen, but whose name, because of that X., I can never forget.

The two-initial ploy has had many fine adherents, among them W. C. Fields, O. J. Simpson, and L. L. Bean. It has been especially strong in the literary line, its adherents including D. H. Lawrence, H. L. Mencken, A. J. Liebling, T. H. White, the T. E.'s, Lawrence and Hulme, the V. S.'s, Pritchett and Naipaul, and T. S. Eliot. The last named gentleman, Mr. Eliot, made things a trifle hot for those who have chosen a first-initial approach to the name problem by his invention of the pathetic Mr. Prufrock, J. Alfred. F. Scott Fitzgerald has doubtless regained some ground for names of the first-initial kind (and much earlier there was a most interesting Numidian named L. Aurelius Augustinius, who later became known as Saint Augustine). But for me there has always been some hint of the con man, the spats-and-weskit-wearing bunko artist—as played by W. C. Fields—in first-initial names. One ought to be very rich, and probably Texan, to walk around with such a name. The editor of the journal *The American Spectator* carries the moniker R. Emmet Tyrrell, Jr., a name that has everything but a hyphen and represents a distinct case, it seems to me, of cognominal overload.

A radical change in one's name seems in most cases a betrayal—of one's birthright, of one's group, of one's own identity. The only classes of people who seem to be able to change their names, to throw off the names they were born with and take on a pseudonym without being subject to the above charge are crooks and authors. As a boy, I used to love to read the Wanted posters in the post office. Wanted: Joseph Gelatso, alias Joseph Gillette, alias Joe Geo, alias Joey Gee. Under which of those names, I used to wonder, did Mr. Gelatso commit his most serious crimes? As Joey Gee, clearly he had his pleasanter moments. Eric Blair, Cicily Fairfield, and Teodor Josef Konrad Korzeniowski became, respectively, George Orwell, Rebecca West, and Joseph Conrad—the first to shuck off the social class into which he was born, the second to name herself after a feminist heroine in Ibsen, the last to simplify his name for an English audience. Yet how right those names now seem, how completely their owners have taken possession of them!

Now a confession. As a magazine editor I once edited, actually changed, a man's name. I am changing his name again here to protect the guilty—myself—and so I shall call him A. Stephen Pottle. Mr. Pottle sent the magazine I worked for quite a good manuscript on a subject that much interested us. We accepted it, though with the proviso that he make certain alterations. Although it was clearly none of my damned business, something about that A. in his name put me off, so when I wrote to him I dropped his first initial in my correspondence. When he wrote to me, he put the A. back in his name. In my response I took it out again. What is more, when I sent his manuscript to the printer, I deleted the A. from his name yet again. If he had chosen to put it back on galley proof, I should of course have let it stand; after all, an author has certain rights, including that to his own name. As it turned out, he didn't, and the article appeared under the unadorned name Stephen Pottle. But if he had queried me about his disappearing first initial, asking what the devil was going on, I had determined to write back to him, "What do you want to be *A.* Stephen Pottle for, when you can be *the* Stephen Pottle?"

I do not say that one necessarily comes to love one's name, but gradually one grows used to it. Like thinning hair, or wide feet, one learns to live with it. From time to time one's name can even seem rather comfortable. One has, after all, worn it for so long; and, unlike nearly everything else in life, it truly isn't any the worse for wear. Still, hearing it so often, one can never altogether cease thinking about it. In *Old Possum's Book of Practical Cats*, T. S. Eliot wrote:

> When you notice a cat in profound meditation,
>   The reason, I tell you, is always the same:
> His mind is engaged in rapt contemplation
>   Of the thought, of the thought, of the thought of
>   his name:
>   His ineffable effable
>   Effanineffable
> Deep and inscrutable singular Name.

But, then, when it comes to our names, we are all rather strange cats.

Bookless in Gaza

WHEN I WAS A BOY OF TEN, perhaps eleven, a
student in the public schools of Chicago, our
class was paid a visit by a woman known as the Library Lady.
My memory of her is not altogether distinct, but I do recall her
being an older woman, large, and heavily made up, with a
bosom of a monumentality such as I believe has since been
rendered extinct by evolution. She was introduced to us as
being from the Chicago Public Library, downtown branch.
This did not unduly impress John Duncan, our class Huck
Finn, who during her visit, with the aid of a mini-slingshot
made of a rubber band and a paper clip, let fly with a spitball
that hit Norman Brodsky in the back of the neck. But I was
impressed as the Library Lady, in a drawl heavy with peda-
gogic drippings, began: "Class, books are your friends. They
will take you to foreign shores and bring you treasures hitherto
undreamed of." She went on to say that since books were our
friends we ought not to bend their spines or earmark their
pages or write in or otherwise deface them. The analogy did
not strike home with me, for I had not, so far as I knew, defaced
any of my friends or earmarked them or bent their spines. But
I did decide then and there that books were not, thank you very
much, any friends of mine.

Not that I was much of a reader before the Library Lady showed up. My problem, I now begin to think, was a happy childhood. As a very young child, my father read to me from a children's Bible and from Andersen's *Fairy Tales* and from *The Adventures of Robin Hood*, and while I liked all these well enough, I saw no reason to go further on my own. Life elsewhere offered too many fine and varied pleasures: the delights of the neighborhood, of sports, of comic books, and, on wintry afternoons and all Saturday mornings, such grand radio shows as *Jack Armstrong, Tom Mix, Frank Merriwell, Captain Midnight, Let's Pretend*, and *Tennessee Jed.* If any of my childhood friends were great readers, they kept it a secret, or at least I did not know about it. Great childhood readers, I have since discovered, were often—though not always—lonely or dreamy or unhappy children. I was none of these, and so books were far from being my idea of a good time.

If I started out with an uninterest in books, the Library Lady turned it into a mild antipathy with her little talk. I did later read the sports stories of John R. Tunis—*The All-American, The Kid from Tomkinsville, Highpockets, The Kid Comes Back*—all of which gave intense pleasure, but chiefly, I think, because they were about sports, which I loved much more than books. Still later, in high school, I read an occasional novel set in the slums—*A Stone for Danny Fisher, Knock on Any Door, The Hoods* are some of the titles that come to mind—but these were read at intervals of perhaps a year between books. Books assigned in school I did not read, and when a book report was due I generally faked it, writing about some great fat novel with the help of a Classic Comic. Books were simply no part of my life. A happy childhood is not easy to overcome.

But overcome it I did, to the point where I think I might be fairly defined as a bookish fellow, at any rate if I am to be judged by what I spend most of my time on. I rise early and, after putting on coffee, begin reading. If I am not reading to earn my living, I read for pleasure. (I am one of those extremely lucky people for whom business and pleasure are nearly indivisible.) When I leave my apartment, I take a book or magazine with me. If I am driving, more often than not I read at stoplights. If I lunch alone, I read while eating. If I need to go to the bank, I read while waiting in line. I am able to read while walking (Macaulay was the great champion at this). Most of the day, when not talking or being talked to, I am reading. I read before dinner and I read after dinner. Unfortunately, I am a person who takes showers, so I forgo the pleasure of reading in the bath. I read while watching television; I read while music is playing in the background. When I recently had a bad cold, an even more bookish friend asked, "Can you at least read?" A list of human functions and activities in which I partake and during which I do not read would be notably short. The Library Lady was wrong. Books are not my friends; they have become much more like family, except that I probably spend more time with books than I do with my family.

Books are an addiction that, when aroused in earnest, is rarely calmed. Gertrude Stein once remarked what a relief it was for her to realize that she did not have to read all the books in the world. Any serious addict will know exactly what she meant, but the problem is that most of us want to read at least all the *good* books in the world—and of these alone there are altogether too many. In one of the world's good books, Maurice Baring's *The Puppet Show of Memory,* Baring writes about the many good books in the pre-revolutionary summer home of his friend Count Benckendorff, and of a particular cupboard full of fine novels. "Before going to bed, we would dive into that cupboard, and one was always sure, even in the dark, of finding something one could read." This reminds me of friends who always put good books, both new and old, in their guest room, usually books suited to the guest's tastes. It is a lovely gesture of consideration, except that, when I have stayed with these friends, I am usually up half the night reading. Self-control around books is a thing I have not been able to learn; and sometimes, in the late hours, groggy and sated from too much reading, I will mutter, in transmuted form, the tag lines from two old Alka-Seltzer commercials of a decade or so ago: "I read too much, I read too fast" and "I guess I read *the whole thing.*"

As for reading too fast—well, that is not quite true, and it gets less and less true all the time. Reading is one of those things at which, beyond a certain point, one does not get quicker with practice. Although I have not always been so, I am now a slow reader; and sometimes—with some books—I cannot read slowly enough. Apologies to Miss Evelyn Wood and her speed-reading institutes, but I see no clear advantage in hastening an activity that gives such pleasure. I find speed-reading an alien concept, certainly when applied to good and entertaining books; one may as well cultivate speed-eating or speed-lovemaking.

Yet the attraction of speed-reading is scarcely difficult to fathom. It panders to the desire to be able to read everything —and yet still be able, as one advertisement directed to college students has it, to go to the big dance. But though the desire to read everything may linger, at a certain age belief in its realization grows dim. One makes accommodations, little adjustments. Kant, as is widely known, used to practice what he called "cerebral hygiene," which meant that he read no journals, though he did, while never traveling much himself, love travel books ("they will take you to foreign shores, . . ."—could the Library Lady have visited eighteenth-century Königsberg?). Kant would have found my own cerebral hygiene dreadfully wanting, for I subscribe to some twelve or fifteen journals—weeklies, monthlies, and quarterlies among them. Justice Holmes comes closer to being my model. A great puritan in these matters, he was unable until in his seventies to marshal "the moral face" not to finish any book he began, and consequently slogged through many a bad book ("empty fortresses," he called them); but he did forgo reading newspapers. This is something that I do for long periods, and, negative pleasure though it is, it brings great happiness.

I have at various times been a three-newspaper-a-day man, the journalistic equivalent of a two-pack-a-day smoker. I grew up extracting first the comics from our family newspaper, then the sports pages. For years I took a newspaper with my morning coffee, habitually, the way other people take toast. I once had a job on a political magazine for which a thorough reading of each day's *New York Times* was a prerequisite to arriving at the office. This experience of enforced newspaper reading may have marked the beginning of the end, though the end itself came when I realized that it is the nature of newspapers to be picked up in a state of anticipated excitement and laid down in disappointment. With newspaper reading generally, I should say, an awful lot goes a very short way. As things stand at present, I tend to miss newspapers grievously when they are shut down by a strike and not to read them when they are publishing.

Not that I have broken the newspaper habit completely. An old friend saves for me each Sunday's *New York Times Magazine* and its *Book Review,* and these I skim through in batches of six or seven at a sitting. A short while ago, with a sigh of real relief, I came to the end of a twenty-week trial subscription to the *Wall Street Journal.* It must be the best edited and least trivial of all current American newspapers; my problem is that it is triviality I crave in newspapers: a little murder, a little gossip, lots of circuses, plenty of fresh evidence of the privileged classes making fools of themselves. Although I crave these things, and the best contemporary newspapers tend to supply them in ample quantities—see any day's *New York Times* or *Washington Post*—I think I probably do better without them. Proust's M. Swann speaks as my alter-superego here:

"The fault I find with our journalism is that it forces us to take an interest in some fresh triviality or other every day, whereas only three or four books in a lifetime give us anything that is of real importance. Suppose that, every morning, when we tore the wrapper off our paper with fevered hands, a transmutation were to take place, and we were to find inside it—oh! I don't know; shall we say Pascal's *Pensées?*" He articulated the title with an ironic emphasis so as not to appear pedantic. "And then, in the gilt and tooled volumes which we open once in ten years," he went on, showing that contempt for things of this world which some men of the world like to affect, "we should read that the Queen of the Hellenes had arrived at Cannes, or that the Princess de Léon had given a fancy dress ball. In that way we should arrive at the right proportion between 'information' and 'publicity.' "

Yet though M. Swann is surely correct, how easy it is to go on a straight news diet. I have spent days on which I have read a newspaper with breakfast; dressed to the morning television news; driven to work while listening to an all-day news broadcast; read another newspaper at lunch; returned home to the blare from the same radio news broadcast; watched the evening national news with a cocktail in hand; then watched the *Mac-Neil-Lehrer Report;* read *Newsweek* after dinner; and switched on the ten o'clock news before turning in at the end of—shall we say?—a highly informative day. I have spent such days, but I hope I never spend another. How many Americans do spend most of their days thus? Many hundreds of thousands, I should guess. Certainly most television and radio broadcasters must, and most newspaper editors as well. For myself, I should rather share the fate of the hero of Evelyn Waugh's *A Handful of*

Dust, who is forced to end his life imprisoned in the Brazilian jungle by a madman to whom he must read, over and over, the novels of Charles Dickens.

Reading Dickens over and over must have been Evelyn Waugh's idea of Hell, but, if I did not have to live in a Brazilian jungle, it comes closer to being my idea of Heaven. Allow me my major premise for a moment: if there is a Heaven, will it contain books? Or will the very need for books be expunged? In Heaven, there may be no need to read about foreign shores or treasures hitherto undreamed of. There may be no need even to dream of such treasures; they will presumably be there, on the premises, so to speak. But if there are no books in Heaven, then—as John Sparrow once remarked of Heaven if his dear friend Maurice Bowra were not there—I do not care to go. My own view is that there *will* be books in Heaven, but only in foreign languages, ancient and modern and even lost, all of which I shall be able to read with perfect ease.

As for Hell, will there be books there? The Abbé Mugnier, friend to Edith Wharton and the artists and intellectuals of the Faubourg Saint-Germain, was once asked if he, gentle soul that he was, believed in Hell. He said that since it was Church dogma that Hell existed, he believed in Hell, though he also believed there was no one in it. But if the sweet-natured Abbé was wrong, it seems unlikely that there will not be something to read in Hell. My own guess is that there will be no actual books, but only bound volumes of the *New York Times* op-ed pages.

But in either place, Heaven or Hell, I hope that there will be more to do than just read. High though reading is on my list of pleasures, I find it is a pleasure I can sustain for only a limited time. While I have, on more than a few occasions, sat up till dawn with a book—most of them novels, many of these Russian—generally two straight hours of reading, three at the utmost, is all I can take without needing a break. Roughly twenty years ago, I was able to read under optimal, or nearly desert island, conditions. I was in the army, stationed in a southern city where I knew no one; I lived in a furnished though by no means dismal apartment, with no radio, phonograph, or television set. On many workdays I was able to knock off at noon, and weekends were completely free. For a serious reader I am describing a situation bordering on the orgiastic. I sent home for books; I bought books; I took books out of the library. My afternoons, my evenings, my weekends, all were booked. Taking time out only for nourishment and hygiene, I read and read and read—and nearly went bonkers. What saved me was the purchase, from the local Sears, Roebuck, of a basketball. As in the joke whose punch line is "Hit the ball and drag Irving, hit the ball and drag Irving," I would read a book and shoot baskets, read a book and shoot baskets. Mae West said that there can't be too much of a good thing, but I think she was wrong.

The Guinness Book of World Records lists no records for reading, either for the most books read in a lifetime or for the longest period of sustained reading. For most books read, I should think that fairly high up on such a list would appear the names Coleridge, Matthew Arnold, Sainte-Beuve, Saintsbury, Edmund Wilson, and V. S. Pritchett. (If there were an annual list of the ten best-read men and women in America, incidentally, it seems unlikely that it would overlap much with those lists for the best-dressed men and women.) As for the longest sustained period of reading, this is even more difficult to guess at. Logan Pearsall Smith was said to disappear into his room and read for days at a time. The late Alexander Gerschenkron, in a fine essay in *The American Scholar* entitled "On Reading Books," mentioned that on two of the fifteen occasions when he finished reading *War and Peace*, he was so reluctant to depart the magic aura of that masterpiece that he turned the book over and started it again. In *The Calf and the Oak,* Solzhenitsyn reports that Alexander Tvardovsky, the editor of *Novy Mir* and a chain smoker, was so absorbed in his reading of Solzhenitsyn's then unknown novel *The First Circle* that he forgot to smoke. But perhaps the record for sustained reading belongs to a fictional character, the young hero of Somerset Maugham's novel, *The Razor's Edge,* who at his club, in a single sitting from morning till night, reads in its entirety William James's *The Principles of Psychology.*

To be able to read *The Principles of Psychology* in a single sitting would require a splendid chair or an iron bottom, preferably both, not to speak of great powers of concentration. Still, the conditions for reading are no trifling matter. Not that serious readers are daunted by rough conditions. I have a friend who has read all the novels of George Eliot on the subway, and all of Jane Austen and much Trollope and Mrs. Gaskell besides. I myself can read standing up, sitting down, on my back, stomach, or side. I read easily in moving cars; I read on beaches; and I find reading on airplanes especially luxurious. The only place I cannot read, in fact, is in libraries. I like libraries; I enjoy roaming about in them, walking through stacks, checking the periodical room, breathing in the atmosphere of them. Yet apart from checking books in and out or looking up an odd fact, I have always used libraries as hotels—that is, whenever I attempt to read in them for any length of time, I fall asleep. It is helpful to me to know that, should I ever develop insomnia, a day at the Bodleian or the Widener or even my local branch library could cure it easily.

Part of my problem is that I frequently find something slightly artificial in the libraries' attempt to make people comfortable: an eagerness to please that, heartfelt though it may be, does not quite come off. (As an example of what I mean, I once asked a librarian of a local library in Texas if she had a copy of Locke's *Second Treatise on Civil Government.* "No," she replied, "I am afraid not. But we have other nice books on government.") One can accommodate oneself to true discomfort, but to work under modern library conditions of quasi or ostensible comfort is more than I can stand. Besides, I like to read with my tools around. I read, for one thing, with a pencil in my hand. If the book I am reading is my own, I mark lightly, with a vertical line along the margin, passages I might want to return to. (That's correct, Library Lady, I mark up my books' pages.) If I come across something connected with other work I am doing, I scribble down a note about it on an index card. If I come across something of general interest (such as this Russian proverb: "Do not call in a wolf when dogs attack you"), I write it in a notebook I keep on the table near my chair. On this table also sits a French and an English dictionary, and more often than not a cup of coffee or tea. Serious business, this reading.

I certainly take it seriously, so much so that I find myself quite unable to read pleasantly trashy things in good conscience. Take detective fiction. Apart from some stories of Conan Doyle and a single novel by Simenon, I have read no other detective fiction in my life. I do not wish to seem sniffy here. In the debate once begun by Edmund Wilson's famous essay about detective fiction, "Who Cares Who Killed Roger Ackroyd?," I used to think myself solidly on the side of the couldn't-care-less crowd. What I found, though, is that I can care all too easily. Georges Simenon is a highly seductive writer, but he is said to have written more than one hundred Maigret novels alone. No, I cannot start up with him. Like a man with a serious weight problem, I cannot keep such candy around the house. I would rather indulge my curiosity about old Ackroyd's demise at the movies, or on television, where only a few wasted hours are involved.

In my reading, as in a few other departments of my life, I have come to hold what many may consider to be a philistine assumption: that everyone dies some day—yes, Maudie, even you and I. As near as I am able to concentrate upon such a dark thought, I hold with Montaigne, who said, "We must be always booted and ready to go, so far as it is in our power." "Booted" to me includes being as well read as possible. I am not sure that I should go so far as Justice Holmes, who used to say that he was worried lest Saint Peter ask whether he had read some dull book that he was supposed to have read. Yet the assumption that time is all the more valuable because limited makes it easier to eschew fat and pretentious volumes whose tendency is easily enough guessed. Saint Peter, surely, is not likely to query anyone about Arthur M. Schlesinger, Jr.'s biography of Robert Kennedy, except possibly Professor Schlesinger himself about why he wrote such a book to begin with.

And now a philistine confession to go with a philistine assumption: I read in the hope of discovering the truth, or at least some truths. I look for truth in what some might deem strange places: novels and poems, histories and memoirs, biographies and autobiographies, letters and diaries. Many of these are literary places, but then, as Desmond MacCarthy once wrote, "It is the business of literature to turn facts into ideas." In reading for truth, you understand, I am not seeking a full game plan, some large system that will explain the world to me, or a patent for bliss. Instead I seek clues that might explain life's oddities, that might light up the dark corners of existence a little, that might correct foolish ideas I have come to hold too dearly, that might, finally, make my own stay here on earth more interesting, if not necessarily more pleasant. When I read in a book by Solzhenitsyn, "No, we must not hide behind fate's petticoats, the most important decisions in our lives, when all is said, we make for ourselves," I sit up and make note of it.

When I read in a line by Marianne Moore that "we must have the courage of our peculiarities," I not only sit up, I want to dance to it.

Not that this grown man dancing with small truths does not take pleasure in the music. I take immense pleasure. So much so that the puritan in me tends to distrust something that I enjoy so much. Part of the pleasure in reading is in the splendor of language properly deployed, but an even greater part comes from satisfying one's curiosity. If lust has an intellectual equivalent, might it not be curiosity which is allowed free rein? Though few are the books I regret having read, much of my reading has been altogether desultory—and continues to be. Gazing upon a shelf of books I have not yet read but soon hope to, I find the following items: *Diaghilev* by Richard Buckle, *Sabbatai Sevi* by Gershom Scholem, *Anthony Trollope* by James Pope Hennessy, *Collected Poems* by Roy Fuller, *The Sitwells* by John Pearson, *Chateaubriand* by George D. Painter, *The Apathetic Bookie Joint* by Daniel Fuchs, *Lermontov* by Laurence Kelley, *A Short Life of Kierkegaard* by Walter Lowrie, and *History of the Idea of Progress* by Robert Nisbet. Separately these books represent many amusing and instructive hours; taken together they do not, as they say down at the gas station, make a whole hell of a lot of sense.

"You can either read books or write them, but you can't do both." I do not know whose *mot* that is, but when I first heard it I thought it clever but without substance. Yet I have since come to wonder if perhaps there may not be some truth in it. One day a few years ago I had lunch with an author of many books, some long and monumental and others short and subtle. In the course of our lunch I mentioned having read a newly published novel. He said that he hadn't. I later referred to Solzhenitsyn's *Gulag* volumes. He had not read them. I brought up a recent biography that had made a stir. Nope, he hadn't read it either. Finally, he said: "Look, I must tell you something. I don't read anything except books and articles that have to do with the two books I am myself currently working on. It isn't that I don't want to read other things, you understand; it's only that I can't find time to do it." I have since noticed the same thing in other productive writers whom I know. They may be intelligent, penetrating, even wise, but they tend not to be very well read. They use books, they scrounge around in them, they dig out from books what they need, but always with a purpose. The writers I mentioned earlier as among the best read—Coleridge, Matthew Arnold, Sainte-Beuve, Saintsbury, Edmund Wilson, V. S. Pritchett— are chiefly known as essayists. Perhaps they read too much to write full-blown books. Like the man said, you can read 'em or write 'em, but you cannot do both.

As someone who for the most part reads 'em, I recently was interested to find Wallace Stevens (in *The Letters of Wallace Stevens*) expressing more than once his distrust of reading. Stevens was far from being anti-intellectual, but he seems to have concurred with the general view set forth in the above paragraph, even to the point of remarking that "that particular vice [reading] is the deadly enemy of writing." Of course Stevens was a poet, with a need for what T. S. Eliot called the "necessary laziness" of the poet, by which he, Eliot, meant a freeing of the mind from things that will "encroach upon his necessary receptivity." Still, it was Stevens who first put the notion in my impressionable mind that reading and thinking are not always coterminous activities. Writing to his young Cuban friend José Rodriguez Feo, Stevens said that he would "try to raise a question in your mind as to the value of reading. True, the desire to read is an insatiable desire and you must read. Nevertheless, you must also think." Stevens advised Feo to spend an hour or two a day at pure thinking, "even if in the beginning you are staggered by the confusion and aimlessness of your thoughts."

Whether Señor Feo took Wallace Stevens's advice is not known, but I did, at least partially and in somewhat exaggerated form. I determined to set aside a day on which I would do no reading—none whatsoever: no books, no magazines, no newspapers, no mail. The only thing I would read, I vowed, would be stop signs. The day I picked for printlessness was a Saturday. I did not expect it to be an easy day to get through. In fact, before turning in on the eve of this day-without-print, I fortified myself with a final snack, a tasty little Henry James essay on George Sand.

I woke Saturday morning with one thought on my mind: how am I going to get through this day? Whereas normally I shuffle into the kitchen to make coffee, then flop into my chair with a book, this morning I merely flopped into my chair. "It adds tremendously to the leisure space of life," Wallace Stevens wrote, "not to pick up a book every time one sits down." Too true. It was not yet 7:00 A.M. and already I had begun feeling the pressure of additional leisure space on my life. I sat in my chair and awaited thought, but it was no more punctual than Godot. After breakfast, since thought or anything remotely resembling it had still not arrived, I went out on errands. I purchased stamps, tea, shoe polish. I had not shined my own shoes for a number of years, and this clearly was the perfect day to do so. Walking about my apartment I noted how no room in it seemed free of reading matter, and I began to feel rather like a man attempting to quit smoking who has been locked in overnight at Dunhill's.

After lunch I listened to music: some Brahms, a Beethoven quartet, an album of songs sung by Lucien Fugère of the Opéra Comique. I watched a bit of a tennis match on television; I dozed in my chair; I arose and went for a short walk. I began to feel a tremor of irritability in myself. I thought about what I might read tomorrow. Somewhere I think I had something resembling an idea, which had to do with a technical solution to a problem I had been having with a piece of writing. But of grand thoughts, sweeping syntheses, I can claim none. As dusk crept up, the day seemed interminable. Time hung heavier than in a Laundromat. What was it that Cornelius Ryan called his book on the invasion of Normandy, *The Longest Day?*

Yet this experiment was not altogether for naught. If nothing else, it demonstrated my dependence on books, which is utter and complete. "It has struck me," wrote Pascal in a famous passage, "that all men's misfortunes spring from the single cause that they are unable to stay quietly in one room." Ah, but Monsieur Pascal, I have sat quietly in one room and to scarcely any avail. I need books, Monsieur. The engine that is my mind will not turn over without a book in my hand. If it comes to that, I am ready to write fewer books in order to read more; besides, in intellectual life perhaps it is better to receive than to give. That I can be happy reading books I count a great blessing. Books have brought me treasures hitherto undreamed of and, I tell you frankly, I want more such treasures. Books have taken me to foreign shores, and I am not keen to return from them. Oh, Library Lady, you were right all along. Please, I beg you, accept my apology.

What Is Vulgar?

WHAT'S VULGAR? Some people might say that the contraction of the words *what* and *is* itself is vulgar. On the other hand, I remember being called a stuffed shirt by a reviewer of a book of mine because I used almost no contractions. I have forgotten the reviewer's name but I have remembered the criticism. Not being of that category of writers who never forget a compliment, I also remember being called a racist by another reviewer for observing that failure to insist on table manners in children was to risk dining with Apaches. The larger criticisms I forget, but, oddly, these goofy little criticisms stick in the teeth like sesame seeds. Yet that last trope—is it, too, vulgar? Ought I really to be picking my teeth in public, even metaphorically?

What, to return to the question in uncontracted form, is vulgar? Illustrations, obviously, are wanted. Consider a relative of mine, long deceased, my father's Uncle Jake and hence my grand-uncle. I don't wish to brag about bloodlines, but my Uncle Jake was a bootlegger during Prohibition who afterward went into the scrap-iron—that is to say, the junk—business. Think of the archetypal sensitive Jewish intellectual faces: of Spinoza, of Freud, of Einstein, of Oppenheimer. In my uncle's face you would not have found the least trace of any of them. He was completely bald, weighed in at around two hundred fifty pounds, and had a complexion of clear vermilion. I loved him, yet even as a child I knew there was about him something a bit—how shall I put it?—outsized, and I refer not merely to his personal tonnage. When he visited our home he generally greeted me by pressing a ten- or twenty-dollar bill into my hand—an amount of money quite impossible, of course, for a boy of nine or ten, when what was wanted was a quarter or fifty-cent piece. A widower, he would usually bring a lady-friend along; here his tastes ran to Hungarian women in their fifties with operatic bosoms. These women wore large diamond rings, possibly the same rings, which my uncle may have passed from woman to woman. A big spender and a high roller, my uncle was an immigrant version of the sport, a kind of Diamond Chaim Brodsky.

But to see Uncle Jake in action you had to see him at table. He drank whiskey with his meal, the bottle before him on the table along with another of seltzer water, both of which he supplied himself. He ate and drank like a character out of Rabelais. My mother served him his soup course, not in a regular bowl, but in a vessel more on the order of a tureen. He would eat hot soup and drink whiskey and sweat—my Uncle Jake did not, decidedly, do anything so delicate as perspire—and sometimes it seemed that the sweat rolled from his face right into his soup dish, so that, toward the end, he may well have been engaged in an act of liquid auto-cannibalism, consuming his own body fluids with a whiskey chaser.

He was crude, certainly, my Uncle Jake; he was coarse, of course; gross, it goes without saying; uncouth, beyond question. But was he vulgar? I don't think he was. For one thing, he was good-hearted, and it somehow seems wrong to call anyone vulgar who is good-hearted. But more to the point, I don't think that if you had accused him of being vulgar, he would have known what the devil you were talking about. To be vulgar requires at least a modicum of pretension, and this Uncle Jake sorely lacked. "Wulgar," he might have responded to the accusation that he was vulgar, "so vat's dis wulgar?"

To go from persons to things, and from lack of pretension to a mountain of it, let me tell you about a house I passed one night, in a neighborhood not far from my own, that so filled me with disbelief that I took a hard right turn at the next corner and drove round the block to make certain I had actually seen what I thought I had. I had, but it was no house—it was a bloody edifice!

The edifice in question totally fills its rather modest lot, leaving no backyard at all. It is constructed of a white stone, sanded and perhaps even painted, with so much gray-colored mortar that, even though it may be real, the stone looks fake. The roof is red. It has two chimneys, neither of which, I would wager, functions. My confidence here derives from the fact that nothing much else in the structure of the house seems to function. There is, for example, a balcony over a portico—a portico held up by columns—onto which the only possible mode of entry is by pole vault. There is, similarly, over the attached garage, a sun deck whose only access appears to be through a bathroom window. The house seems to have been built on the aesthetic formula of functionlessness follows formlessness.

But it is in its details that the true spirit of the house emerges. These details are not minuscule, and neither are they subtle. For starters, outside the house under the portico, there is a chandelier. There are also two torch-shaped lamps on either side of the front door, which is carved in a scallop pattern, giving it the effect of seeming the back door to a much larger house. Along the short walk leading up to this front door stand, on short pillars, two plaster of paris lions—gilded. On each pillar, in gold and black, appears the owner's name. A white chain fence, strung along poles whose tops are painted gold, spans the front of the property; it is the kind of fence that would be more appropriate around, say, the tomb of Lenin. At the curb are two large cars, sheets of plastic covering their grills; there is also a trailer; and, in the summer months, a boat sits in the short driveway leading up to the garage. The lawn disappoints by being not Astro-Turf but, alas, real grass. However, closer inspection reveals two animals, a skunk and a rabbit, both of plastic, in petrified play upon the lawn—a nice, you might almost say a finishing, touch. Sometimes, on long drives or when unable to sleep at night, I have pondered upon the possible decor of this extraordinary house's den and upon the ways of man, which are various beyond imagining.

You want vulgar, I am inclined to exclaim, I'll show you vulgar: the house I have just described is vulgar, patently, palpably, pluperfectly vulgar. Forced to live in it for more than three hours, certain figures of refined sensibility—Edith Wharton or Harold Acton or Wallace Stevens—might have ended as suicides. Yet as I described that house, I noted two contradictory feelings in myself: how pleasant it is to point out someone else's vulgarity, and yet the fear that calling someone else vulgar may itself be slightly vulgar. After all, the family that lives in this house no doubt loves it; most probably they feel that they have a real showplace. Their house, I assume, gives them a large measure of happiness. Yet why does my calling their home vulgar also give me such a measure of happiness? I suppose it is because vulgarity can be so amusing—other people's vulgarity, that is.

Here I must insert that I have invariably thought that the people who have called me vulgar were themselves rather vulgar. So far as I know I have been called vulgar three times, once directly, once behind my back, and once by association. In each instance the charge was intellectual vulgarity: on one occasion a contributor to a collection of essays on contemporary writing that I once reviewed called me vulgar because I didn't find anything good to say about this book of some six hundred pages; once an old friend, an editor with whom I had had a falling out over politics, told another friend of mine that an article I had written seemed to him vulgar; and, finally, having patched things up with this friend and having begun to write for his magazine again, yet a third friend asked me why I allowed my writing to appear in that particular magazine, when it was so patently—you guessed her, Chester—vulgar.

None of these accusations stung in the least. In intellectual and academic life, vulgar is something one calls people with whom one disagrees. Like having one's ideas called reductionist, it is nothing to get worked up about—certainly nothing to take personally. What would wound me, though, is if word got back to me that someone had said that my manners at table were so vulgar that it sickened him to eat with me, or that my clothes were laughable, or that taste in general wasn't exactly my strong point. In a novel whose author or title I can no longer remember, I recall a female character who was described as having vulgar thumbs. I am not sure I have a clear picture of vulgar thumbs, but if it is all the same, I would just as soon not have them.

I prefer not to be thought vulgar in any wise. When not long ago a salesman offered to show me a winter coat that, as he put it, "has been very popular," I told him to stow it—if it has been popular, it is not for me. I comb my speech, as best I am able, of popular phrases: you will not hear an unfundamental "basically" or a flying "whatever" from these chaste lips. I do not utter "bottom line"; I do not mutter "trade-off." I am keen to cut myself out from the herd, at least when I can. In recent years this has not been difficult. Distinction has lain in plain speech, plain dress, clean cheeks. The simple has become rococo, the rococo simple. But now I see that television anchormen, hairdressers, and other leaders in our society have adopted this plainer look. This is discomfiting news. Vulgar is, after all, as vulgar does.

Which returns us yet again to the question: What is vulgar? *The Oxford English Dictionary,* which provides more than two pages on the word, is rather better at telling us what vulgar was than what it is. Its definitions run from "1. The common or usual language of a country; the vernacular. *Obs.*" to "13. Having a common and offensively mean character; coarsely commonplace; lacking in refinement or good taste; uncultured, ill-bred." Historically, the word vulgar was used in fairly neutral description up to the last quarter of the seventeenth century to mean and describe the common people. Vulgar was common but not yet contemned. I noted such a neutral usage as late as a William Hazlitt essay of 1818, "On the Ignorance of the Learned," in which Hazlitt writes: "The vulgar are in the right when they judge for themselves; they are wrong when they trust to their blind guides." Yet, according to the *OED,* in 1797 the *Monthly Magazine* remarked: "So the word *vulgar* now implies something base and groveling in actions."

From the early nineteenth century on, then, vulgar has been purely pejorative, a key term in the lexicon of insult and invective. Its currency as a term of abuse rose with the rise of the middle class; its spread was tied to the spread of capitalism and democracy. Until the rise of the middle class, until the spread of capitalism and democracy, people perhaps hadn't the occasion or the need to call one another vulgar. The rise of the middle class, the spread of capitalism and democracy, opened all sorts of social doors; social classes commingled as never before; plutocracy made possible almost daily strides from stratum to stratum. Still, some people had to be placed outside the pale, some doors had to be locked—and the cry of vulgarity, properly intoned, became a most effective Close Sesame.

Such seems to me roughly the social history of the word vulgar. But the history of vulgarity, the thing itself even before it had a name, is much longer. According to the French art historian Albert Dasnoy, aesthetic vulgarity taints Greek art of the fourth and third centuries B.C. "An exhibition of Roman portraits," Dasnoy writes, "shows that, between the Etruscan style of the earliest and the Byzantine style of the latest, vulgarity made its first full-blooded appearance in the academic realism of imperial Rome." Vulgarity, in Dasnoy's view, comes of the shock of philosophic rationalism, when humankind divests itself of belief in the sacred. "Vulgarity seems to be the price of man's liberation," he writes, "one might even say, of his evolution. It is unquestionably the price of the freeing of the individual personality." Certainly it is true that one would never think to call a savage vulgar; a respectable level of civilization has to have been reached to qualify for the dubious distinction of being called vulgar.

"You have surely noticed the curious fact," writes Valéry, "that a certain *word*, which is perfectly clear when you hear or use it in *everyday* speech, and which presents no difficulty when caught up in the rapidity of an ordinary sentence, becomes mysteriously cumbersome, offers a strange resistance, defeats all efforts at definition, the moment you withdraw it from circulation for separate study and try to find its meaning after taking away its temporary function." Vulgar presents special difficulties, though: while vulgarity has been often enough on display—may even be a part of the human soul that only the fortunate and the saintly are able to root out—every age has its own notion of what constitutes the vulgar. Riding a bicycle at Oxford in the 1890s, Max Beerbohm reports, "was the earmark of vulgarity." Working further backward, we find that Matthew Arnold frequently links the word vulgar with the word hideous and hopes that culture "saves the future, as one may hope, from being vulgarized, even if it cannot save the present." "In Jane Austen's novels," Lionel Trilling writes, "vulgarity has these elements: smallness of mind, insufficiency of awareness, assertive self-esteem, the wish to devalue, especially to devalue the human worth of other people." Hazlitt found vulgarity in false feeling among "the herd of pretenders to what they do not feel and to what is not natural to them, whether in high or low life."

Vulgarity, it begins to appear, is often in the eye of the beholder. What is more, it comes in so many forms. It is so multiple and so complex—so multiplex. There are vulgarities of taste, of manner, of mind, of spirit. There are whole vulgar ages—the Gilded Age in the United States, for one, at least to hear Mark Twain and Henry Adams tell it. (Is our own age another?) To compound the complication there is even likeable vulgarity. This is vulgarity of the kind that Cyril Connolly must have had in mind when he wrote, "Vulgarity is the garlic in the salad of life." In the realm of winning vulgarity are the novels of Balzac, the paintings of Frans Hals, some of the music of Tchaikovsky (excluding the cannon fire in the 1812 Overture, which is vulgarity of the unwinning kind).

Rightly used, profanity, normally deemed the epitome of vulgar manners, can be charming. I recently moved to a new apartment, and the person I dealt with at the moving company we employed, a woman whose voice had an almost strident matter-of-factness, instructed me to call back with an inventory of our furniture. When I did, our conversation, starting with my inventory of our living room, began:

"One couch."

"One couch."

"Two lamp tables, a coffee table, a small gateleg table."

"Four tables."

"Two wing chairs and an occasional chair."

"Three chairs."

"One box of bric-a-brac."

"One box of shit."

Heavy garlic of course is not to every taste; but then again some people do not much care for endive. I attended city schools, where garlic was never in short supply and where profanity, in proper hands, could be a useful craft turned up to the power of fine art. I have since met people so well-mannered, so icily, elegantly correct, that with a mere glance across the table or a word to a waiter they could put a chill on the wine and indeed on the entire evening. Some people have more, some less, in the way of polish, but polish doesn't necessarily cover vulgarity. As there can be diamonds in the rough, so can there be sludge in the smooth.

It would be helpful in drawing a definitional bead on the word vulgar if one could determine its antonym. But I am not sure that it has an antonym. Refined? I think not. Sophisticated? Not really. Elegant? Nope. Charming? Close, but I can think of charming vulgarians—M. Rabelais, please come forth and take a bow. Besides, charm is nearly as difficult to define as vulgarity. Perhaps the only safe thing to be said about charm is that if you think you have it, you can be fairly certain that you don't.

If vulgarity cannot be defined by its antonym, from the rear so to say, examples may be more to the point. I once heard a friend describe a woman thus: "Next to Sam Jensen's prose, she's the vulgarest thing in New York." From this description, I had a fairly firm sense of what the woman was like. Sam Jensen is a writer for one of the newsmagazines; each week on schedule he makes a fresh cultural discovery, writing as if every sentence will be his last, every little movie or play he reviews will change our lives—an exhibitionist with not a great deal to exhibit. Sam Jensen is a fictitious name—made up to protect the guilty—but here are a few sentences that he, not I, made up:

The great Victorian William Morris combined a practical socialism with a love for the spirit of the King Arthur legends. What these films show is the paradox democracy has forgotten—that the dream of Camelot is the ultimate dream of freedom and order in a difficult but necessary balance.

The screenplay by Michael Wilson and Richard Maibaum is not from an Ian Fleming novel; it's really a cookbook that throws Roger Moore as Bond into these action recipes like a cucumber tossed into an Osterizer. Osterization is becoming more and more necessary for Moore; he's beginning to look a bit puckered, as if he's been bottled in Bond.

From these sentences—with their false paradoxes, muffed metaphors, obvious puns, and general bloat—I think I can extrapolate the woman who, next to this prose, is the vulgarest thing in New York. I see teeth, I see elaborate hairdo, much jewelry, flamboyant dress, a woman requiring a great deal of attention, who sucks up most of the mental oxygen in any room she is in—a woman, in sum, vastly overdone.

Coming at things from a different angle, I imagine myself in session with a psychologist, playing the word association game. "Vulgar," he says, "quick, name ten items you associate with the word vulgar." "Okay," I say, "here goes:

1. Publicity
2. The Oscar awards
3. The Aspen Institute for Humanistic Studies
4. Talk shows
5. Pulitzer Prizes
6. Barbara Walters
7. Interviews with writers

8. Lauren Bacall
9. Dialogue as an ideal
10. Psychology."

This would not, I suspect, be everyone's list. Looking it over, I see that, of the ten items, several are linked with one another. But let me inquire into what made me choose the items I did.

Ladies first. Barbara Walters seems to me vulgar because for a great many years now she has been paid to ask all the vulgar questions, and she seems to do it with such cheerfulness, such competence, such amiable insincerity. "What did you think when you first heard your husband had been killed?" she will ask, just the right hush in her voice. "What went on in your mind when you learned that you had cancer, now for the third time?" The questions that people with imagination do not need to ask, the questions that people with good hearts know they have no right to ask, these questions and others Barbara Walters can be depended upon to ask. "Tell me, Holy Father, have you never regretted not having children of your own?"

Lauren Bacall has only recently graduated to vulgarity, or at least she has only in the past few years revealed herself vulgar. Hers is a double vulgarity: the vulgarity of false candor —the woman who, presumably, tells it straight—and the vulgarity provided by someone who has decided to cash in her chips. In her autobiography, Miss Bacall has supposedly told all her secrets; when interviewed on television—by, for example, Barbara Walters—the tack she takes is that of the ringwise babe over whose eyes no one, kiddo, is going to pull the cashmere. Yet turn the channel or page, and there is Miss Bacall in a commercial or advertisement doing her best to pull the cashmere over ours. Vulgar stuff.

Talk shows are vulgar for the same reason that Pulitzer Prizes and the Aspen Institute for Humanistic Studies are vulgar. All three fail to live up to their pretensions, which are extravagant: talk shows to being serious, Pulitzer Prizes to rewarding true merit, the Aspen Institute to promoting "dialogue" (see item 9), "the bridging of cultures," "the interdisciplinary approach," and nearly every other phony shibboleth that has cropped up in American intellectual life over the past three decades.

Publicity is vulgar because those who seek it—and even those who are sought by it—tend almost without exception to be divested of their dignity. You have to sell yourself, the sales manuals used to advise, in order to sell your product. With publicity, though, one is selling only oneself, which is different. Which is a bit vulgar, really.

The Oscar awards ceremony is the single item on my list least in need of explanation, for it seems vulgar prima facie. It is the air of self-congratulation—of, a step beyond, self-adulation—that is so splendidly vulgar about the Oscar awards ceremony. Self-congratulation, even on good grounds, is best concealed; on no grounds whatever, it is embarrassing. But then, for vulgarity, there's no business like show business.

Unless it be literary business. The only thing worse than false modesty is no modesty at all, and no modesty at all is what interviews with writers generally bring out. "That most vulgar of all crowds the literary," wrote Keats presciently—that is, before the incontestable evidence came in with the advent and subsequent popularity of what is by now that staple of the book review and little magazine and talk show, the interview with the great author. What these interviews generally come down to is an invitation to writers to pontificate upon things for which it is either unseemly for them to speak (the quality of their own work) or upon which they are unfit to judge (the state of the cosmos). Roughly a decade ago I watched Isaac Bashevis Singer, when asked on a television talk show what he thought of the Vietnam War, answer, "I am a writer, and that doesn't mean I have to have an opinion on everything. I'd rather discuss literature." Still, how tempting it is, with an interviewer chirping away at your feet, handing you your own horn and your own drum, to blow it and beat it. As someone who has been interviewed a time or two, I can attest that never have I shifted spiritual gears so quickly from self-importance to self-loathing as during and after an interview. What I felt was, well, vulgar.

Psychology seems to me vulgar because it is too often over-bearing in its confidence. Instead of saying, "I don't know," it readily says, "unresolved Oedipus complex" or "manic-depressive syndrome" or "identity crisis." As with other intellectual discoveries before (Marxism) and since (structuralism), psychology acts as if it is holding all the theoretical keys, but then in practice reveals that it doesn't even know where the doors are. As an old *Punch* cartoon once put it, "It's worse than wicked, my dear, it's vulgar."

Reviewing my list and attempting to account for the reasons why I have chosen the items on it, I feel I have a firmer sense of what I think vulgar. Exhibitionism, obviousness, pretentiousness, self-congratulation, self-importance, hypocrisy, overconfidence—these seem to me qualities at the heart of vulgarity in our day. It does, though, leave out common sense, a quality which, like clarity, one might have thought one could never have in overabundance. (On the philosophy table in my local bookstore, a book appeared with the title *Clarity Is Not Enough;* I could never pass it without thinking, "Ah, but it's a start.") Yet too great reliance on common sense can narrow the mind, make meager the imagination. Strict common sense abhors mystery, seldom allows for the attraction of tradition, is intolerant of questions that haven't any answers. The problem that common sense presents is knowing the limits of common sense. The too commonsensical man or woman grows angry at anything that falls outside his or her common sense, and this anger seems to me vulgar.

Vulgarity is not necessarily stupid but it is always insensitive. Its insensitivity invariably extends to itself: the vulgar person seldom knows that he is vulgar, as in the old joke about the young woman whose fiancé reports to her that his parents found her vulgar, and who, enraged, responds, "What's this vulgar crap?" Such obvious vulgarity can be comical, like a nouveau riche man bringing opera glasses to a porno film, or the Chicago politician who, while escorting the then ruling British monarch through City Hall, supposedly introduced him to the assembled aldermen by saying, "King, meet the boys." But such things are contretemps merely, not vulgarity of the insidious kind.

In our age vulgarity does not consist in failing to recognize the fish knife or to know the wine list but in the inability to make distinctions. Not long ago I heard a lecture by a Harvard philosophy professor on a Howard Hawks movie, and thought, as one high reference after another was made in connection with this low subject, "Oh, Santayana, 'tis better you are not alive to see this." A vulgar performance, clearly, yet few people in the audience of professors and graduate students seemed to notice.

A great many people did notice, however, when, in an act of singular moral vulgarity, a publisher, an editor, and a novelist recently sponsored a convicted murderer for parole, and the man, not long after being paroled, murdered again. The reason for these men speaking out on behalf of the convict's parole, they said, was his ability as a writer: his work appeared in the editor's journal; he was to have a book published by the publisher's firm; the novelist had encouraged him from the outset. Distinctions—crucial distinctions—were not made: first, that the man was not a very good writer, but a crudely Marxist one, whose work was filled with hatreds and half-truths; second, and more important, that, having killed before, he might kill again—might just be a pathological killer. Not to have made these distinctions is vulgarity at its most vile. But to adopt a distinction new to our day, the publisher, the editor, and the novelist took responsibility for what they had done—responsibility but no real blame.

Can an entire culture grow vulgar? Matthew Arnold feared such might happen in "the mechanical and material civilisation" of the England of his day. Vladimir Nabokov felt it already had happened in the Soviet Union, a country, as he described it, "of moral imbeciles, of smiling slaves and poker-faced bullies," without, as in the old days, "a Gogol, a Tolstoy, a Chekhov in quest of that simplicity of truth [who] easily distinguished the vulgar side of things as well as the trashy systems of pseudo-thought." Moral imbeciles, smiling slaves, poker-faced bullies—the curl of a sneer in those Nabokovian phrases is a sharp reminder of the force that the charge of "vulgar" can have as an insult—as well as a reminder of how deep and pervasive vulgarity can become.

But American vulgarity, if I may put it so, is rather more refined. It is also more piecemeal than pervasive, and more insidious. Creeping vulgarity is how I think of it, the way Taft Republicans used to think of creeping socialism. The insertion of a science fiction course in a major university curriculum, a television commercial by a once-serious actor for a cheap wine, an increased interest in gossip and trivia that is placed under the rubric Style in our most important newspapers: so the vulgar creeps along, while everywhere the third- and fourth-rate—in art, in literature, in intellectual life—is considered good enough, or at any rate highly interesting.

Yet being refined—or at least sophisticated—American vulgarity is vulnerable to the charge of being called vulgar. "As long as war is regarded as wicked," said Oscar Wilde, "it will always have its fascination. When it is looked upon as vulgar, it will cease to be popular." There may be something to this, if not for war then at least for designer jeans, French literary criticism, and other fashions. The one thing the vulgar of our day do not like to be called is vulgar. So crook your little finger, purse your lips, distend your nostrils slightly as you lift your nose in the air the better to look down it, and repeat after me: *Vulgar! Vulgar! Vulgar!* The word might save us all.

The End of Moviegoing

HE TENSEST MOMENT AT THE MOVIES nowadays rarely takes place on the screen or even while the movie is being shown. No, tension is greatest between showings, at that moment when the people who have seen the movie are leaving the theater and the people who are about to see it are still waiting behind the thick velour cordon. There they scrutinize the faces of those on the way out for clues to whether the movie has evoked satisfaction or apathy, pleasure or anger, delight or rage. The problem is that going to the movies today one doesn't really know with any certainty what one is getting into. One may have read reviews of a particular movie, had friends extol its many splendors, but neither of these is quite so trustworthy as the pure physical reaction of those who have seen it only a moment before—or what I think of as "word of face."

I know that, when behind the cordon, I look for word of face. And when I emerge from a movie I try to arrange my own wrinkles, pouches, jowls, and dewlaps into an appropriate critical statement. To word of face I sometimes add word of mouth. "Don't worry," I have been heard to say, "it's not that bad." Or "A fine flick." Or, more often these days, "God-awful, hideous, and terrible." Of course these little reviews come too late, for the people behind the cordon have already bought their tickets. Yet when departing especially bad movies, I have been known to approach people at the box office, advising them to return home, to give their ticket money to the Salvation Army instead, to cut and run while there is still time —usually, I regret to report, to no avail. Most people are not susceptible to sound advice, particularly from a raving stranger, but seem to need to see truly dreary movies for themselves.

No wrath like that of a lover spurned—and because I count myself a lover of movies, when they spurn me by bringing forth inferior goods I tend to show my wrath. Wrath expressed gives pleasure of a sort, though I should much prefer the more substantial pleasure of a good movie. But this is a pleasure I find in shorter and shorter supply. Whereas once I was at least a movie-a-week moviegoer, I now see, apart from movies shown on television, six or eight or at most ten movies a year. Sweet but unserious music, elegant food, lovely movies—these are among the shaded water holes in the desert of life; and now one of them, the movies, is drying up. I find myself filled with resentment.

As a member of the last generation in America to grow up without television, I am, in the nature of the case, a movie man. If there were any Saturdays when I was growing up in the 1940s on which I did not go to the movies, I do not remember them. I remember going to the movies in the evenings with my father, especially on hot summer nights in the age before air-conditioning. I am old enough to remember when they gave away dishes at the movies, when certain neighborhood theaters had double seats for lovers, when downtown theaters combined movies with stage shows. If you don't remember any of these things, then, dearie, you're much younger than I.

I remember, too, going to the movies during those years without even bothering to ask what was showing. One might enter a movie somewhere in its middle, sit through the rest of it, then stay up to the point at which one had entered. It didn't seem a bad thing to do then, though now, for some reason, it does. At half price, movies for children cost twenty cents, at some places a quarter, but one of the theaters in our neighborhood, the Coed, charged only eleven cents. Another, the Bertha, specialized in children's matinees, which usually meant cowboy movies, eight or ten cartoons, a serial or two, and charged only a dime. There were no ratings, no X, R, PG, G, et cetera. I do, though, recall being turned away from another neighborhood movie theater, the 400, when it showed *The Best Years of Our Lives,* which was considered adult fare because it had, as I have since learned from seeing it, an almost anti-aphrodisiac bedroom scene.

Mention of the name 400, modest little theater though it was, reminds me of the grand names movie houses of those days carried. None of the current Cinema I, II, and III. Exotic place-names were a specialty in the city where I grew up: the Riviera, the Tivoli, the Valencia, the Oriental, the Granada. Moorish names, many of them, and Moorish names got Moorish settings: turrets and minarets, sculptures and tapestries, and kilometers of fake Oriental rugs. The interiors of many of these theaters made Hearst's San Simeon look like an attached house in Astoria. The Granada, a theater that in its design was two or three jumps beyond rococo and seemed slightly larger than the country of Liechtenstein, had a vast blue ceiling in which light bulbs, star-like, blinked on and off. It was all, in the word of Theodore Dreiser's Clyde Griffiths in *An American Tragedy,* "Aladdinish."

As a boy of impressionable years, nothing impressed me more than the movies. After seeing a movie I would generally change my hair style. One Saturday evening I would pomade it heavily à la Clark Gable; another I would attempt a pompadour à la Van Johnson. My pals and I would swing through the trees of empty lots in imitation of Errol Flynn as Robin Hood; and once, after seeing a movie with a medieval setting, we mounted our bicycles, tore off fairly large tree limbs, and jousted. How we avoided a maiming I do not know.

From the movies of those days I acquired a rich mine of misinformation. For a very long time, for example, I believed that the United States was a Catholic country; this was a result of the large number of movies—*The Bells of St. Mary's, Going My Way, Boys' Town, The Keys of the Kingdom*—in which Bing Crosby, Spencer Tracy, Pat O'Brien, or Gregory Peck played a priest. Riding the buses or subways I used to take special pleasure whenever I could rise up to ask, "Would you like my seat, Father?" This was also the age of World War II movies, bits from which still stick in my mind, such as the one—from *Thirty Seconds Over Tokyo?*—in which the Chinese actor Richard Loo, who played so many villainous Japanese commanders, exposes the American lieutenant disguised as a Japanese officer, then announces, "You see, Lieutenant, I, too, went to Harvard. Perhaps you do not remember me. . . ." I myself have always regretted not having gone to Harvard, for I know I could have found dozens of occasions in which to use those same lines.

In my adolescence, movies became linked with sex. The movie theaters were where, in late grammar school years, one met girls. The movies were the scene of necking; later there were drive-ins (or passion pits, as they were called). From the movies one also picked up social-sexual tips on stylish kissing, how to light a cigarette, what drink to order. One learned what glamour was supposed to be. Movie actors and actresses had it —glamour, the great glowing thing itself. Many of the great stars of the period—Gary Cooper and Edward G. Robinson, Bette Davis and Katharine Hepburn—played essentially the same role (chiefly, one gathers, themselves) over and over; yet

that didn't seem to matter in the least, for when they were on
the screen they filled it so interestingly. (Evelyn Waugh, himself an old moviegoer, wrote to Nancy Mitford in 1965 that he
had lost his interest in plays and movies: "The girls all seem
hideous and the men common.") One of the reasons movie
stars could maintain their allure was that they did not go on
television talk shows, as movie stars do now, there to reveal—
almost all of them—the utter commonplaceness of their minds.
Who was it who said that Shakespeare could not have written
the plays attributed to him because there is conclusive proof
that he acted in them?

At university, movies did not become less interesting to me,
but my motives for going to them changed somewhat. Increasingly a paramount motive was entailed—escape. The movies
were a great form of escape. (Which reminds me of a very good
movie, with the late Steve McQueen, called *The Great Escape*,
a title that plays wonderfully on itself, almost as if Picasso had
painted a picture entitled "An Expensive Picasso.") The movies became a fine place to hide out while shirking one's stu-
dently duties. One night, owing a paper the next day on the
Nicomachean Ethics, I thought a movie would be just the warm-
up needed for writing about Aristotle. Like Mr. Hulot, I
treated myself to a brief holiday and went off to see a movie
whose title I did not know but which turned out to be *The
Killing*, Stanley Kubrick's first film. About a racetrack holdup,
The Killing was then a true sleeper, an unheralded and hence
unknown little classic. Coming upon a sleeper, a very rare
experience today, was one of the great delights of moviegoing.
Nowadays a person would have to be either a true movie addict
or a complete naif to go into a movie without getting some
rough idea of its content beforehand. A movie theater is less
and less an oasis, a safety island, an escape hatch from worldly
cares. Edmund Wilson, in *Upstate*, tells of feeling the strains

of his bad heart while walking in Manhattan, when he "went into the nearest movie in order to go to the men's room. I did not notice the signs in front, which in any case were not explicit; but when I was coming out and saw what was on the screen, I sat down and watched the performance. It was an enormous human vagina which an actress in various ways was showing off. . . ." Enough—and more than enough—said.

Is the moviegoer a distinct psychological type? I do not say that everyone who goes regularly to the movies falls into the pattern of a psychological type, but true movie addicts do, I think, have certain qualities in common. They tend to be people who feel a deep if not well-defined longing; to be somewhat passive; to be romantic, a bit dreamy perhaps, with an ample capacity for fantasy. Movies make up a disproportionate share of their experience, and nothing is quite so real to them as an event or relationship that has an analogue in some movie. Often they can be spotted, like alcoholics who drink alone, going into movie theaters unaccompanied. Their memories are drenched in movies. In the hero-narrator of his novel *The Moviegoer*, Walker Percy has created a stellar example of the type.

Other people, so I have read, treasure memorable moments in their lives: the time one climbed the Parthenon at sunrise, the summer night one met a lonely girl in Central Park and achieved with her a sweet and natural relationship, as they say in books. I too once met a girl in Central Park, but it is not much to remember. What I remember is the time John Wayne killed three men with a carbine as he was falling to the dusty street in *Stagecoach*, and the time the kitten found Orson Welles in the doorway in *The Third Man*.

The one period in my life when I qualified as a serious moviegoer was during a ten-month stretch in the army while stationed at Fort Hood, Texas. Movies at Fort Hood were shown at 7:00 and 9:00 P.M. at three different post theaters, and

I went off to them four or five evenings a week, usually alone, sometimes going by post cab to two different theaters on the same night. This may sound bleak, but the alternatives available in the nearby town of Killeen, Texas, were bleaker: a cheeseburger, a dozen or so beers, a tattoo. I would see anything (but *anything*) showing at the post theaters, with the exception of horror movies, toward which I had—and retain —a horror. Moviegoing was a most workable mode of killing slow Texas time, of in effect dreaming with my eyes open. Dreaming rightly describes the feel of heavy moviegoing, and I can recall scarcely any of the movies that I saw during this period, with the exception of a less than trivial movie entitled *Running Wild* starring the not late but nonetheless unlamented Mamie Van Doren.

At this same time I became the movie critic for the post newspaper, the weekly Fort Hood *Armored Sentinel*—but a movie critic with a difference. The difference was that, because new movies arrived at the post on Thursday and the newspaper's copy had to be at the printer's in Tyler, Texas, the preceding Wednesday, I reviewed movies without first seeing them; or at least most of them, for an occasional second-run movie, which I had seen earlier in my well-spent youth, was shown. But not being able to see the majority of the movies I reviewed proved, I found, no real disadvantage. Written from studio publicity releases, with my own gaudy phrasings added, my reviews were chiefly wise-guy summaries. When I did make a judgment, though, I was pleased to discover, upon seeing the movie after having written about it, how seldom I went far astray. This is not a testament to my acuity but to the predictability of most movies. After all, a movie with John Wayne or Debbie Reynolds, Jerry Lewis or Jayne Mansfield does not exactly suggest limitless possibilities. Years later I was offered a job as a movie critic on rather a more serious publication than the Fort Hood *Armored Sentinel.* But the thought of watching movies with a notebook, pen, and pocket flashlight in hand was not, I decided, my idea of a flaming good time. Besides, having to deal with flashlight, notebook, and pen, how would I be able to eat my popcorn?

Certain feelings, moods, and activities are to me everlastingly associated with moviegoing. The smell of popcorn—when they used to make it fresh in the theater and it still had a smell—is one of them. Special brands of candy, too, seem unthinkable outside a movie theater: Milk Duds, Snow Caps, Dots, Jujubes, Raisinettes, and other confections of goo and rock that have helped make American dentists among the leading money earners of our time. Then there is the oddly disoriented feeling which results from having gone into a movie in daylight and emerging from it into the night; and the connected feeling of slight, not necessarily unpleasant, confusion upon coming out of a movie in a strange city. There is something sinfully delicious about going off to the movies in the afternoon in the middle of the week. I always made it a point to sneak off to the movies at one time on every job I have ever held, lest anyone ever accuse me of being a completely responsible and mature person.

On the subject of maturity: is there, I wonder, an age beyond which too regular attendance at the movies is a bit unseemly? I note for example an odd discrepancy in the fact that, while the majority of movies seem to have been made with the young in mind, our leading national movie critics—Pauline Kael and Stanley Kauffmann, John Simon and Andrew Sarris, Vincent Canby and Judith Crist—are all past fifty years old. Of course, one might argue that going to the movies is a way of staying young. The hot movie critic in the city in which I live, though he must by now be forty, continues to look like someone in his late adolescence. He is a man with a nearly boundless appreciation for movies of all kinds: serious, horror, science fiction, good, and bad. Thinking about him leads me to believe that the secret of remaining youthful in appearance is to remain immature.

Still, the most intelligent people I know beyond forty go less and less to the movies. This may have to do with the fact that at a certain age one ceases to learn much from the movies. One feels that one knows more about life than almost all the men and women who make movies. So while one continues to look to the movies chiefly for pleasurable escape, one is no longer quite so able as formerly to depend upon finding it. Movie reviewers are less and less helpful. The daily press reviewers in my own city are men of too skimpy general culture to be trusted. Vincent Canby in the *New York Times* is a bit too dull to be read. Pauline Kael in *The New Yorker* is no longer quite to be believed. While she is doubtless the most talented of the people who regularly write about the movies, one too often feels that the movies are not a sufficient subject for her —so that reading Pauline Kael prattling away page after page on, say, the movie *Popeye* becomes a spectacle akin to listening to someone play "Mares Eat Oats and Does Eat Oats" on a Stradivarius. Of regular movie reviewers I tend to prefer Stanley Kauffmann, in the *New Republic*, because he has, in the general run of his judgments, the profound good sense to agree with me, and Vernon Young, in the *Hudson Review*, because he writes the most consistently interesting prose.

A large part of the problem may inhere in the job of movie critic. Anyone who reviews movies regularly must see something on the order of 150 new movies a year, not to speak of movies seen at film festivals and conferences. Too much of a bad thing, I should say; too much time spent in the dark, the effect of which, on movie reviewers, seems to push them to want to find a good thing every now and again—and then, traditionally, to make too much of it. Yet if one were to review only serious or even interesting movies, then one could probably do so, at best, no oftener than quarterly, for there are probably not enough such movies to keep a reviewer busy on a weekly, let alone a daily, basis.

James Agee is generally considered to have been the best movie reviewer to have practiced the trade in this country, and it is true that when he was good he was very, very good. (And when he was bad—as in a fast, flip paragraph he wrote putting down *Casablanca*—he could be horrid.) But what made Agee so good was his understanding that much of movie reviewing has to do with discriminating between the fourth- and the third-rate—and his additional and crucial understanding that the fourth- and even the fifth-rate movie could be oddly pleasurable. Conversely, serious things in the movies can be oddly dreary. Thus, in one of his 1943 reviews, Agee wrote: "*Ox-Bow* is one of the best and most interesting pictures I have seen for a long time, and it disappointed me. *Bataan* is incomparably less of a picture, and I liked it verymuch." Agee seems to have been quite without intellectual snobbery—imagine affirming in the pages of a sniffy journal like the *Nation,* as he did, that he rather liked *Lassie Come Home*—and the candor to own up to the fact that the trashy could be nonetheless fascinating. His reviews often contain lines like this on a dog of a 1943 movie entitled *Old Acquaintance:* "The odd thing is that the two ladies [Miriam Hopkins and Bette Davis] and Vincent Sherman, directing, make the whole business look fairly intelligent, detailed, and plausible; and that on the screen such trash can seem, even, mature and adventurous."

How to account for this strange condition in the movies whereby the patently junky can nevertheless often hold one's interest? It can be accounted for in large part, I think, by the fact that we ask less of the movies than we do of other forms of art and entertainment. To say of a movie that it has a fine chase scene or a few witty moments is generally to say that, on the whole, one approves of it. But who would be satisfied with a novel that had one good chapter, or a symphony with, say, thirty-two bars of striking music? Because one also puts out less mental effort in watching a movie than in reading a book or listening to serious music, one is the more willing to settle for less. Besides, a movie, unlike a bad book or wretched music, is scarcely ever completely boring. Something is always going on; some tidbit holds the attention. A few years ago I saw an entirely superfluous movie entitled *Interlude;* it was a crude update of *Intermezzo,* the older sentimental-passion classic with Ingrid Bergman and Leslie Howard. *Interlude* had nothing to recommend it but its star's, Oskar Werner's, raincoat. Yet when Werner wore that raincoat, a finely tailored piece of goods, the clichés, incredible emotions, and idiot conflicts at the heart of the movie seemed somehow bearable. Oskar Werner's raincoat, I thought, should have won that year's Oscar for best performance in a supporting role.

Spectacle, which Aristotle thought the "least artistic of all the parts of tragedy and the least to do with the art of poetry," has always for me been a large part of the attraction of the movies. I am, for example, a sucker for any movie in which men wear the uniforms of the British in India or of the French Foreign Legion; a patsy for any movie having to do with Napoleon; and an absolute pushover for any movie having to do with the Confederacy or the antebellum South. Certain subjects, similarly, seem to me foolproof fodder for movies— among them movies set in prisons or having to do with boxing or with the attempt to bring off a perfect heist. Adaptations from second-rate literature—B. Traven's *The Treasure of Sierra Madre,* Dashiell Hammett's *The Maltese Falcon*— seem often to make finer movies than adaptations from first-line literature, though it depends on who is doing the adapting: Aldous Huxley's movie version of *Pride and Prejudice* has always seemed to me excellent. Good writers when left alone to do their work —which I gather they only infrequently are—make the best recipe for a winning movie: Graham Greene's scenario for *The Third Man*, for example, or James Agee's for *The African Queen*. Every time I prefer to trust men and women with literary, rather than film, culture.

Film cultists, cineasts, and others will, or at any rate should, be appalled by much of what I have written here. For them the movies are preeminently a visual business, and a very serious one indeed. Others may agree with Voltaire, who said that "the spirit that reigns in the theater is the faithful image of the spirit of a nation"—substituting the word "movies" for "theater"— for they find the movies, and popular culture generally, invaluable for understanding the national character. Still others may side with Madame du Châtelet, Voltaire's mistress, who said of the arts generally, "One may have preferences, but why exclusions?" and find this remark especially applicable to the movies. There is much to be said for all these views, but since much has already been said for them, perhaps I can be excused for not saying it again.

No, I am more interested in trying to discover what has happened to all but ruin the charming pastime of moviegoing. It is difficult to date such things, but I have the feeling that the decline set in sometime in the early 1960s when (I haven't checked the date) Susan Sontag, writing in *Partisan Review*, remarked that going to the movies was a much more casual and pleasurable activity than going to the theater. For the movies one needn't dress or buy tickets in advance or plan dinner out. "Let's catch a flick" was all one needed to say, and delight awaited. This was of course perfectly true, but all the same I wish Miss Sontag hadn't said it. The effect was rather as if a restaurant critic, writing in the Sunday *New York Times*, praised a quaint, inexpensive restaurant for its superlative food: the place instantly becomes noisy and costly, and the quality of the food goes down.

Earlier than this there had been people who took movies very seriously. Universities had film societies, and every major city had at least one little art house, where a pallid young woman smoking a Russian cigarette looked up contemptuously from her Baudelaire long enough to sell you a ticket for a Peruvian film that opened on a scene of peasant boys slaughtering a vicuña. Cultish stuff, really, but sometime in the middle 1960s the cult went national. Movies, alas, turned into film. Art—and highly artful—films had been made right along; such men as Kurosawa, Ray, Fellini, Antonioni, De Sica, and the young Orson Welles had, after all, been at it for decades. Yet now nearly every movie was thought to be, potentially, an art work. In a memorable phrase Frank Sinatra, Old Blue Eyes himself, speaking at an Oscar awards ceremony, said it was time for Hollywood to get back into "the Mona Lisa business."

Movies, in short, had become a highly serious and even more highly self-conscious matter. Wherever I went during that time movies were topic number one. Joining a small, amiable-looking group in the corner of an upper-middle-class living room, one was likely to be told that they were discussing the moral dimension of *Alfie*, and no one was likely to be welcome there long who said he hadn't noticed that it had any. Everywhere one was polled for one's opinion of the latest Altman, Friedkin, Scorsese. Around dinner tables, on couches, in faculty lounges many a sentence began, "Pauline Kael thinks . . . ," "John Simon says . . . ," "Andrew Sarris feels. . . ." I recall the wave of nausea that swept through me one evening when I was out with a couple who asked what did I think of *Annie Hall*—and in a tone of voice that implied an invitation to talk about Woody Allen as if he were Dante. And, lo, it wasn't long thereafter that Woody Allen, judging from pronunciamentos he made in many a portentous interview, began to talk as if he had come to believe he truly was Dante.

Meanwhile the universities, in their continuing effort to be first with the worst, inaugurated film-studies courses and programs, for which parents could pay upward of ten thousand dollars a year to send their sons or daughters to the movies. English professors toted around essays in their briefcases with snooze-inducing titles like "Ingmar Bergman and Women." "Kael feels . . . ," "Simon thinks . . . ," "Sarris says. . . ." Movies were being called the Now art. Clearly, things had gotten out of hand; it was almost enough to make an old moviegoer consider taking up bridge.

I do not mean to say that, in the midst of all this glut of chat and chaff, good movies weren't, and still aren't, being made. The forty-or-so-minute sequence between the young boy and his horse on the Greek island in *Black Stallion* left me aswoon. I disco-danced in my seat at *Saturday Night Fever.* I gave my sloppy housekeeping seal of approval to *Raging Bull* and to the performance of Robert De Niro, who seems to me well on his way to becoming the actor of the age. Better news yet: some of the tumult seems to be dying down. In the college curriculum film studies appear to be slipping. One scarcely ever hears "Simon says . . . ," et cetera. It has long since become clear, as Hilton Kramer has put it, that "Pauline Kael is not going to be the Edmund Wilson of our time." The Now art is beginning to look a little Then.

But even as the wave rolls back, much detritus is left on the shore. Movies continue to be greatly overrated, and one must pick one's way around them carefully as across a mine field. Some of the most dangerous among them are those that take themselves, and are taken by others, most seriously. I chose, for example, to step around both *The Deer Hunter* and *Apocalypse Now*. I saw *Star Wars* but took a pass on *The Empire Strikes Back*. I wouldn't see *The China Syndrome* with the aid of a Guggenheim grant; nor, for all my admiration of Laurence Olivier, *The Jazz Singer* on a Rockefeller. I would sooner undergo exploratory surgery than see any movie by Ken Russell. But I'm afraid I stepped right in the middle of *Kramer vs. Kramer*. I also stepped on—perhaps the metaphors here ought to be switched from mine fields to cow pastures—*The Marriage of Eva Braun*, which I thought ought to be annulled. Seeing two or three such dogs in a row, I understand the feeling of a friend of mine, a woman of sure taste and a strong antipathy to nonsense, who one night emerged from a bad movie to announce to her husband, "I don't ever want to see a movie that I haven't already seen before."

Still, old habits do not die so easily, and I continue to search for movies that are at least not directly offensive. On my personal moviegoing front, there have been setbacks and gains. As for setbacks, my nearest neighborhood theater, in walking distance from home, went porno, showing movies with such titles as *800 Fantasy Lane*, *Sweet Secrets*, *Pussycat Ranch*, and *Teddy Bare*. (This theater has since returned to what, on its marquee, is announced as "Family Entertainment.") On the credit side, another neighborhood theater has become a rerun house, changing its bill of fare fully four times each week, and showing such lush offerings as Greta Garbo, Humphrey Bogart, and Jean Renoir double features. (Not that I can any longer sit through a double feature; as legs are the first thing to go in an athlete, so it is an old moviegoer's bottom that gives way first.) This theater also runs some pretty putrid double features as well, such as Sam Peckinpah's *The Wild Bunch* and *Straw Dogs*, an evening that has all the allure of riding on a whiplash roller coaster after having been in a spaghetti-eating contest.

Theaters are also cropping up that show not reruns but what I think of as late or second runs—that is, movies that have played around but have not yet been shown on television. Where the glitzier new theaters charge $4.00 or $5.00 for a movie, these theaters charge $1.50 or $2.00. Having gone to the latter, I have discovered that certain movies I would hate at $4.00 I find tolerable at $1.50. Although I haven't yet seen it, Goldie Hawn in *Private Benjamin* seems to me possible at $1.50 but a cheat at $4.00. *Ordinary People,* which I haven't seen either but which strikes me as having that *Kramer vs. Kramer* middlebrow dog-dead earnestness, I don't think I should care to see for nothing. It's not, you understand, the principle of the thing; it's the money.

Moviegoers today seem to me in a condition similar to that of lovers of novels. If their appetite is to be satisfied, it will have to be fed largely on a diet of older movies; and it is quite possible to do this, for there is by now a large enough backlog of good older movies just as there is a sufficient backlog of nineteenth-century novels to keep the novel lover off the streets. Hope, however, lingers on. Perhaps at this moment Billy Wilder is directing Walter Matthau and Jack Lemmon in an urbane comedy; or François Truffaut is planning a series of movies adapted from the novels of Simenon; or Albert Finney and Audrey Hepburn are on location shooting a contemporary remake of *The Thin Man.* Ah, would it were so. But I fear the likelihood is greater that production is already well underway on a movie, starring Charles Bronson and Farrah Fawcett, in which a killer shark, on the rampage in Florida, is swallowing up condominiums—a disaster movie, in every sense of the term.

Disremembrance of Things Present

I T WOULD BE an exaggeration to say that I have long wanted to write an essay on the subject of memory but keep forgetting to get around to it. It is closer to the truth, though, to say that if I intend to write about memory, I had better do so soon, while I still have any of my own left. A slow leak in memory, the conventional wisdom has it, is an almost ineluctable part of growing older. But I have undergone a number of blowouts, in the course of which I have discovered that my memory, this faculty for remembering and recollecting, is not exactly steel-belted. Examples abound. Let me see if I can remember any.

In the lobby during the first intermission at the opera— Pavarotti in *Rigoletto*—I notice someone staring at me. He approaches. "Excuse me," he says, "but aren't you Joseph Epstein?" "I am," I answer. "We went to high school together," he says. I search his face for some clue that will allow me to recall his name, but none is forthcoming. "I am sorry," I say, in surrender, "but I am afraid I do not remember you." He then tells me his name, which I do recall, though I cannot put his high school face to it. Later, leaving the opera house, I am greeted by a former student of mine, who says she didn't think she would ever see Pavarotti upstaged but he certainly was tonight, by the man who played the title role. I agree, numbly and more than a bit dumbly, because, though I recall her face, her personality, even certain of the papers she wrote in my course, I cannot come up with her name. A name without a face, a face without a name: I suppose such little blackouts are common enough. Yet I seem to be suffering them more frequently as time goes on. If there is an art of instant recall, I appear to be a practitioner of its reverse: the art of instant oblivion.

Recently, over a forty-eight-hour period, I made a little list —journal of a forgetter, it might be called—of items that I know very well but that, when the time came to call them up, simply disappeared. The list starts with the word for the kitchen utensil used to drain fruits and vegetables (colander); the name of the town outside San Francisco where my brother lives (Tiburon); the unit of currency in Turkey (lira); the name of the offense made famous by the University of Oklahoma football team (the wishbone). These items all came up in conversation. Others came up on the street during the same period. In a shoe store I encountered a local television johnny, a man I see nearly every night on the television news and drew a blank on his name. I met a student who had been in a course I taught less than a year ago. While I could remember almost all the nuances of his behavior as a student—he specialized in displaying a certain mild boredom provoked by his presumed (though unproven) intellectual superiority—I could recollect only his last name, and I am not sure I had that quite right. (Did it or did it not have an *s* on the end?) Finally, in a shopping center, I saw the younger brother of a boyhood friend. He saw me as well, though I think he was not sure I was the person he thought I was, so we did not greet each other. I could not recall his name, but I did remember that his brother's first name was Burt and that, while the family was Jewish, there was nothing Jewish about its last name. This meeting—or, rather, non-meeting—occurred at roughly two o'clock in the afternoon; at eleven that night, after I put down my book and was about to turn off the bed lamp, I smiled as the right name, David Sherman, slid into my mind.

That smile, you may be sure, did not last long, for the next day I was up and about and forgetting again. These episodes —fits?—of forgetfulness are troubling in the extreme. Not that I have ever prided myself, as many people do, on a superior memory. Still, until fairly recently I should have rated my own memory at somewhere between adequate and quite good. When, in schoolboy years, feats of memory were required— for learning batting averages or biological phyla—mine never let me down. Certain things I have never been able to remember: how to spell rhythmn (?), whether women I have known named Ann have an *e* on the end of their names, the definition of teleology, the subjunctive conjugation of *savoir*. Nor can I ever quite recall if it's good fences or the absence of them that make for good neighbors, or whether it is better to cast thy seed upon a rock or into the belly of a whore, though, since I live happily married in an urban setting, neither of these confusions has thus far proved to be a serious problem.

What does irritate me is this endless minor forgetting, this inability to call up information on demand, these illogical blockages and blot-outs. Where did it all start? Difficult for me to pinpoint. As my life has become rather more crowded with small responsibilities and the manifold details that go along with them, I began some four or five years ago to make daily lists of things to do. Although I should like my lists to include items like "Lead raid on Aqaba," "Send letter to General Allenby," "Begin writing book on Arab revolt," mine generally reads: "Pick up laundry," "Cash check," "Buy stamps," "Cook chicken." Occasional slips have occurred: the unmailed letter found three weeks later in the raincoat pocket, the forgotten birthday, the usual Dagwood Bumsteadian husbandly absent-mindedness. But thus far my forgetfulness has not entailed anything exotic or privately humiliating. I have not yet shown up for a dinner party on the wrong night, forgotten my own telephone number or last name, brushed my teeth with shaving cream. But then I am still relatively young.

There are, I gather, people who have what is known in computer science as "random access memory"; they have not only well-stocked minds but a nearly perfect retrieval system. An apposite quotation, an obscure date, a past private experience—they need only call out for it and it is there, like the most faithful and efficient of family retainers, never sick, on duty twenty-four hours a day, working for room and board only. I, on the other hand, begin to resemble a dowager in a shabby bed jacket, pulling on a frayed bell cord and ringing for servants who often arrive two or three hours later, when my need for them is gone. Alas, I have begun to feel rather like the man in the old joke who tells a psychiatrist that he has the terrible problem of not being able to remember anything. "When did this problem first arise?" the psychiatrist asks. To which the man replies, "What problem?"

Yet when it comes to memory, "What problem?" turns out not to be such a dumb question. Many are the theories of memory, for nearly every philosopher has held one. (I think especially of poor Henry Bergson, whose book on laughter furrows most brows and whose book on memory, *Matter and Memory,* is so forgettable.) Many are the experiments devoted to investigating memory, for it has long been one of the great subjects in psychology, especially in connection with pedagogy. Yet the theories often conflict—who, by the way, can remember them all?—and the experiments seem to have more to do with describing the malfunctions, skewings, and tricks of memory than with memory itself. J. Z. Young, the eminent English neurophysiologist, has remarked that we still have scant information about "the principles of the operation of the memory." Research proceeds; language grows more technical ("nucleotide change," "RNA base ratios," "presynaptic inhibition" are but a few of the key phrases required if one is to sit in on a scientific discussion of memory); but the question of how a particular record is written in the memory remains, essentially, a mystery. No one can yet tell me why I am able to forget what I wrote in articles and reviews that I once felt passionately about and yet am able to recall the entire lyrics of "Some Enchanted Evening."

Medieval philosophers, and Greek philosophers before them, often believed the human soul to be linked externally to the five senses and internally to imagination and memory. The importance of memory to Plato, for whom the most truly important knowledge was the soul's recollection of Ideas, can scarcely be overestimated. In the ancient world, where printed material was scant, memory was decisive to all learning, and the subject of memory was part of the more general study of rhetoric. In *The Art of Memory*, Frances A. Yates discusses in scholarly detail the inner gymnastics of memory and its history, which is said to have begun in the sixth century B.C. with Simonides of Ceos—who was also the first poet to be paid for a poem (and hence the unacknowledged patron saint of all free-lance writers). Cicero wrote about memory. Seneca was famous for his memory, and was said to have been able to repeat two thousand names in the order in which they were given to him. Augustine, himself a teacher of rhetoric, speaks of a friend, one Simplicius, who was supposed to have been able to recite all of Vergil backward. Saint Thomas Aquinas was himself not only supposed to have had a prodigious memory, but was, in addition, a great authority on the subject. The most famous classical work on memory is a how-to-do-it volume entitled *Ad Herennium* (c. 86–82 B.C.) by an author who for some centuries was thought to be Tullius but whose true name, according to Professor Yates, is now acknowledged to be lost to history. Forgotten, then, is the author of the world's most influential book on memory—only the first of endless ironies on this matter of memory.

Too bad, really, for memory is a subject about which it would be good to have clear and uncomplicated information —the straight poop, as they used to say in the army. Instead we are thrown back on common sense, which is usually not such a bad thing to be thrown back on, except that memory so frequently demonstrates itself to be un- or non- or even anti-commonsensical. Take the vexing question of memory and aging. What makes it vexatious, of course, is the fear that as we grow older our minds, quite independent of our wishes, aspire toward a condition of tabula rasa. Such, at any rate, is the received opinion: as we grow older our memories inevitably grow dimmer. Yet scientific opinion, I gather, seems to run contrariwise. A Dr. Leslie Libow, who is a specialist in geriatric care, was not long ago quoted in the *Wall Street Journal* as saying that only 10 percent of the population over the age of sixty-five shows some mental deterioration, such as partial memory loss. I believe you, Doctor, but, even though I am only in my forties, I cannot promise to remember your name.

Most people do, I suspect, believe that memory fades with age. Although I know a number of persons in their seventies with superior memories, I think that, for the general run of people, their concern with remembering becomes less. Trollope, in his *Autobiography*, says that for the novelist "there comes a time when he shuts his eyes and shuts his ears. When we talk of memory fading as age comes on, it is such shuttings of eyes and ears that we mean. The things around us cease to interest us, and we cannot exercise our minds upon them." This seems to me persuasive, and not restricted to novelists alone. Most of us, as we grow older, have a sharper sense of what truly does interest us—and, concomitantly, what does not. If we liken life to a trip, memory might be considered a suitcase, and after a certain age an experienced traveler becomes rather more discriminating about packing it.

The first time I noticed my memory beginning to slip in any consistent way was some six years ago, when I began university teaching and found how quickly I forgot the names of the students in my classes, excepting only the excellent and the truly egregious ones. I do not *intend* to forget students' names, but evidently they do not go into my suitcase. (When I meet some of them years afterward, I usually pretend to remember their names; to me, dishonesty in this matter is almost always the best policy.) Where do they go, these names? Possibly off into the same empyrean into which strains of music fade.

But then perhaps I oughtn't to mention music, for I have scarcely any musical memory at all. I buy records, I go to concerts, I listen to a fair amount of music. Yet my pleasure, though it can be intense, is not of a lingering kind, for it ends with the music itself, and afterward I cannot recollect it in either tranquillity or agitation. I suppose this is because I do not have a good ear, and so can remember no music but the most timeworn classical war-horses and the least subtle popular tunes. As some people are blessed with splendid auricular memories, others have astonishing ocular memories and are able to recall nearly everything they have once seen, including whole pages of print. A. R. Luria, the Soviet psychologist, in his book *The Mind of a Mnemonist,* reports the case of S., a man who could memorize lengthy lists of numbers or stretches of poetry written in a language he did not know, and be able to repeat them forward or backward or (in the case of the rows of numbers) diagonally, not merely on the next day but five, ten, even seventeen years later. This is further than most of us would care to go.

The specialty of my own memory, I am beginning to discover, is literary. I wish this meant that I have stored up long patches of poetry, from Pindar through Pound, that I could quote either for my own pleasure or for use in driving unwanted visitors from my home by force of sheer boredom. But no. When I say my memory is literary I mean that it seems to work toward literary ends almost exclusively. First, I tend to remember things that might be useful for my own writing. Second—and more dangerous—I tend to shape my memories, to edit them, rewrite them even, working with the facts of past experience less like a historian or a biographer than like a novelist. But an instance is wanted.

I have a dear friend who has a brilliant and mischievous sense of humor. More than once I have attempted to explain the rare quality of his humor to other people; for part of it has to do with the fact that he does not seem to require an audience, or at least an immediate one, for some of his best jests. In this respect he is rather like a highly polished pianist who plays chiefly for his own pleasure. But to make more vivid my friend's sly wit, I have found myself telling the following anecdote about him:

A woman came up to my friend at a party to tell him how charming she thought his wife was. He thanked her, allowed that he had to agree with her, then added that most people were surprised to learn that his wife was deaf, indeed had been from birth. The fact is, of course, that his wife hears very well, and always has. His own private pleasure was to watch that woman, during the remaining hours of the party, speak to his wife very loudly and with most emphatic pronunciation.

Now the only thing wrong with this story is that it is completely untrue. I do not know quite why, but I felt a creeping doubt about it, and so one day queried my friend about its truthfulness. He replied that, no, he had never told anyone his wife was deaf, but suggested that I might have confused this incident with another that also took place at a party. There, a man, a famous local talker, was holding forth with great passion, causing a young lady to remark to my friend about the man's extraordinary conversational powers. Yes, my friend replied, and the wondrous thing is that, gregarious fellow and raconteur that he is now, he was an autistic child who lived in an igloo of self-chosen silence for the first twenty-five years of his life. This was, of course, the sheerest invention. The next morning, when the young woman told her boyfriend about this remarkable phenomenon and from whom she had heard it, he instantly recognized it as a piece of my friend's handiwork, and set her straight.

In its essentials, my memory's rewriting of this incident is not entirely false to the spirit of my friend's humor. Whether it is an improvement over the true happening I do not know. What I do know is that I did not intend it as an improvement. I did not intend it at all; I thought I was reporting, as they used to say on the old *Dragnet* television series, "just the facts, ma'am." But I am afraid that it all comes perilously close to the kind of literary embroidery that the late London drama critic James Agate—himself a great improver upon the facts—often referred to as "the higher truth."

It may well be that the memories of writers are to be trusted least of all. Truman Capote used to brag about his memory and, in connection with his book *In Cold Blood*, claimed that he required neither tape recorder nor even a notebook for recollecting and recording ample chunks of conversation. Not long after the book appeared, an article about Capote published in *Esquire* reported that while Capote was being interviewed in a restaurant, someone came up to his table but Capote could not remember his name; the man turned out to be Capote's own lawyer. Willie Morris once told a newspaper reporter that he thought writers tended to drink heavily to blunt the edge of memory, which they felt, according to him, more sharply than others. (One can almost hear the tinkle of ice cubes accompanying that observation.) More convincing to me is the notion put forth by the Canadian novelist Mordecai Richler, who maintained that there is a distinct difference in the very nature of experience before and after a person decides to become a writer. Before the decision to write, one experiences things directly; after the decision to write, nearly all experience becomes grist for writing, and thus is often colored and twisted and pounded into literary shape. My favorite title for a memoir, *What Little I Remember* by the physicist Otto Frisch, could never have been chosen by a writer. One of the occupational chores of being a writer, in fact, is that one is expected to remember nearly everything that one has experienced. Memory, for any writer, is the bank on which he must draw. Mencken was on target when he said the writer's task was to "essay to invent new ideas, to precipitate novel and intellectual concepts out of the chaos of memory and perception."

Yet the memory problem is scarcely a writer's problem alone. Someone—will it surprise you to learn that I have forgotten who?—has said that the human consciousness, in its daily ramblings, tends to spend roughly 40 percent of its time in the past, roughly 40 percent in the future, and the remainder in the present. As one grows older, I suspect that the portion of time spent thinking about the past lengthens even as the past itself lengthens, and that portion spent thinking about the future diminishes even as the future itself diminishes. All the more frustrating, therefore, does the idea of a faulty memory loom. The very notion of spending an increasing amount of time dwelling on a past that never did quite exist is, to put it gently, highly disturbing. It is bad enough that we cannot know the future; that we have, into the bargain, forgotten or gotten askew large segments of the past is appalling.

Worse news: William Maxwell, a novelist now in his seventies and one whom I greatly admire for his literary delicacy and temperamental balance, reveals that he holds even bleaker views about the accuracy of memory than I. This is doubly interesting, I think, because William Maxwell is a writer whose materials seem to derive chiefly from his own past. *The Folded Leaf, Time Will Darken It,* and his most recent novel, *So Long, See You Tomorrow,* are all works soaked in memory—in what Proust (the Homer and Freud and Clausewitz of the subject of memory) called "a nostalgic longing for impossible journeys through the realms of time." In *So Long, See You Tomorrow,* Maxwell, speaking through a narrator who seems clearly to be the author himself, says:

What we, or at any rate what I, refer to confidently as memory—meaning a moment, a scene, a fact that has been subjected to a fixative and thereby rescued from oblivion—is really a form of storytelling that goes on continually in the mind and often changes with the telling. Too many conflicting emotional interests are involved for life ever to be wholly acceptable, and possibly it is the work of the storyteller to rearrange things so that they conform to this end. In any case, in talking about the past we lie with every breath we draw.

"In speaking about the past we lie with every breath we draw." Is this dire declaration true? When our own personal past is entailed, I rather suspect it is true. Proust would agree with William Maxwell, at least to the extent of believing that we cannot will, or command, our memories. "And so it is with our own past," he wrote in the "Overture" to *Remembrance of Things Past.* "It is a labour in vain to attempt to recapture it: all the efforts of our intellect must prove futile. The past is hidden somewhere outside the realm, beyond the reach of intellect, in some material object (in the sensation which that material object will give us) which we do not suspect. And as for that object, it depends on chance whether we come upon it or not before we ourselves must die." Proust himself, of course, found his material object, the plump little cakes called *petites madeleines.* For many the material object has been the couch in the psychoanalyst's office, for psychoanalysis, whatever else it may or may not be, is a determined—some would say a predetermined—journey in search of memory lost.

But a distinction must be made between the memory for one's own past (in which one is too thoroughly implicated, usually as a plaintiff, but sometimes as a defendant) and the memory for objects, events, and ideas outside oneself. It is masterful memory of this latter kind that is required in serious scholarship, along, of course, with keen intelligence. Benjamin Jowett, Master of Balliol College—who is the subject of the poem that begins, "First come I. My name is Jowett. / There's no knowledge, but I know it"—used to maintain that the absence of a really first-class memory was what kept him from being a great scholar. Wallace Stevens similarly remarks in one of his letters, "I could never possibly have any serious contact with philosophy because I have not the memory." Henry James, totting up Sainte-Beuve's literary virtues, mentions "his marvelous memory." And William James, in his chapter on memory in *The Principles of Psychology,* wrote that any example of "your quarto or folio editions of mankind must needs have amazing retentiveness of the purely physiological sort."

Yet William James would have agreed, I expect, with the author of the *Ad Herennium,* who claimed that in mnemonics brute rereading was often necessary, and that in matters having to do with memory "theory is almost valueless unless made good by industry, devotion, toil and care." This is borne out elsewhere. The Talmud shuls of Eastern Europe used to train young boys in the daily memorizing and explication of a folio of the Talmud, and an old rabbinic doctrine holds that knowledge of a text is only assured by rereading it 101 times. William Lyon Phelps, who used to allow students in his Shakespeare course to substitute accurately quoted Shakespearean passages for answers to examination questions, quotes President Charles Eliot of Harvard who admitted that his "gift" for never forgetting a name came from repeating half a dozen times in his mind the name of each new person he met, while looking that person in the face. Many famous feats of memory, in short, have hard work behind them. This perhaps explains why the English used to say that a gentleman is not someone who knows Greek but someone who has forgotten it.

There are people who are born with extraordinary memories (idiot savants among them), and there are people who train their memories into a condition of extraordinariness (fellows who have memorized the Manhattan telephone directory or can name twenty-seven films in which Akim Tamiroff did not play a character named Mohammed), but memory at its most impressive is that of the truly superior mind, whose memory is owed to study, to thoughtfulness, and to the integration of all the forces of intellection. William James put it nicely: "The one who thinks over his experiences most and waves them into systematic relations with each other, will be the one with the best memory." And so it has seemed to me among the few powerful scholars I have known. They have only to press the button of memory to call up the most wondrous network of associations. Their suitcases, to return to my earlier metaphor, have a great deal more in them because they are so much more intelligently packed.

Next to them I think of myself as a man in a crowded railway station, schlepping three shopping bags, out of which obtrude bits of tissue, comic books, soiled linen. A cigarette is perched behind my ear, even though I do not smoke; a train ticket is held between my teeth; and my raincoat pockets are stuffed with sheet music and old socks. Such at any rate is the self-view of one man whose memory is giving him difficulty. This view is not so very discrepant from reality. A few more details: I will find myself opening a linen closet to hang up my overcoat; I will begin to dial a telephone number, and three digits into the dialing forget who it is I am calling; I will, in conversation, have a pertinent point to interject, but when it comes my time to speak, the point has eluded me. These things do not happen always, but often enough to be highly disconcerting.

I should think myself a little mad, in fact, if I did not observe so many of my contemporaries—even people ten years on either side of my age—who seem to be going through similar little *maladies de la mémoire*. I telephone an acquaintance who suggests that I get back to him that same evening. I ask for his home telephone number. He cannot produce it. A friend accepts an invitation in the early afternoon for an informal dinner that very night—and fails to show up because, in a few hours' time, he has completely forgotten about it. At a New York university I enter an elevator with a literary critic of some fame; in the elevator is a historian of equal fame, a woman he has known for perhaps thirty years. It is incumbent on him to introduce her to me. "You are not going to believe this," he says to her, "but I'll be damned if I can remember your name."

Which leads me to a theory. It is the thoroughly untested theory (no polls, no laboratory work, no systematic surveys) that memory loss is often most acute, or at least acutely felt, in one's prime. I put this theory forth on the ground that while one's prime is usually, by definition, the time of the height of one's powers, it is also the time of the height of distraction in one's life. I have no intention of dragging in that Tootsie Roll cliché of popular psychology, the mid-life crisis, but the fact remains that so very much is swirling about in the years of one's prime. The suitcase of memory—filled with all that has gone before, filled with all that is happening currently—strains at the straps. Most of us wish to pack in everything. It cannot, for most of us, be done. William James quotes a French writer, a M. Ribot: "We thus reach the paradoxical result that one condition of remembering is that we should forget." And James himself adds, "In the practical use of our intellect, forgetting is as important a function as recollecting."

On the need for forgetting, or the problem of too keen a memory, Jorge Luis Borges has written a wonderful little story entitled "Funes the Memorious." Ireneo Funes is a young man living in a small Uruguayan town, who has a knack for recalling names and also for telling the time of day without aid either of a clock or of the sun. One day he falls from his horse and is left paralyzed, but also with the gift of "infallible perception and memory." He could thus, among other things, learn a new language in a day. Borges writes: "He could reconstruct all his dreams, all his half dreams. . . . Funes remembered not only every leaf of every tree of every wood, but also every one of the times he had perceived or imagined it. He decided to reduce each of his past days to some seventy thousand memories, which would then be defined by means of ciphers." And deeds even more astonishing than these are recounted. Yet Borges's narrator notes: "I suspect, however, that he was not very capable of thought. To think is to forget differences, generalize, make abstractions." Reading Borges's eight-page story, one realizes what an absolute hell remembering everything would be. "Funes the Memorious" ends on this flat sentence: "Ireneo Funes died in 1889 [at age 21], of congestion of the lungs." But the real cause of death, one gathers, was drowning by data.

The powers of memory are mysterious. Dwelling on the finest memories cannot relieve a toothache or alter a low mood induced by foul weather. But not to have fine memories to dwell upon seems an unbounded sadness. Vast though the differences between two persons' memories may be, no one, it seems, can quite comb his memory clean of oddments. (Only the other evening I, who yield to nearly everyone in my knowledge of jazz, was able to call up immediately the name of the wife of Dick Haymes who was herself a cabaret singer —Fran Jefferies—when no one else at table could recollect it. But, then, who doesn't have such toys stored in his mental attic?) Santayana thought "inheritance and memory make human stability," and in *The Life of Reason* he wrote: "In endowing us with memory nature has revealed to us a truth utterly unimaginable to the unreflective creation, the truth of mortality." Others have felt that memory, with the ability it bestows to allow a person to live vividly away from his body and immediate environment, is a possible sign of the ability to continue to live after the body has disappeared. I am not ready to argue that this is true, but it is a point I do not intend to forget.

Penography

A FETISH—FINALLY. Ah, sweet mystery of life at last I've found you. And just in time. I have for so long liked a lot of things a little that it is exhilarating to like a little thing a lot. I speak of fetish neither in the primitive nor the sexual meaning, but rather in the sense of fetish as an object for which one has an obsessive devotion, a slightly irrational reverence. My fetish speaks for me and I through it. It is for pens, fountain pens specifically, and I tell you straight out, Doctor, I have this thing for fountain pens—I am nuts about them, Doctor, do you hear me, absolutely bonkers!

Evidently I am not alone in this madness. I am told that fountain pens are currently making a small comeback in popularity. Magazines carry advertisements for them; department stores and office-supply and stationery stores display them prominently. Not that fountain pens are exactly sweeping the country. Few drugstores any longer carry ink, though once they all did. I doubt if many schoolchildren at present use fountain pens. Whole generations have by now grown up inkless, learning to write with ball-point pens and felt-tipped markers. Some members of those generations are discovering the pleasures of the fountain pen for the first time. For me, it's the second time.

I returned to using fountain pens roughly five years ago. But I am old enough to have used wooden penholders and steel nibs in grade school, and to recall teachers coming round to fill our inkwells from gallon jugs of board-of-education ink. I spoke above of pleasures, but what a spectacular mess those ancient instruments could make! Blotting paper was in the pencil box of every child. The rigid metal of the nibs combined with the drippings from the ink could make writing a wretched business. Only a few years later—around fifth grade —did I come to use my first fountain pen, an Esterbrook, a rather blunt-looking instrument, which came in an orange-brown color over something akin to a herringbone pattern. The Esterbrook was a sturdy pen, a Model A among pens; it did not leak—much—and I believe it then cost $1.49.

By this time, age eleven or so, my handwriting was already quite ruined. At least I myself never cared for it. Nor did any of my grade-school teachers. The slant of my letters was erratic; letters that should have been closed (*s*'s, *p*'s, *d*'s) were often left open; neither my ascenders nor my descenders were of a uniform height or depth; my capitals were pretentious in the extreme; even my periods lacked authority. Graphologically speaking, I was a disaster.

This was no minor disaster, either; for penmanship, as instruction in handwriting was called, was one of the important grade-school subjects. Every child had a penmanship manual offering instruction in something called the Palmer Method, and daily we practiced the loops and slants of what was felt to be classical cursive handwriting. One day an instructor from the company that published the manuals visited our school. A tall slender woman with a southwestern accent, she did capital *O*'s and *S*'s at the blackboard. "Swat, swat, swat that skeeter!" she called out as she made the long slanted line of the *S*, then looped it at its top for the trip down and back.

Her aim, and that of the manuals, was to give us clear, regular, and quite uniform handwriting.

This was, of course, an enterprise destined for failure. A person's handwriting is one of the distinctive things about him, and no two handwritings, like no two sets of fingerprints, are the same. There is something about handwriting that seems to cry out for the expression of idiosyncrasy. Circles for dotting *i*'s, Gothic touches on capitals, swooping flourishes at a word's end—there is no graphic stunt people won't try in the effort to be elegant and individual. Handwriting is tied up with what people nowadays are pleased to call their "identity." It is a most intimate matter, and richly complicated.

If a graphologist were to have examined my youthful handwriting, he might well have diagnosed an identity crisis. (Family therapy, he might even have concluded, was indicated.) Perhaps it is in one's handwriting that one first sets out to create a style for oneself. The handwriting of my childhood was part Palmer Method, part imitation of my father's handwriting, part Declaration of Independence signature—and what was left was me. It didn't, if I may say so, come off. I secretly thought that my poor handwriting was a sign of poor character. Had I been a girl, I should have been in serious trouble. Some boys did have nice handwriting, but boys were not really expected to have nice handwriting. Girls, though, were under an *obligation* to write beautifully. To fail in that regard was tantamount to failing hygienically. A girl with poor handwriting seemed nearly a slut. I don't recall any girls in our class with poor handwriting. It wasn't allowed.

I brought an additional difficulty to the job of handwriting. I was precocious in one thing only: I learned to print letters before I went to school. In doing so I taught myself to hold a pencil—and, later, a pen—in a manner I can only describe as highly individual. It involved an odd bunching of fingers around the writing instrument, a bunching that resembled nothing so much as the bout-ending hold of a wrestler named Cyclone Anaya, which he called the Cobra Twist. Added to this was an odd turning inward of my wrist, which led most people to think I wrote left-handed. Naturally I hid this unorthodox grip from my grade-school teachers, though I refused to give it up for my serious writing (and have only finally done so a few years ago). Wicked friends were always amused by this grip; kind strangers, when first seeing it, assumed I had a debilitating muscular disease.

Holding a pen as I did, no pen was my friend. Fountain pens were, though, a very big item when I was young. A comedy record, spinning a joke off the fact that fountain pens were so frequently given as bar mitzvah gifts, had a young Jewish boy announce in his bar mitzvah speech, "Today I am a fountain pen!" Many were the manufacturers of fountain pens: Eversharp, Sheaffer, Parker, Waterman, Wearever. Owning an expensive pen-and-pencil set seemed a mark of very great distinction. Such a set was part of an elegant man's accoutrement, which in those days might include cuff links, a key chain, a money clip, a small gold pen-knife, perhaps a signet ring. But the expensive fountain pen was knocked out of the box—or, rather, pocket—by the ball-point pen. The first ball-point pen was invented by a Hungarian named Laszlo Jozsef Biro and patented in 1939. But it rose to prominence when it was marketed in this country by a man named Milton Reynolds, who produced a pen called the Reynolds Rocket. The Reynolds Rocket sold for $12.50—a big figure in 1945— and the claim made for it was that it could write underwater, which it could. Above water, though, it was scarcely any good at all. Nonetheless, on October 29, 1945, the first day it was marketed at Gimbels in New York, ten thousand were sold.

Ball-point pens rose even higher in popularity as they fell

in price. They had much in the way of convenience to recommend them: they didn't blot, they didn't require refilling, they were eminently disposable, rather like toothpicks. Being for the most part made of plastic, ball-point pens became part of that body of items one used and threw away. Or if one didn't exactly throw them away, it was no great heartbreak if they became lost, because, first they were not very expensive, and second one had developed no attachment to them. It is difficult to imagine anyone, even a child, feeling saddened because he has lost his favorite ball-point pen.

To the degree that ball-point pens rose in popularity did the general interest in handwriting seem to fall off. The early ball-points tended to skip, and even the more expensive ones seemed to run away with one's handwriting. A fit analogy here might be that of driving a car with a gearshift or driving one with an automatic transmission. The automatic transmission (the ball-point) had much to recommend it, but the gearshift (the fountain pen) gave you a great feeling of control. My own handwriting, poor with fountain pens, became fully hideous with ball-point pens.

"What is handwriting but silent speech?" Erasmus wrote. "How warmly we respond whenever we receive from friends or scholars letters written in their own hands." And he continued: "An elegant script is like a fine picture; it has a pleasure of its own which engages the author of a letter while he is composing it no less than the recipient when he is studying it." Thus, thank-you notes, letters of condolence, and other missives of a personal kind seem to call for handwriting, as if handwriting is the most personal, and hence most sincere, form of communication. When Henry James began to dictate his novels and letters to a series of typists, he mounted elaborate Jamesian apologies to his correspondents for "this cold-blooded process," also referring to it as this "fierce legibility" and "the only epistolary tongue of my declining years."

Of course, there is something talismanic about handwriting. How else can one account for the attraction of autographs and the passion of autograph hunters, be they either children or hardened professionals? Writing that comes from the hand of an admired or famous person is perhaps as close as one can get to touching that hand. The apostle Paul was supposed to have written to the Galatians in his own hand. Imagine what the autograph of Jesus of Nazareth would bring on the open market! One way of calibrating contemporary fame might be to find out whose signature among contemporaries fetches the highest price among autograph collectors.

An author's signature is felt to enhance the value of a book. On a few occasions I have been asked to sign a hundred or so copies of books I have written. It sounds a charming thing to do, one of the triumphant rites of authorly achievement. In fact, after signing the first half-dozen copies, it becomes inexpressibly boring. In a used-book store I once came across the book of a well-known critic, affectionately inscribed to a famous novelist; the affection was evidently less than reciprocal, else what would the book be doing in a used-book bin? At first, I found this highly amusing; then I thought that perhaps I had seen something I oughtn't to have seen. The novelist would probably have done better to rip out the signature page before he sold the book. Selling the book with the inscription seemed, somehow, slightly sacrilegious, almost as if the recipient were selling a part of the author's spirit, or the man himself.

Few novelists still consider a person's handwriting part of his or her character—something, in any case, to be noted, like the color of a person's eyes or his smile. Thackeray, though, was a novelist who did, whenever the chance permitted, note his characters' handwriting. In *Vanity Fair*, one of his characters writes "a fine mercantile hand," another writes a "schoolboy hand"; of yet another character Thackeray remarks that he had "the best of characters and handwritings." As for their own handwriting, many writers surprise. Proust, for example, wrote a loose and inelegant hand, where one would have expected quite the reverse. Max Beerbohm's handwriting is just as one would have expected: compact, clear, with very little slant. Wordsworth wrote in a small, cramped hand. But the smallest handwriting is that of Aleksandr Solzhenitsyn, who trained himself to write as small as possible so that his books would come to fewer manuscript pages and thus would be easier to hide and smuggle out of the Soviet Union. Evelyn Waugh wrote a clear hand with many an interesting idiosyncrasy—in an otherwise cursive handwriting he wrote his *r*'s as if they were printed capitals—and, with his penchant for marching backward, ever backward, he wrote with a wooden penholder and steel nib.

As some people imagine what a writer looks like, I think of what his or her handwriting looks like. William Plomer, the English man of letters, has filled in some of these blanks for me. In his memoirs he not infrequently describes a person's handwriting. Christopher Isherwood's handwriting he calls "imperturbable." Lady Ottoline Morrell's proclaimed her "not a type but an individual." Virginia Woolf's handwriting, "sharp, delicate, and rhythmical as her prose, was pleasing in itself." Of the blanks that remain blanks, I could be quite wrong, but I imagine writers of voluminous works—Balzac, Dickens, Tolstoy—to have had scrawling, untidy handwriting, with little or no interest in crossing *t*'s and dotting *i*'s. In this connection I recall a charming scene in Henri Troyat's biography of Tolstoy. Troyat pictures the great writer in his upstairs study at Yasnaya Polyana, turning out page after page of *War and Peace*, while downstairs his wife and older children are reworking each page into "fair copy." It is a scene worthy of a Russian Jane Austen. As for Jane Austen, I imagine her handwriting to have been very neatly formed indeed—exquisite crewelwork, like her novels. But then I tend to think—quite without any knowledge to back it up—of eighteenth-century handwriting as small and elegant, of nineteenth-century handwriting as strong and sprawling.

As for twentieth-century handwriting, allow me, solipsistically, to put forth my own. It is a hodgepodge, a cacophony on the page. Erasmus had it that elegance of handwriting is primarily based on four things: the shape of letters, the way they are joined, their linear arrangement, and their proportion. Of these four, I should say that I do only one, joining letters, passably well. Of the remainder, I make a frightful botch. Inconsistency is the chief difficulty. In the same word I will loop the descender of the letter *p* and then bring the same descender down a few letters later without a loop. I may end one word with a flourish tantamount to a deep bow from the waist, then end the next without so much as a by-your-leave. What is more, I am not even consistently inconsistent: every so often I will turn out two or three beautifully formed words in a row. At forty-six I continue to fool around with my signature. If I hold up two of my own signatures, they sometimes seem to me as if written by two different people. I am surprised that by now my bank hasn't reported me for forgery of my own name.

I am what people schooled in the rude jargon of Vienna call an anal type—or, more precisely, I aspire to anality, insofar as that Freudian term means a love of tidiness, a rage for order. I say aspire, for this love, this rage, has remained an aspiration only. Still, applied to handwriting, it is for neatness that I yearn. What I desire is endless elegant notebooks filled with penetrating observations, all written in a fine script. As it happens, I do keep a journal, but not in elegant notebooks. I fear that the reason for this is that my handwriting is not up to expensive paper. My handwriting on costly stationery would be like chili on Limoges china.

What, I wonder, would graphologists make of my handwriting? What, I further wonder, do I make of graphology? The purpose of graphology is to relate elements of a person's handwriting to traits of his personality. Sometimes this is done in a most general, and therefore most unhelpful, way, as when large handwriting is said to characterize a large-spirited, ambitious person and small handwriting to characterize a mean-spirited, pedantic person. But when graphologists get more specific they do not necessarily get more persuasive. Here, for example, is Huntington Hartford, an ardent graphologist and author of a book entitled *You Are What You Write*, on the significations of dotting the *i:*

An "i" dot before the letter means procrastination, for example, and beyond it, impatience; a club-shaped "i" dot, temper, brutality. There are three or four meanings peculiar to the "i" dot, however, about which most graphologists agree. For some reason they often link the dot precisely placed above the "i" with a good memory and a wavy dot with a sense of humor. (I am not 100 percent convinced!) They ascribe a critical faculty to those who, in superior scripts like those of Einstein, Lessing, and Pasteur, connect the dot with either the preceding or the following letter. Finally, there is the "i" dotted with a complete little circle. Before the days of Walt Disney, with the circular dot over the "i" in his famous signature, Louise Rice informed us . . . that the users of this sign are "the adapters of art."

Important if true; if not true, then amusing. I at any rate find it amusing, but many eminent intellectuals and artists have found graphology more than amusing; among its adherents have been Madame de Staël, Goethe, Poe, Leibniz, and, in our day, Randall Jarrell. Foolish though graphology may seem in its particulars, most of us, I suspect, believe in it a little, if only in an ex post facto way. A book review editor, speaking of a writer who had failed to meet a deadline, not long ago said to me, "From his creepy handwriting I should have known not to trust him." Similarly, if I show you a handwriting filled with energy and obvious confidence, then tell you that this is the handwriting of Sigmund Freud—whose handwriting, very rhythmic, does so seem—you are likely to say, "How appropriate!"

Can madness be revealed in a person's handwriting? Graphologists tend to think so, and so did the late John Cheever, who, in his story "The Five-Forty-Eight," uses handwriting as a clue to mental breakdown. The chief character in this story notes of his secretary, with whom he is to enter into a love affair, that "he had found only one thing in her that he could object to—her handwriting." Cheever continues:

He could not associate the crudeness of her handwriting with her appearance. He would have expected her to write a rounded backhand, and in her writing there were intermittent traces of this, mixed with clumsy printing. Her writing gave him the feeling that she had been the victim of some inner—some emotional—conflict that had in its violence broken the continuity of the lines she was able to make on the paper.

On the other hand, judgment by handwriting must clearly be guarded against. In his novel *Lament for the Death of an Upper Class,* Henri de Montherlant puts the case for the antigraphology point of view very neatly, when of a meek and terrified character he notes: "It is amusing to observe that M. de Coantré's writing, very upright, well formed and weighty, the signature, heavily underlined and the lines rising, would, according to the rules of graphology, have made one attribute to the writer all the qualities of character in which he was most certainly and most completely deficient."

Yet, within very strict limits, handwriting can reveal traits, if not of character, then of personality. In a person's handwriting, one can often read his aspirations—toward orderliness, elegance, grandeur. Handwriting can also reveal pretentiousness, affectation, exhibitionism, and many another minor ex-cess. Or take illegible handwriting. What does it say about a person that his handwriting is illegible? I should say that it speaks to a sense of self-importance. American physicians are famously illegible. Horace Greeley wrote in a hand so illegible that letters of dismissal from him were often used by fired employees as recommendations for new jobs, for all that new employers could usually make out was Greeley's signature.

Illegibility has never been my problem; legibility has been. My clear dissatisfaction with my clear handwriting has brought about my fairly recent interest in fountain pens. My hope here is for a technological solution: a better writing instrument will make for a better handwriting—or so I reason. Thus far, though, I have been forced to conclude, in the fashion of the public-relations wing of the National Rifle Association, that pens don't kill handwriting, people do.

Meanwhile I am building up quite a nice arsenal of fountain pens. I have the little dears on my desk before me. Let me take inventory: two rather dud Sheaffers, one maroon with gold trim, one black with silver cap; two Parkers, one a 1932 model in black and gray horizontal stripes with a dull silver clip, the other sleek black, with a cap in two different shades of gold and a beige stone at its tip; a dark red Waterman, silver trim, a slender little jobby with a stainless steel point; a Pelikan, black with gold trim and a removable point; and, finally, in my hand at the moment, the fine Swiss pen, a Mont Blanc, No. 24, black with gold trim and Mont Blanc's traditional six-point star at both top and bottom. Owning so many pens may seem extravagant, but I myself think this is a quite modest collection. My family, I know, is grateful that I do not go in for skywriting.

Different strokes for different folks, and different pens for different yens. Sometimes I have a yen for the streamlined feel of my gold-capped Parker; sometimes I have a yen for my Pelikan, which is feathery light; sometimes I have a yen for my

1932 Parker, which, along with its being half a century old, gives off a delicious smell of ink (I warned you we were talking here of a fetish). My Mont Blanc is most serviceable for writing lengthy things. Sheaffers are often my choice for writing checks. I tend to travel with my Waterman, which is the only one of my pens with a cartridge ink supply. I am not, I should say here, one of those gents who walks about with nine pens, a six-inch ruler, and an air gauge in his shirt pocket, all tucked into a plastic shield that has Fergusson's Hardware & Supply printed on it. No, I prefer to pick out and wear a single pen to fit the mood of the day, rather like picking out and wearing a necktie.

I continue to look for the perfect pen—the pen, you might say, ultimate. I read catalogues from pen companies with an intensity similar to that with which men, long at sea, read *Playboy*. I check stationery shops; at antique stores I inquire whether they have any old pens in stock. Who knows, I may come across a Waterman Patrician, first manufactured in 1928, or the splendid plastic and rolled gold Mont Blanc of the mid-1960s, or the costly French-made S. T. Dupont at a vastly cut-rate price. What I am looking for, of course, is a pen that feels exactly right, that will flow along in exact cadence with my thoughts—indeed, whose even flow will cause ideas to flow in me. Choice of a fountain pen, after all, entails the same meticulous attention to individual preference as does, say, choice of a tennis racquet: weight, grip, balance—each can affect performance crucially. As for ink, I find myself regularly buying new brands, trying out new colors, mixing like a mad chemist one with another . . . but I had better not get started on the subject of ink.

Since we are talking here about a fetish, allow me to report a recent dream. In this dream a friend of mine produced from his suit-coat pocket a pen—a somewhat battered Mont Blanc

with a partially translucent green top—which, he announced
with a smile, had once belonged to Rudyard Kipling. Even in
my sleep I was ill with envy for his ownership of that pen. But
I arose the next morning with what I feel is a winning market-
ing idea. Why not autograph model fountain pens, on the
order of Chris Evert tennis racquets, Jack Nicklaus golf clubs,
Pete Rose baseball gloves? Why not, in other words, Dante,
Shakespeare, Jane Austen pens? True, fountain pens did not
come into use until 1884, when the firm of L. E. Waterman
produced the first usable ones, but this is a mere technical
difficulty that can be surmounted. Patent, meanwhile, pend-
ing.

The market for this particular item might be severely limited to one—me. I have always been inordinately interested in
the conditions of composition. Whenever I read a literary
biography I linger lovingly over the descriptions of the rooms
in which writers work, of their oddities and idiosyncrasies in
the actual act of writing. Hemingway, for example, wrote
standing up at a high desk; W. H. Auden amidst a clutter of
paper and cigarette ash; William Faulkner in a shed behind his
house in Oxford, Mississippi. (Faulkner, incidentally, had a
most deceptive handwriting; it was straight up and down,
small, fine, and extremely tidy, when, given his flights of rhetoric, one would have expected thick strokes, slashes really,
strewn messily about the page.) Theodora Bosanquet, Henry
James's secretary-typist, wrote a charming little book on
James's work methods; in it she compared taking dictation
from James to accompanying a fine singer on the piano.

Nothing so facilitates writing as actually having something
to say, yet the conditions under which, and the tools with
which, writing is done can contribute to facility—or to difficulty. From my own experience, the one time I can recall
having a truly wretched time getting writing done—the one

time, that is, when the problem was neither knowing what I wanted to say nor knowing how to say it—was after I had recently bought an Olivetti portable typewriter with italic type. No sooner had I brought that machine home than I realized I had made a mistake. How I loathed the look of that type on my pages! Everything I wrote seemed, in that type, arrhythmic, dull, stupid. I put the typewriter to the test by typing out a paragraph from E. M. Forster, a few sentences from Orwell, and four or five lines from a poem by T. S. Eliot —all of which seemed to me, in that type, arrhythmic, dull, stupid. This machine, I concluded, must go. And go presently it did. I traded it in—traded down, as they say on the used-car lot—for a Royal standard twenty years older than the Olivetti. We, the Royal standard and I, have lived happily ever after.

As for pens, the search goes on. I note those among my acquaintances who use fountain pens and those who do not. In movies my interest peaks whenever someone writes a letter. In a film about the life of Gustav Mahler, Mahler, when composing, used a long and elegant black pen of a kind I have never seen before or since. Do composers and choreographers, I wonder, use special pens? In a television series made from the memoirs of Albert Speer, whenever the actor who plays Hitler signs a document he uses the large Mont Blanc Diplomat (current U.S. price $250). This is a pen I have long admired yet do not quite covet. The pen is almost a bit too grand, a bit too pretentious. I myself would be embarrassed to take it out in public, for it seems unsuitable for anything less momentous than, say, signing a declaration of war—something I do not often do. Putting such a pen into the hand of Hitler, however, seemed an altogether appropriate touch. Give that propman an Emmy.

Some people wish to live surrounded by art, others require high-powered and finely mechanized automobiles. All I ask for is a pen. True, I am looking for a perfect pen, a Bucephalus, a Joe DiMaggio, a Sarah Vaughan of a pen. This would be a pen that would make my handwriting worthy of the approbation of the sniffiest Jane Austen heroine. From it ideas would flow in orderly profusion. It would blot when breaches of good sense, self-deceptions, and lies were written with it. Held loosely, it would toss off charmingly witty sentences; pressed down upon, it would touch the profound. It would permit no dull patches; only brilliance would issue from it: penetrating insights, fantastic formulations. Writing with such a pen would be like cantering along the Pacific Ocean on a palomino, instead of what writing really is—stopping and starting in a junk wagon down a thousand broken-up alleys. What a glory it would be to own such a pen! I keep searching, ever hopeful, even as I am confident that, were I to find such a pen, no ink for it would be available.

But I Generalize

As a university teacher, I don't normally call students "Honey," yet not long ago I not only called a student "Honey," but, in a state of complete exasperation, I invited her to dance. It happened, as scandalous things frequently do, out of town. I was lecturing at a school in Ohio, and during a session with a group of freshmen students, one of them, an earnest young woman, asked if I didn't think I sometimes engaged in dangerous generalizations. I allowed as how I generalized but that I was not aware of doing so dangerously. Could she give me an example? Reading from one of my sacred and profound works, she adduced the following instance on the behavior of immigrants to America: ". . . Greeks ran restaurants, the Jews went into retailing, the Italians sold produce and became florists, the Irish (along with being policemen) worked as waiters and owned neighborhood bars, the Germans did a bit of everything." Well, those were certainly generalizations, but what, I asked, was dangerous about them?

"Wouldn't they be offensive to the people about whom you say these things?" she answered.

"Why?" I rejoined. "I myself, a member of the Hebrew extraction, as a black sergeant of mine once referred to Jews, am not in the least offended that my co-religionists went into retailing in this country. Nor do I think that the Greeks, Irish, Germans, and Italians would be in the least offended by my generalizations about them."

"Still," she said, "what you wrote isn't true of *all* Greeks, Jews, Italians, and Irish."

"True enough," I said, "Einstein didn't go into retailing but relativity, Fermi didn't go into flowers but fission. But there is enough general truth to my statements to hold up. At least I believe there is."

"Even if there is," she said, "I don't think you're entitled to say things like that."

And then it happened: "Honey," said I, "if I can't say things like that, then we may as well turn on the stereo and start dancing, because all conversation becomes impossible."

Along with demonstrating my ability to overpower an eighteen-year-old girl in argument, this incident reminds me not only of my own love of generalization but of its importance to civilized discourse. Generalization, especially risky generalization, is one of the chief methods by which knowledge proceeds. In science such generalizations are called hypotheses, and eventually these scientific generalizations have to be backed up. Apparently, though, this is not even true of all scientific generalizations; I recently learned, for example, that Gödel thought that "not everything that is true is provable." And Valéry spoke of that body of items that "are neither true nor false—in fact they could not be either." Outside of science, not all generalizations have to—or indeed can—be backed up. I sometimes think risky generalizations are the only kind that are of interest. Safe generalizations are usually rather boring. Delete that "usually rather." Safe generalizations are quite boring. But I generalize.

Generalizations have had a very bad press. Part of the reason they have been so roundly contemned is that they can so readily be pressed into service for inimical causes. What else is racism, what else anti-Semitism, but faulty generalizations organized and systematized? The most thoughtful writers have implored those who generalize to knock it off. "All general judgments are loose, slovenly, imperfect," noted Montaigne. "General notions," wrote Lady Mary Wortley Montagu, "are generally wrong." And Blake, never noted for the light touch, added, "To generalize is to be an idiot." Yet all these attacks on generalization—it will not have been missed by close readers—are themselves generalizations.

There are generalizations and there are generalizations—which is not only a generalization but very close to a tautology. Allow me to elaborate. I myself have a sharp distaste for large social generalizations, those, that is, whose pretense is to take in all of society. Lonely crowds, affluent societies, organization men are not for me. I am not too wild about Me Decades or Future Shocks either. To pass muster with me, a generalization must not be too roomy, or cover too vast an area, or even be on too significant a subject. I despise, for instance, the notion that we are living in something called "a culture of narcissism," but I like very much John O'Hara's observation that "almost no woman who has gone beyond the eighth grade ever calls a fifty-cent piece a half-a-dollar." For me a generalization, like a friend, has to have a little modesty.

This doesn't mean that I am interested in modest generalizations exclusively. Not at all. I am afraid that I am one of those people who continues to read in the hope of sometime discovering in a book a single—and singular—piece of wisdom so penetrating, so soul stirring, so utterly applicable to my own life as to make all the bad books I have read seem well worth the countless hours spent on them. My guess is that this wisdom, if it ever arrives, will do so in the form of a generalization.

My hope is that I am not dozing when it appears. Opportunity, to cite a generalization that is perhaps even more boring than it is false, knocks but once.

Meanwhile, I have an unrepentant fondness for authors who generalize. This would naturally include the great writers of aphorisms, many of them French (La Rochefoucauld, La Bruyère, Chamfort), a few German (G. C. Lichtenberg, Karl Kraus, Meister Eckhart), an occasional Englishman (Horace Walpole), and no Americans (Emerson, for me, does not qualify). Although novelists are supposed to show and not tell, I take particular pleasure in novelists who take a few moments off now and again to generalize. George Eliot goes in for this sort of thing, Proust does it rather more frequently, and, among living novelists, Anthony Powell, in his twelve-novel cycle, *A Dance to the Music of Time,* can almost be said to specialize in it. Not only does Powell himself, through his narrator Nicholas Jenkins, generalize, but so do other of his characters (the composer Moreland notably among them); and sometimes whole scenes will be given over to characters who generalize back and forth with one another. These generalizations are often a touch oblique, but unfailingly interesting.

"Nothing dates people more than the standards from which they have chosen to react," is a fair though modest sample of Anthony Powell's work in this line. But it can—and does—get much richer. Of a woman in one of the novels, the narrator asks, "Was she determined, in the habit of neurotics, to try to make things as bad for others as for herself?" Generalization, in Powell's hands, can be used even in the process of description. Walking into an apartment, for example, one of his characters smells "the fumes of unambitious cooking." Or he can create a general type and then go on to generalize upon his generalization. Such a general type, for Powell, is the "habitual role-sustainer," of whom he writes:

Habitual role-sustainers fall, on the whole, into two main groups: those who have gauged to a nicety what shows them off to best advantage: others, more romantic if less fortunate in their fate, who hope to reproduce in themselves arbitrary personalities that have won their respect, met in life, read about in papers and books, or seen in films. These self-appointed players of a part often have little or no aptitude, are even notably ill equipped by appearance or demeanor, to wear the costume or speak the lines of the prototype. Indeed, the very unsuitability of the role is what fascinates.

The power of this, as of most generalizations, depends upon the experience one brings to it. I, in my experience, have known a number of Powellian habitual role-sustainers, not the least a contemporary who, though born in the Middle West, when in his early twenties became a kind of Englishman, a role he has sustained for more than a quarter of a century now. He is of the second type of Powell's habitual role-sustainers—that is, he is unsuitable for the role he has chosen. It doesn't come off. What is intended as elegance plays as pompous, even faintly comic. But it is too late to change roles. All one can hope for him now is knighthood or a plaque in Westminster Abbey.

Again, Anthony Powell notes of another of his characters that he spoke a number of foreign languages with facility, and that, as with all people who speak foreign languages easily, he was not quite to be trusted. Now here is an extraordinary generalization. So extraordinary is it that a reader needs to rub his eyes and read it again. To speak foreign languages easily, Mr. Powell is saying, is to be not altogether reliable. This seems wild, possibly a little mad. However, it presents a problem, at least for me, because almost everyone I have known who has had great facility in speaking foreign languages has been something less than reliable. Perhaps this gift of fluency is a form of linguistic adaptation: nature, in its inscrutable wisdom, has known that these men, because of their unreliability, will be asked to cross many borders and hence speak many languages and has equipped them accordingly, as in equipping certain tree-dwelling monkeys with prehensile tails.

As in the above instance, personal experience of the subject being generalized about is often essential to one's judgment of the quality of a particular generalization. Experience is the developing solution in which many of the most interesting generalizations are exposed, revealing some to be blurry, some botched, some perfectly precise. A quick call to the consulate may be enough to determine whether there are, say, any minia-ture golf courses in Mozambique, but only a certain longevity can help one to judge Proust when, generalizing, he writes, "After a certain age, from self-esteem and from sagacity, it is to the things we most desire that we pretend to attach no importance." A twenty-two-year-old student cannot hope to know if that statement is or is not true.

Sometimes one can have rather too much experience to judge a generalization. A few years ago, in *The New Yorker*, I read in a story by Cynthia Ozick about a character who was described, in a generalized detail, as the sort of man who car-ried in his pocket a Swiss army knife. Now the author clearly did not think well of this character, and the Swiss army knife was meant to be emblematic of his stuffiness and smugness, his superficiality and self-conceit. Did this generalized detail hold up? I thought about it, one hand scratching the back of my head, the other, in my pocket, fingering my two-blade Swiss army knife.

"Women," I recently heard an acquaintance opine, "are able to eat enormous quantities of ice cream." Are women able to eat enormous quantities of ice cream? I have neither strong views nor ample data on the question, but I rather like the spirit of disinterested wonder behind the generalization. I also approve its fine undemonstrability. True, I have known a number of women who were not otherwise great (how to put it?) trencherpersons who could nevertheless dispatch large quantities of ice cream. But not to like ice cream, it seems to me, is show oneself uninterested in food. I wish this generalization to apply indiscriminately to women and men both.

Women, I suspect, must provide the single greatest subject for generalizations, and I am much too cunning and cowardly to attempt to add here to the already vast stockpile of these generalizations. In a too-brief essay entitled "What a Lovely Generalization!" James Thurber claimed that women themselves go in heavily for generalization and that a woman's "average generalization is from three to five times as broad as a man's." That is a statement that fits fairly snugly into the category of highly dubious generalization, with some overlap into that of broad generalization. Highly dubious generalizations, in my view, are often more interesting than broad generalizations—or they tend, at least, to be more amusing. ("Often," "at least," "in my view," "tend,"—my, that is an uncharacteristically qualified statement; I shall try not to let it happen again.) Such an amusing, highly dubious generalization is to be found in the reason Evelyn Waugh offered for the worsened quality of proofreading in his lifetime: "I am told that printers' readers no longer exist because clergymen are no longer unfrocked for sodomy."

Broad generalizations, with their companions sweeping statements and comfortable conclusions, are almost always less felicitous. There is usually something lumpy about them, something intellectually indigestible; one cannot quite, as generalizations ask you to do, swallow them whole. Henry Adams went in for such generalizations. Edmund Wilson once said of Adams that he "esteemed him without being too crazy about him." Among living contemporaries, Malcolm Muggeridge, a writer I happen to be crazy about without much esteeming, has come more and more to specialize in the broad generalization, an example of which, from Muggeridge's diaries, *Like It Was*, follows:

Civilizations grow weak because in them power becomes divorced from the mob in the form of wealth and hereditary privilege, or even constitutional authority. Its everlasting fount is the envy of the poor for the rich, the desire of the humble and meek that the mighty should be pulled down and they installed in their place. This is the essence of politics, and everything else is phoney.

The sentiments do not disgust me. I rather like the snap of the last sentence, with its authoritative air of cutting through intellectual frills and fustian. It is that *s*, that use of the plural in civilizations, that does it in. A single civilization ought, it seems to me, to be the legal limit of the scope of any generalization.

Clearly, a number of interesting issues, problems, questions arise in connection with generalizations. But if any of them is to be dealt with in a serious manner, codification will be required, and codification takes time and money. I have, therefore, put in for a grant from the National Endowment for the Humanities on behalf of a little not-for-profit organization I run, which I call The Center for Things on the Periphery and to which the codification of generalizations seems, as noted in my application, a perfect project. My grant, I have been given to understand, is still being processed, but the problem of codification of generalizations presses, and so, grantless, I beat on, boats against the current, borne back ceaselessly, et cetera, et cetera.

The first category is the most dangerous of generalizations and is called, fittingly, the dangerous generalization. Among dangerous generalizations, surely the most dangerous of all is the one that runs: "People who threaten suicide never do it."

More common dangerous generalizations are those that have to do with racial and religious groups. To cite only a mild instance of such a generalization: in recent years I have more than once heard it said that, "Orientals are terrible drivers." Can this be true? Generalizations have this extraordinary self-fulfilling propensity. Since hearing the generalization about Orientals being terrible drivers, I have duly noted a great deal of terrible driving by Orientals. Hence the danger of racial and religious generalizations. Minority groups have enough problems without them. Let us, then, adopt the policy of only positive generalizations about racial and religious groups, so that we shall have only intellectual Jews, dignified blacks, cultivated Orientals, and so on. The blandness of this will soon become so boring that in time perhaps these generalizations will die out altogether.

Generalizations that are close to racial and religious generalizations and that I hope will stay around are those about nations, their character and the conduct and quality of their citizens. There is something about the tone and tenor of these generalizations that I prize, even though they tend overwhelmingly to be malicious. At their most malicious, they run along the lines of the joke which has it that both the Hungarian and the Rumanian will sell you his grandmother, but the (I forget which) is worse because he cannot be trusted to deliver. Stendhal, who was a world-class generalizer, scarcely ever seems intellectually happier than when generalizing about a nation. Early in the pages of his *Life of Rossini*, Stendhal reports that the citizens of the nations of the southern part of Europe do not have the patience and perseverance to become first-rate violinists and flautists, and "instrumental music has wholly taken refuge among peaceful, patient folk beyond the Rhine." The reason that France has produced no great opera, according to Stendhal, is that French composers "have chosen blindly to imitate the Italian conception of *love,* whereas love, in France, is nothing but a feeble and second-rate emotion, entirely overwhelmed by *vanity* and stifled by the witty subtleties of *intellect.* " Good old Stendhal, like a superior billiard player, he was not above kissing one generalization off against another. Thus, after writing about love being but a feeble and second-rate emotion in France—a generalization lovely both in its amplitude and its specificity—he rolls right on to write: "Now, whether or not there be any truth in this impertinent generalization, I think it will be universally acknowledged that music can achieve no effect at all save by appealing to the imagination."

The authority for Stendhal's generalizations was that he had visited the countries about which he had generalized so ex cathedra-ly. He could answer in the affirmative the question, "Vas you der, Henri?" One of the great pleasures of travel, surely, is the right it confers on the traveler to generalize about the places he has visited. Generalizations about a foreign country or strange city are a form of intellectual slide show, and it is difficult not to bring these slides out to show to friends back home. One is, though, under an obligation not to bring back boring slides—not to show the intellectual equivalent of pictures of the kids atop the Eiffel Tower or of Ethel on a donkey in front of the pyramids. Generalizations about places must be fresh and neatly formulated. A friend, back from a week in Houston, recently remarked, "Everything vicious that has ever been said about Los Angeles is true of Houston."

The farther away the country or city about which one is generalizing, the more sweep and grandeur one may inject into one's generalizations. I much admire the travel essays of Jan Morris, but even in my admiration I am amused by the sheer width of her generalizations. She can write, "Indians, of course, love to reduce the prosaic to the mystic." That "of course" is, of course, a splendid touch. Again: "Delhi is a city of basic, spontaneous emotions: greed, hate, revenge, love, pity, kindness, the murderous shot, the touch of the hand." Couldn't that sentence, with just a bit of fine tuning, be written about Chicago? It could, but Chicago is perhaps too close to home for one to dare it. Or yet again: "Iowans are marvelously free of grudge or rancor; violence is not really their style. . . ." If that generalization seems fairly sound to you, think again, for in its original form it was written not about Iowans at all but about Egyptians. As someone who himself goes in for generalizations, it's enough to take my breadth away.

"There are two categories of people," wrote Kleist, "those who think in terms of metaphors and those who think in terms of formulas." I used to have a stronger taste for this kind of generalization than I now do. There is something appealing in the finitude of them. If there are only two types or categories or kinds—or even if there are four or five—then the world suddenly seems so much more intellectually manageable. Whole works have been built on such generalizations. The late Philip Rahv's most famous essay, "Paleface and Redskin," is one example; another is Isaiah Berlin's *The Hedgehog and the Fox.* Do people, I not long ago found myself saying to myself, divide between those who wish to survive life and those who wish to master it? Not bad, eh? Or so I thought, until it occurred to me that I fell into neither of my own two lovely categories. I wish neither to master life nor merely to survive it; I wish to understand it (more than I do) and to enjoy it (even more than I have).

Can it be that there are finally only two kinds of generalization: those that are true and those that aren't? Isn't it enough that a generalization be stately and finely formulated? Isn't it almost too much to ask that it also be true? Flannery O'Connor writes in a letter, "I have never met anyone with a stutter who was not nice." Now here is a generalization one wants to be true; something deep yet obscure makes one want to think that people put to the torture of the perpetual frustration of stuttering are, somehow or other, sainted. Alas, I have met people with stutters who are not nice, which for me does in that generalization. Other generalizations, especially those written in French, seem to call for assent; no language seems to me better suited for the flashy but false generalization than French. Thus, an anonymous Frenchman observes that translations are like beautiful women: *"Si elles sont fidèles elles ne sont pas belles; si elles sont belles elles ne sont pas fidèles."* [If they are faithful, they aren't beautiful; if they are beautiful, they aren't faithful.] Sorry, but I have met a few beautiful and faithful translations and even more beautiful and faithful women. Ah, me, another generalization goes down the tubes.

Permit me now to suggest that there are not two but four basic kinds of generalization. In order of their popularity in the world, these are: Generalizations that are (1) commonplace but false; (2) commonplace and true; (3) original but false; and (4) original and true. An original but false generalization, in my opinion, is E. M. Cioran's remark that "people who are in love agree to overestimate each other," while an example of an original and true generalization, again in my opinion, is Sir Herbert Grierson's remark that "witticisms are never quite true." As it happens, I adore witticisms, and it wounds me to acknowledge that I think Sir Herbert Grierson's remark both original and true. Yet true in my heart I know it is, and I take it as bad news.

But then so many of the best generalizations—that is, the original and true generalizations—seem to convey bad news. I take as bad news, for example, G. C. Lichtenberg's observation that "people who have read a great deal seldom make great discoveries." Of such discouraging generalizations, there is no shortage. Another term for a discouraging generalization is an aphorism. An aphorism need not be discouraging, but the best ones, again, usually are. Along with being assertive and aristocratic, aphorisms tend also to be world-weary. The Viennese writer Karl Kraus, who wrote some of the most devastating aphorisms, said of the form, "An aphorism need not be true, but it should surpass the truth. It must go beyond it with one leap." An example from Karl Kraus: "No ideas and the ability to express them—that's a journalist."

Do nations or cultures get the aphorists they deserve? Many of the aphorisms of Karl Kraus ("Social policy is the despairing decision to undertake a corn operation on a cancer patient") as well as many of those of Lichtenberg ("What they call 'heart' is located far lower than the fourth waistcoat button") are imbued with anger and disgust. Although Lichtenberg died in 1799 and Kraus in 1936, both men were raised and worked in Teutonic cultures. Can it, then, be that these men, though born more than a century apart, are expressing a similar cultural taste in generalization? If Teutons seem to go in for rage and loathing in their generalizations, the French seem to prefer an amused puncturing of pretensions, at least to judge from their aphorists—from La Rochefoucauld ("One would not know how to count up all the varieties of vanity"), to La Bruyère ("Favor places a man above his equals, the loss of it below them"), to Paul Valéry ("I introduce here a slight observation which I shall call 'philosophical,' meaning simply that we can do without it").

If a nation or a culture gets the kind of aphorists it deserves, why has the United States had no first-class aphorists? Instead we have supplied the fodder for fine generalizations by foreign visitors, from Tocqueville to Bryce to Santayana to Huizinga. But of ambitious aphorists we have chiefly Emerson. "Nothing great was ever achieved without enthusiasm," said Emerson, but perhaps he might have done better to temper his own. Emerson said everything. If he said one thing ("I hate quotations"), he could often be relied upon to have said the reverse ("By necessity, by proclivity—and by delight, we all quote"). Covering himself, he also said, "A foolish consistency is the hobgoblin of little minds. . . ." Emerson's generalizations are more like pronunciamentos. His tone is too vatic, his formulations are devoid of charm. As generalizations go, Emerson's are in many ways a model of how not to do it.

How, then, does one do it? How best does one fashion a generalization? The saying of it, when it comes to generalizations, is usually everything. Generalizations are of that body of knowledge known as unsystematic truths, and they may, as John Stuart Mill says, "be exhibited in the same unconnected state in which they were discovered." Still, it will not do to come on too high, or too sweepingly. Generalizations that begin "Man is . . ." or "Woman is . . ." seem almost to command dissent. Even for generalizations they are too general. "Nature" is another word I recommend pruning from all generalizations, and for largely the same reason: it is too vague, too ethereal, too much. Even God is more comprehensible than Nature. Man, Woman, Nature, God—these things, being general enough, stand in no need of further generalization.

"The most dangerous moment for a bad government is when it begins to reform itself." Now that generalization—it is by Tocqueville—seems to me splendid. It comes at things at a near perfect level of generality, neither too high nor too low. It calls up all those governments, from Roman to French to Russian, whose last-minute attempts at reform only made easier the way for the revolutions that toppled them. Its tone, authoritative and slightly ironic, seems to me near perfect as well, being neither dogmatic nor hesitant—dogmatism and hesitancy being the Scylla and Charybdis between which any seaworthy generalization must sail. If you can find objections or exceptions to Tocqueville's generalization, that is all right, too. Mill said of such propositions that "they are very seldom exactly true; but then this, unfortunately, is an objection to all human knowledge."

That most human knowledge is not exactly true I find rather comforting, as long as I keep in mind that some knowledge is a good deal more exact than other knowledge. The lesson in this for those of us who love generalizations and wish to keep on generalizing is fairly clear; it comes—no one, surely, will be surprised—in the form of a generalization: Always seek the general and never quite trust it. If you don't think this makes any sense, just put another record on the stereo—make it something with a driving beat—and turn it up loud so that you don't have to think about it. We, I regret to say, have nothing further to discuss.

Balls-Up

THREE FANTASIES:

Primo: A Manhattan town house at a quite good address. The women in the room are very smartly dressed; the men are in dinner clothes. My hostess comes up to ask if I will agree to play. I demur, thanking her all the same. "Oh, please do," she says, with an earnestness I cannot find it in my heart to refuse. As I move toward the piano, a well-polished Baldwin grand, I hear a woman say, "He's going to play." Across the room, another woman murmurs, "He's going to play—I was so hoping he would!" I rub my hands together briefly, bend and unbend my fingers, and proceed to toss off a flawless rendering of "Rhapsody in Blue." As I finish, I notice that everyone seems to have gathered round the piano. Ice cubes tinkle; cigarette smoke wafts to the ceiling. I play and sing two Cole Porter songs, then follow up with Noel Coward's "Imagine the Duchess's Feelings," which has everyone in stitches. I move on to play and sing—first in English, then in French— "I Won't Dance." I close, gently and with just a touch of profundity, with "September Song." Applause envelops me. "Now that," says my hostess, handing me a fresh drink, "was simply unforgettable!"

Secondo: A hill overlooking the Loire Valley. I appear over the crest of the hill in white linen trousers, a chambray shirt, a wide-brimmed straw hat of the kind Pope John XXIII used to wear when he would go into the streets of Rome. It is a perfect day: the sun shines, flowers are everywhere in bloom, the river is a serene azure. I set up my easel, my canvas chair, and, before beginning to mix my palette, eat a lunch of what Henry James once called "light cold clever French things." After lunch, working in watercolors, I begin to paint the vista before me in a strong line and with a use of color that falls between that of Degas and Dufy. I achieve a work that is obviously representational yet, such is the force of my character, my sensibility, my vision, is just as obviously a small masterpiece. When I am done, I put away my materials with the confidence of a man who, though he knows he is out of step with the times, knows that his own time will come.

Terzo: A large empty room, good wood floors, clean light flowing in from the windows along its north wall. On the south wall is a mirror reaching from floor to ceiling. I enter, remove my suit coat, loosen my tie. I stretch my arms out to the side, turn my head first clockwise, then counterclockwise. I bend over to pick up three rubber balls, one red, one yellow, one blue. I toss the red ball from my right hand to my left, then back again to my right hand. I feel the heft and balance of each of the balls in my hands. I begin to juggle them, flipping a new ball into the air each time the previous one reaches its peak and begins its descent, all the while softly humming to myself the strains of "Lady of Spain." After three or four minutes of this, I add a fourth ball, a green one, which joins the cascade I create by juggling the balls gingerly from hand to hand. Then I add a fifth ball, orange; later a sixth, purple. Six balls in the air! The cascade has now become a rainbow revolving before me. My control is complete, my pleasure in this control no less. My only regret is that there is not room in my hands for a seventh ball. Perspiring lightly, effortlessly keeping all these balls in the air, I smile as I hum "Over the Rainbow."

Now of these three fantasies, two are not merely improbable but, for me, utterly impossible. Although I spend a goodly amount of time listening to records and going to concerts, I can neither read music nor play a musical instrument. Worse, I was one of those children who, in grade school, was asked not to sing but just to mouth the words, lest my naturally off-key voice carry the rest of the class along with me into the thickets of dissonance. My drawing was of roughly the same discouraging caliber. In school periods devoted to art, teachers who walked up and down the aisles checking their students' sketches and paintings never stopped, or even hesitated, to gaze at mine, which were so clearly beyond help or comment. If there were an artistic equivalent to mouthing words—a colorless crayon, say, or disappearing paint—I would, I am certain, have been asked to avail myself of it.

Denied these two gifts, of song and of drawing, I have, in life's rather arbitrary lottery, been allotted a third. I am reasonably well coordinated. Delete that "reasonably": I am extremely well coordinated. ("Don't be so humble," Golda Meir once said, "you're not that great.") I was never big or fast or physically aggressive enough to be a first-class athlete, but, as a boy, I could catch anything, or so I felt. Grounders, liners, fly balls—I gobbled them up. Throw a football anywhere within fifteen yards of me, and I would be there to meet it. In tennis I was most notable for flipping and catching my racquet in various snappy routines. In my teens I mastered most of the ball-handling tricks of the Harlem Globetrotters: spinning a basketball on my index finger, rolling it down my arm and catching it behind my back, dribbling while prone. Quite simply, I had quick and confident hands. Perhaps I should be more humble about these playground skills, for I make myself sound pretty great.

Great and humble though I apparently am, juggling is something I have never been able, yet have long yearned, to do. It is one of those fantasies possible of fulfillment, like going to Greece. Besides, juggling seemed a harmless enough fantasy, involving neither the disruption of the ecosystem nor the corruption of children. And then one day not long ago, in the produce section of the grocery store where I shop, I saw the owner's wife, an Irishwoman of great high spirits, juggling three navel oranges. So filled with envy was I that I determined then and there to learn to juggle.

When an intellectual wants to learn something he goes to the library. He reads up. But it turned out that at my library there was not much to read on the subject of juggling. The library's two books on juggling had been taken out. The library also had a novel entitled *The Juggler* by Michael Blankfort, but it, too, was gone from the shelves. Doubtless this novel is not about juggling at all but instead uses the word metaphorically, as does the final entry in the library's catalogue on the subject, *Juggling: The Art of Balancing Marriage, Motherhood, and Career.* No help there. It was beginning to look, as the English say, like a bit of a balls-up.

I remembered that Hazlitt wrote an essay entitled "The Indian Jugglers," which I reread. It starts magnificently: "Coming forward and seating himself on the ground in his white dress and tightened turban, the chief of the Indian Jugglers begins with tossing up two brass balls, which is what any of us could do, and concludes with keeping up four at the same time, which is what none of us could do to save our lives, nor if we were to take our whole lives to do it in." Hazlitt proceeds to describe the Indian juggler's act, noting that the juggler astonishes while giving pleasure in astonishment. "There is something in all this," he writes, "which he who does not admire may be quite sure he never admired really anything in the whole course of his life." Reading this I felt one of the keenest delights that reading offers: the discovery that someone more intelligent than yourself feels about a given subject exactly as you do.

Hazlitt then moves on to compare the juggler's skill with brass balls to his own skill with words—and finds the latter paltry in comparison. Nothing in his own work is so near perfection as that which the Indian juggler can do. "I can write a book: so can many others who have not even learned to spell," Hazlitt writes. His own essays—some of the greatest written in English—he calls "abortions." "What errors, what ill-pieced transitions, what crooked reasons, what lame conclusions. How little is made out, and that little how ill!" The juggler can keep four balls in the air, but for Hazlitt "it is as much as I can manage to keep the thread of one discourse clear and unentangled." The juggler, through patient practice, has brought his skill to perfection, something which Hazlitt feels unable to come anywhere near doing with his. "I have also time on my hands to correct my opinions and polish my periods: but the one I cannot, and the other I will not do."

Anyone who does intellectual work will instantly recognize the cogency of Hazlitt's comments. So little does such work allow for a true sense of completion, or a satisfying feeling of perfection. Every artist has felt this, and the better the artist the more achingly has he felt it. "A poem is never finished," said Valéry, "but only abandoned." If Hazlitt and Valéry, two workers in diamonds, felt this way about their works, imagine how those of us who labor with zircons feel about ours! As an old costume jeweler, I must say, I appreciate the possibility that juggling holds out for perfection—for doing the small thing extremely well.

For me, though, more is involved. Within very serious limits I am a self-improvement buff, if only a failed one. Of myself in this connection I can say, every day in every way I stay pretty much the same. A few years ago, for example, I set out to learn classical Greek. Aglow with the luster of self-betterment, I enrolled myself in a course in Greek at the university where I teach—and lasted a cool and inglorious two weeks. Walking into the room on the first day of class, I was taken for the teacher, a natural enough confusion since I was more than twenty years older than anyone else in the course (except for the actual teacher, who turned out to be roughly twenty years older than I). Being the old boy, I felt a certain obligation not to appear stupid. The option taken by a likable fellow named Fred McNally, who more than two decades ago sat next to me in an undergraduate French class, and who whenever called upon answered through an entire semester, "Beats me, sir," did not seem an option open to me. Given my natural ineptitude with foreign languages and my fear of having to avail myself of the McNally ploy, I found myself studying Greek two hours a night. Add to this another hour for class and yet another hour for getting there and back, and nearly one fourth of my waking life was given over to this little self-improvement project. The result was the general disimprovement of everything else in my life. In the end I decided that learning Greek would have to be on that long list of items I must put off until the after-life.

Juggling balls is surely less time-consuming than juggling Greek paradigms, but is it really self-improving? Having thought a bit about this, I have concluded that it is not a whit self-improving. Juggling is in fact the recreational equivalent of art for art's sake. It is not good exercise; you do not do it in the sunshine; it is not an excuse for gambling; it does not simulate the conditions of life; it teaches no morality (you can't even cheat at it, a prospect which lends so many games, from golf to solitaire, a piquant touch). Unlike, say, playing in the outfield, you cannot even think of anything else while doing it. Juggling is all-absorbing and an end in itself: *le jeu pour le jeu.*

Juggling is play, almost with a vengeance. "We may call everything play," writes Santayana, "which is useless activity, exercise that springs from the physiological impulse to discharge energy which the exigencies of life have not called out." Juggling also satisfies some of the criteria Huizinga lays down for play in *Homo Ludens.* It does, as Huizinga puts it, "create order, *is* order. Into an imperfect world and into the confusions of life it brings a temporary, a limited perfection." And juggling is certainly, to quote Huizinga again, "invested with the noblest qualities we are capable of perceiving in things: rhythm and harmony." Excluding people who use it to make a living by entertaining others, however, juggling is neither a fine nor a useful art, but rather a delicate, slightly perverse activity. No self-improvement, no end other than itself, sheer play, exquisitely useless—these are among the qualities that endear juggling to me.

Some people can do entirely without play, but I am not one of them. Neither is Georges Simenon, who, I was surprised to learn while recently reading his journal, *When I Was Old,* is of all things a golfer. Nor was Hazlitt, who was a dedicated player of fives, an English version of handball. Matthew Arnold was an ice skater. Ezra Pound enthusiastically—as, unfortunately, he did everything—played tennis. Edmund Wilson was a passionate amateur magician. Other artists and intellectuals, if not themselves players, were devoted followers of games: G. H. Hardy, the Cambridge mathematician, of cricket, and Marianne Moore of baseball. While I am unable to report that T. S. Eliot had a bowling average of 192 or that Einstein was a pool shark, my guess is that among the most serious mental workers there is many a hidden player.

My own small problem is that sources of play have been drying up on me. For many years now I have been unable to take any interest in mental games: crossword puzzles, chess, bridge, Scrabble. Even poker, a game I once loved, no longer retains much interest for me, unless the stakes are high enough to frighten me. Basketball, another former love, is now too vigorous a game for me, and I can today walk under a glass backboard without even wistfully looking up. As a boy, I was a quite decent tennis player, but I find I have no appetite for being a mediocre player in a game I used to play well. I do play the game called racquetball, yet if a week goes by in which I do not get on the court, I do not weep.

The reason I no longer take any interest in mental games, I have concluded, is that I do mental work, and consequently seem to have little in the way of mental energy left for mental play. I have noticed, by the way, that many people who have a great deal of zest for such games, and who are very good at them, are often people of real intelligence whose work does not require them to make strenuous demands on their mental powers. For myself, I would rather be thinking of phrases or formulations to be used in essays than of how best to get off a blitz or of a four-letter word that means payment in arrears.

As for my loss of interest in physical games, here the problem, I think, is that I have lost the power to fantasize while playing. When playing tennis or basketball, for example, I find I can no longer imagine myself at center court at Wimbledon or in the final game of the NCAA at Pauley Pavilion, the sort of thing I invariably did as a boy. Nor am I sufficiently competitive to enjoy winning for its own sake, even though on the whole it is rather better than losing. The friend with whom I play racquetball and who is a much better athlete than I—as a boy he was an all-state football player and later a Big Ten wrestling champion—is even less competitive than I. Sometimes I wonder how either one of us ever manages to win the games we play against each other, and it usually turns out that not the better man but the least tired man wins.

Nor have I ever had the discipline or concentration to play solitary games. Running, still much in vogue, is out of the question for me. I have never been able to take calisthenics of any sort seriously. I own a bicycle, which I ride occasionally and which gives me pleasure, but this is scarcely a game. In fact, it has become most useful to me as part of a riposte. Lately, when people suggest I must be making a lot of money as a fairly productive writer, I reply, "If I am doing so well, how come I'm still riding a reconditioned three-speed Huffy?"

All this makes it the more interesting to me that I am so keen about juggling—a form of play that is both solitary and requires real discipline. Despite such drawbacks, juggling thrills me. In the phrase of the bobby-soxers of the late 1940s, it really sends me. Another drawback is that juggling, unlike other games and sports—if juggling is indeed a game or a sport —does not have an established lore, a pantheon of heroes. It is, of course, a very old form of play: court jesters, I believe, had juggling in their repertoires. But if there was a Babe Ruth, a Jim Thorpe, or a Joe Louis of juggling, I have not heard of him.

True, many of the silent-movie stars, who came out of vaudeville, juggled. Charlie Chaplin did and so did Buster Keaton. I recall a hilarious Buster Keaton movie—which of his movies isn't hilarious?—in which Buster is a contestant on a radio amateur hour whose talent turns out to be juggling. Juggling, mind you, over the radio. In the movie Keaton, deadpan as always, is blithely tossing balls in the air while in their homes the members of the listening audience are banging away on the sides of their Philco consoles, certain that the silence is attributable to a loose tube. A splendid bit.

W. C. Fields broke into show business as a juggler, a skill at which he is said to have been consummate. In Robert Lewis Taylor's biography, *W. C. Fields: His Follies and Fortunes,* Fields is said to have begun juggling at the age of nine, inspired by the vaudeville performance of a group calling itself the Byrne Brothers. Fields's father hawked fruit and vegetables in Philadelphia, and Fields practiced on his father's wares. "By the time I could keep two objects going," he said, "I'd ruined forty dollars worth of fruit." He later worked with cigar boxes, croquet balls, Indian clubs, and odd utensils. In his early adolescence he was obsessed with juggling. He worked hours and hours at it, teaching himself to keep five tennis balls in the air, catching canes with his feet, and performing any other kind of trick he could dream up.

Field's specialty as a juggler was to appear to fumble, then recover from what had all the marks of a disastrous error. He never lost his relish for this artful bumbling. Later in life, while serving his guests at large dinner parties, Fields would fill a plate, preferably for a comparative stranger, and, as he would begin to hand it down the line, drop it, "provoking," as his biographer tells it, "a loud concerted gasp. With consummate nonchalance he would catch it just off the floor, without interrupting whatever outrageous anecdote he was relating at the moment." But the best juggling story Robert Lewis Taylor tells is about the night Fields was working on some new trick in a hotel room in Pittsburgh, when his continual dropping of a heavy object disturbed the tenant in the room below, a bruiser who came up to complain. The complainant recognized Fields as the juggler he had seen earlier that evening at a local theater. To calm the man down Fields taught him a simple trick calling for juggling two paring knives. "I hope he worked at it," Fields said in recounting the story, "because if he did, he was almost certain to cut himself very painfully." Fieldsian, absolutely Fieldsian.

Juggling today appears to be undergoing a small renaissance. Street jugglers appear in profusion along Fisherman's Wharf in San Francisco. In Manhattan they mingle among the multitudes of street vendors. Although I myself have not seen the act, there is at work nowadays a group known as the Brothers Karamazov that is said to give great satisfaction. Along with other odd-shaped objects, the Brothers K juggle running buzz saws and, most astonishing of all, live cats. A few new juggling books have recently been published: *Juggling for the Complete Klutz* is the title of one and *The Juggling Book* that of another. Have we the makings here of a wildly popular fad?

My guess is that we do not. For one thing, juggling is just too damned difficult to catch on—if you will pardon the expression—with great numbers of people. For another, it lacks manufacturing possibilities. Balls can still be bought at dime stores (if not quite, lamentably, for dimes). So far as I know, Adidas, Nike, Puma, and other sports-equipment manufacturers have yet to produce juggling shoes, juggling shorts, or juggling watches. Certainly there is no need for them. I myself, when juggling, wear the simplest costume: buskins turned up at the toes, gold pantaloons, a leathern jerkin, and a cap with bells.

But the time, surely, has come to get some balls in the air. How good a juggler am I? In two words, not very. In trying to explain my quality as a novice juggler I feel rather as Buster Keaton must have felt while juggling over the radio. I can keep three balls in the air for roughly two minutes. I do the conventional beginner's pattern known as "the cascade," in which the balls appear to be flowing over a perpetual waterfall. While juggling I can go from a standing to a kneeling position; I can juggle sitting down. I can vary the cascade pattern with the pattern known as "the half-shower," in which. . . . But I hear you banging on your Philco. Let me conclude then by saying that, as a juggler, I am far from ready for Vegas, television, or even small family parties.*

Yet such limited prowess as I have I owe to my mentor, a man who calls himself, on the title page of *The Juggling Book*, Carlo. His real name is Charles Lewis. Mr. Lewis has done a bit of this and a bit of that, from teaching math and science in public schools to leading encounter groups to founding a spiritualist newspaper to organizing a small circus troupe. From the photograph of him on the back of the book—long dark hair, a gray beard, corduroy jeans, loose-sleeved East Indian shirt—he looks rather guruish, and guruish he turns out to be. The Carlo Method, as Mr. Lewis styles his teaching, is not without a large measure of current psychobabble. Given half a chance—and as the author of his own book, he has more than half a chance—Carlo will babble on about "levels of awareness," "great possibilities for creativity," "control and direction of body forces," "inner states," "healing effects on your psyche," and, natch, that old rotting botanical metaphor, "growing." Juggling, Carlo advises, will help me "continue to grow." Thank you, Carlo, but I was growing before I read your book: growing older, growing feebler, growing closer to death—growth enough, I should think.

When Carlo knocks off the psycho-spiritual palaver, which I find so *antipatico*, he is an excellent teacher. He writes clearly, and he takes the novice through each step slowly. He

---

*Here I cannot resist bragging. Since writing this essay, I have learned all the fundamental tricks of juggling with three balls. I can also do a number of four-ball tricks, and have only recently begun to learn to juggle with plastic clubs. I am, therefore, ready for small family parties, but only useful, I fear, to end especially dull ones, as someone once suggested that two-long-play records of the late Ludwig Earhart explaining the German economic miracle was, similarly, good for ending dull parties.

had me worried at first, though, when he said that juggling, like riding a bicycle or whistling, is something everyone can learn to do, since I, after repeated attempts to learn, can whistle only pitiably. Juggling turns out to be one of those activities (tennis is another) in which one benefits greatly from professional instruction at the outset. Fundamentals—how to position your body, how to hold the balls, how to toss them—are decisive. Unlike almost any other ball game, for example, you do not use your fingertips in juggling but instead toss the balls from your palms. In all these matters Carlo is very helpful. Sometimes, too, he will strike off a delicately humorous sentence, as when he advises not to reach up to catch the balls but rather to let them fall into your hands. "The balls will come down," he writes, "which I can guarantee from long experience." Sometimes he will hit exactly the right lyrical note, as when he writes: "Somehow there is a ball up there that's never going to come down. You realize suddenly that you never have to stop; you can juggle forever." He is right about that, and when it occurs, it is a golden moment. On the day it finally happened to me, after more than a week of practice, I felt sheer exhilaration and wanted to shout, "Look, Ma, both hands!"

Earlier I said that juggling does not provide much in the way of exercise. Let me amend that by saying that at the beginning you do get quite a bit of exercise—chasing the balls you drop. To cut down the chasing I began practicing in my wife's and my bedroom, juggling over the bed and thereby, as a friend remarked, turning a conjugal into a conjuggle bed. Not long afterward, by turning on our clock-radio, I added music to my practice sessions and discovered that the piano rags of Scott Joplin are particularly nice to juggle to. As my juggling began to improve, so did the music. Stan Getz's saxophone makes for fine juggling accompaniment and so do Haydn's piano trios and Telemann's wind concertos. Juggling to Strauss waltzes and Glenn Miller swing is lovely. Opera is no good at all.

Part of the delight of juggling is the rhythmical pleasure created by the clear and steady beat of the balls slapping against the palms. This gives a satisfaction roughly analogous to that which a beginning pianist must feel when running through rudimentary practice exercises. Tossing the balls first high, then low, then in wide, then in narrow arcs, I can also create pleasing if altogether ephemeral designs of a kind I could never achieve with a crayon or paintbrush. In these small ways, then, juggling has compensated me for two common pleasures—those of rhythm and design—that my natural inaptitudes have hitherto prevented me from enjoying.

To drift slightly into metaphor, juggling has supplied the possibility, however small, of chaos in my life. Since beginning to juggle I now realize how exceedingly well ordered my life has become. I read, I write, I teach, I live among family and friends whom I love. Nor would I have it otherwise. At the same time I have always marveled at, without necessarily admiring, those people who seem to have so high a threshold for chaos in their lives: people who can simultaneously carry on love affairs while behind in their alimony payments, have government liens on their businesses, and undergo chemotherapy—people who, to use a juggling metaphor, somehow manage to keep a lot of balls in the air. One such chaos merchant of my acquaintance, a man in his early fifties, recently married a woman of twenty-three while concurrently acquiring a mistress in her late forties, a brilliant reversal of the norm that had his friends surmising that he married for sex and kept a mistress for conversation. Whatever the case, the man is obviously a juggler.

At the same time, juggling is an exercise in subduing chaos. Keeping the balls in the air, making of them a fluid pattern, one achieves a pleasing kind of order. As with much art, the trick in juggling is to make the difficult look effortless. As Samuel Butler once put it,

> As lookers-on feel most delight,
> That least perceive a juggler's sleight,
> And still the less they understand,
> The more th' admire his sleight of hand.

Yet in juggling many are the moments—when a ball slips loose, when two balls collide in midair—when chaos wins and panic, for an instant, clutches the heart. At such moments one hears the knock of the house detective, feels the unopened IRS letter in the hand, sees the X ray being slid dramatically from its envelope.

While the balls are in the air, describing their arcs, slapping gently against my hands, with everything under control, I am happy. Perhaps this happiness comes from my complete preoccupation with what I am doing. Perhaps it comes from the thrill of beginning to master a skill, however small and insignificant. It is a thoughtless happiness, an almost animal happiness, but no less real for all that. With the balls flying about me, I am happy but not, I must confess, altogether content. Even in my happiness I wonder if it is not time to move on and learn new tricks. Ought I to begin to master juggling four balls? What about rings and then Indian clubs? My man Carlo says that juggling on your back while on a trapeze is just about as far as one can go with this sort of thing. "Man thou art a wonderful animal," says Hazlitt, "and thy ways past finding out." William, I say, you don't know the half of it.

The Crime of
a Happy Childhood

I SOMETIMES THINK I may have peaked in my seventeenth year. Life had not yet started to seem complicated. I had no notion that I would one day earn my living doing intellectual work, and consequently hadn't begun to live in my mind. Fear of death was not allowed to curdle joy in living. I smoked like Gary, Indiana, ate like a cossack, and followed wherever instinct and laughter led. When school wasn't in session I went to bed at five in the morning, woke at two or three the following afternoon, and in between slept like a rutabaga. My daddy was rich, my ma good-looking, and even in bleak Chicago it seemed perpetually like the summertime of Gershwin's song. Or so I have come to imagine.

But have I only imagined it? Were my childhood and youth really as happy as they are in my memory? Optimism, it has been said, is the preferred philosophy for viewing the past: every day further away seems better and better. "There is nothing fine about being a child," Cesare Pavese writes, "it is fine, when we are old, to look back to when we were children." And is it not in any case rather boorish to claim a happy childhood in the first place? The modern scenario for human development does not call for a happy childhood. (Screenwriters here include Sigmund Freud and, among others, Ernest Hemingway, who once said that the first requisite for a writer was to have an unhappy childhood.) The modern scenario calls for a childhood filled with frustration, rebellion, alienation. Childhood, in this script, is the time for being awkward, misunderstood, spiritually wounded. It is a fine time, too, for building up psychological gripes: father didn't show me enough love, mother showed me too much. Not that everyone had to have had an unhappy childhood. It is commonly agreed that childhood may well have been extremely pleasant for, say, bullies, cheerleaders, the indelicate, and the great galloping hordes of the insensitive. But for anyone with the least sensitivity, for those unhappy few (millions), growing up had to be, let's face it, hell.

George Orwell had an unhappy childhood, if his essay "Such, Such Were the Joys . . ." is any evidence, and so most likely did J. D. Salinger, judging by his character Holden Caulfield in *The Catcher in the Rye.* Nearly all modern stories or memoirs of growing up are accounts of sadness, loss, secret terror. This being so, my own relatively happy childhood—note that I have already begun to qualify it—is increasingly coming to seem an embarrassment. A colleague of mine seems much more in the main flow. He had recently been made a member of his high school's distinguished alumni hall of fame, and at the festivities at which he was installed he read a poem he had composed for the occasion. Much of this poem is given over to misgiving recollected in tranquillity. "Most of us hated it, you know. High school," the first line of the second stanza begins. There is also a certain amount of belated pleasure at the ill fortune of those who, when young, seemed to fit in, who are dealt with thus:

It's not the world. And what I have to say
to those who don't fit in is, don't despair.
The best jock of my time now has a bay
window, an ugly wife, almost no hair
and sells used cars and probably is gay.
So is the cutest girl, that cheerleader.
I do not mock their choice of what lust is
But only note there is some kind of justice.

That stanza makes me a bit edgy. Although I was far from
the best jock in my high school class, I did, I fear, fit in,
smoothly and even joyously. Will I, as the logic of this stanza
implies, one day have to pay for this? Today, in my forties, I
still retain quite a lot of my hair, am married to a beautiful
woman, and when last tested checked out heterosexual—and,
mutatis mutandis, prefer to keep things this way.

When the poem was read and its author had stepped down,
he was roundly congratulated by students at his old high
school, many of whom told him that the poem spoke for them.
This is not altogether surprising to me, for the sentiments in
the poem, I believe, express the received opinion on the subject
of growing up in our time. Growing up is nowadays officially
understood to be a bad job.

Perhaps the reason it is thought to be a bad job is that so
many artists and intellectuals seem to have had unhappy childhoods. Here an interesting question crops up. Is it because
their childhoods were unhappy that these men and women
became artists and intellectuals? Did their unhappiness as children force them into the dreamy world of the artist, to hide in
the books of the intellectual? And if there is anything at all to
this, is it possible, further, that their unhappy early years have
given so many artists and intellectuals what one thinks of as
their adversary disposition toward the society in which they

live and toward life in general? Roomy questions, these, with a great deal of space for disagreement about their answers.

Notions about when one is and is not supposed to be reasonably happy can be tyrannous. Once word of them gets around, people seem to do their damnedest to live up to them. We have for some time now been told that old age is not exactly a barrel of laughs; childhood is weighted with many miseries; and adolescence is even worse. In middle age we can look forward to the thing called "the mid-life crisis." One's twenties and thirties are not without their own special perils: loneliness, confusion, conflict. If all of this is so, then it means, if my calculations are correct, that we can figure on roughly thirty-five to forty minutes of enjoyment in a normal life span.

And yet for most of us, at least in this country, life is not so dire an affair. To be sure, in childhood one can fall under the sway of a despotic parent; one can suffer sorely from physical problems such as bad skin or early obesity; one can be placed under the lash of extreme shyness or a sad stutter or one of a hundred other exacting psychological trials. But most of us have been lucky enough to elude these various afflictions, and not everyone who has been visited by them has allowed them to spoil the days of his or her childhood. True, in childhood and adolescence it seems as if one has less control over one's life than at any other time. Constraints on external freedom are never greater: one cannot come and go as one pleases; one cannot readily indulge one's interests or desires; one feels, in fine, less in charge of one's destiny than perhaps one ever will again. And yet, and yet. . . . "Junior year in high school," a friend of mine recently remarked, aping a beer commercial, "it don't get no better than that."

I am not ready to go quite so far, but I must say that whenever I think of my youth it seems to me to have passed very pleasantly. And I think of it a good deal. Among the things I think about in connection with it is that I had one enormous advantage: parents who put no special pressures on me; who asked only that I be a decent fellow; who labored under no theories of child rearing but apparently merely trusted their instincts; and who, finally, had lives of their own to live and felt very little need to insert themselves more than was necessary in mine, yet nonetheless never for a moment allowed me to feel other than certain that, should I need them, they would be there to help. I don't quite know how my parents were able to bring this off, but I am immeasurably grateful that they did. Unable to do likewise when it came to raising my own children, I have to add to my gratitude my admiration.

I may have a closer connection to my childhood than many other people because I continue to live in the city in which I grew up. In fact, I now live only a few miles from the neighborhood in which our family lived during the better part of my childhood and adolescence. Proust had his *madeleine*, but I have my Chevy, in which I find myself often driving through my old neighborhood, filled with a complex combination of yearnings and regrets. Two of my closest boyhood friends are still among my closest friends. At restaurants, movies, cultural and sports events I fairly frequently run into acquaintances from school days. Some, it is true, I would as soon not run into. But most give pleasure, and reassurance that life retains some continuity. I recall, in this connection, a meeting at a pro basketball game with a friend with whom as a young man I used to play cards and whom I hadn't seen for roughly twenty years. "Can you believe it!" he said, as if twenty years had never happened. "The Bucks are four-and-a-half-point dogs!"

H. L. Mencken was a man who lived in the city in which he grew up. The city, of course, was Baltimore, and Mencken lived much the better part of his life in the very house in which he was born at 1524 Hollins Street. Mencken was a rooted man, and rootedness was a quality he admired. In "On Living in Baltimore" he wrote: "Human relations, in such a place, tend to assume a solid permanence. A man's circle of friends becomes a sort of extension of his family circle. His contacts are with men and women who are rooted as he is. They are not moving all the time. Thus abiding relationships tend to be built up, and when fortune brings unexpected changes, they survive those changes." You can't go home again, it has been famously said, but who said you had to leave in the first place?

A few years ago I had impressive evidence of H. L. Mencken's continuing connection with the city of Baltimore, when I gave the H. L. Mencken Memorial Lecture at the Enoch Pratt Free Library in downtown Baltimore. On a sunny Saturday September afternoon some four hundred people showed up to listen to a talk about Mencken—and less to listen to the particular lecturer than to honor the lecturer's subject. The audience was not mostly made up of academics, either, but of an interesting assortment of young and old from a variety of social classes, all of whom seemed to be united by their regard for Henry Louis Mencken, their city's last great writer. A number of people in the audience knew Mencken personally —among them were a member of the old Saturday Night Club and Mencken's old bartender at the Rennert Hotel—or were distant cousins or friends of friends of the writer. Since Mencken had been born (1880) nearly a century before and had then been dead (1956) nearly twenty-five years, I found this testimony to Mencken's rootedness extremely moving.

One of the consequences of living in the city of one's upbringing is that it throws one back upon one's youth more than if one lived elsewhere. Streets, buildings, even empty lots have interesting associations. I have gone to certain of the same restaurants for thirty years, to the same theaters and ball parks for forty years, man and boy. I have never used that phrase "man and boy" before, or quite comprehended its meaning. But as I travel about my old neighborhood, about the streets of my city, I realize that this is what I am, man and boy—and both simultaneously.

I turn a corner and am in front of the house of a grade-school girl friend. Downtown in the city I pass a theater and recall having seen Nat "King" Cole in it when I was fifteen. Driving down a block of a street called Fairfield in the old neighborhood I mentally click off the names of all the kids who lived on it; and I recall, too, the car of the father of a friend of mine, a creamy beige Packard convertible, one of the last models of its kind before Packard went out of business, soon to be followed by my friend's father, who has been dead for more than a quarter of a century now. I begin to sound like some Faulkner character—and of a rather boring kind—whose family has lived on the same land for seven generations. Do I, I sometimes wonder, give way to nostalgia too readily? If nostalgia be a disease, then I, so near my old neighborhood, am practically living in a contagious ward.

My friends and I talk endlessly about the old days. It is our great subject, topic number one. When four or five of us get together, we bathe in it: "Remember the time that Goldy. . . ." "Didn't the Goss have his mother's paneled Chrysler convertible on that trip? . . ." "Dan passed out in the back seat. . . ." "Frankie Summers was the tailback on that team. . . ." Every one of us has heard these stories, some of them countless times, and the purpose in retelling them is less to convey information than to refuel memory. As we sit around a restaurant table, or in one of our apartments, going over these stories yet again, what we really want is to recapture the past, if only fleetingly. Sometimes we will sit for three, four, five hours, one story of the old days leading into another, someone offering a correction of a small detail, someone filling in a bit of additional material, someone else bringing a story up-to-date ("She married some guy from Houston, and still lives there, last I heard").

I love these sessions, which do not come about at regular intervals. Usually they are called together when a friend is in from out of town; so sometimes we do not meet for ten months or for a year. Laughter is always among us when we do meet; on occasion laughter that hurts, it comes in such great gusts. Yet for all our laughter, for all the joy in these meetings, when they are over and I drive home, usually alone, I tend to feel a tinge of sadness. It is sadness of the sort I associate with a phrase Proust's father once used: "the poetry and melancholy of memory."

Why this sadness? Sometimes it occurs to me that these sessions with my old friends resemble nothing so much as cheerful wakes. We sit around and talk about the deceased. We remember what a grand fellow he was. This is no time for petty criticisms, or ungenerous recollections. Not that we lie, exactly. We tell the truth and nothing but the truth, yet not quite the whole truth. Exaggerations have a way of creeping in. An old friend recalls the time he and I, at seventeen, left his parents' apartment in the middle of the night to join an all-night card game in progress, returning home at six in the morning, having won four hundred dollars. I recall the figure at closer to fifty dollars, but then it may be that his memory is merely allowing for inflation, and I would not think to contradict him, except in print. At these wakes we are dedicated to calling up, respectfully, the deceased's best moments. Fortunately, there were a great many of these—enough to stage many a wake. The deceased in this perhaps overly elaborate metaphor is, of course, our youth. How wondrous it is to recall! How sad to know it is gone!

And it is gone, we all know that. Looking around at one another—at our graying hair, receding hairlines, thickening middles, lined faces—how could we possibly know otherwise? All we want is to get our youth in some sort of reasonable focus. The older we grow the blurrier it becomes. Like the only remaining photograph of someone once loved, none of us wants completely to lose sight of our early years, a time we all loved. So we talk about it, often, nearly every chance we get. Doing so makes us happy. For better or worse, looking back is, as they nowadays say, our drug of choice.

If looking back be a drug, I have in recent months had two very generous fixes. Not one but two reunions linking me to my past had been organized. One was for the members of a college fraternity I had joined at a state university at which I had spent a year; the other was a reunion of my grammar school graduating class, a group that dispersed, lo, some thirty-odd years ago. These two reunions were to be held less than a month apart. I signed up to attend both. With my steady backward glance, with my love of lingering in the past, I should have hated to miss either one.

Reunions are by now a standard American institution. Schools at all levels have them: at ten-, twenty-five-, and fifty-year intervals. Military units—companies, regiments, divisions—have them. So do fraternities and sororities. So, too, people trained at a certain time or in a certain line of work. The *New York Times* not long ago reported on a convention that also served as a reunion for people who have worked in intelligence—a reunion, that is, of spies. Among the other functions they perform, reunions are a great balm to the itch of curiosity. Attending them is rather like going through the pages of an album of before-and-after photographs. The reunion provides a chance to discover whatever happened to the girl you adored and the boy you despised; to observe if the good flourished and the wicked went under; to acquire, with a good deal of luck, a clearer sense of what you yourself were like when young.

Of my two reunions, I had more complicated feelings about the one being put on by my old fraternity. It was during that year at the state university I attended that I changed more radically than I ever expect to change again. In that time I had gone from someone who greatly valued his popularity to someone who had replaced geniality with iconoclasm; from someone fairly secure in his notions about life to someone quite uncertain about the purpose of life; from someone confident about the future to someone who knew only that he felt utterly ill at ease about proceeding down the same track he had been traveling. In that year books and a passion for ideas had interposed themselves between me and my comfortable outlook upon the world. One of the things I had come to dislike was being a member of a fraternity; that mine was, moreover, the best fraternity of its kind only made it worse. I longed to be a freer, more independent spirit. Still, when many years later I told an extremely intelligent woman that I was in a fraternity in college, not only was she not surprised but she was able to name the very fraternity to which I belonged. "Of course," she said, "you were a Phi Ep—one of the elite effete." Dismaying.

Because I didn't feel I belonged, and felt it less and less with every passing year, I felt a bit of a fraud attending this reunion. Fraternity members used to call one another "brother," but spiritually I felt I had long since ceased to be part of this particular family. I was going to this reunion less out of warm feeling than out of voyeurism. I felt, as an older friend once wrote to me on a very different occasion, that these people worshiped different gods than I. They also drove different cars, and the way I found the place of the reunion was by following a fellow, driving an elegant blue Mercedes, who looked like yet another of the elite effete—and turned out to be exactly that.

Mercedes there seemed to be in plenty in the parking lot of the expensive health club at which the reunion was held; also no shortage of BMW's, Jaguars, Cadillacs, Lincolns, and an occasional ample Buick or Oldsmobile. It would have been difficult to have found a nonleather seat in the parking lot. For the most part these men, or at least the majority of them, spent the better part of their waking hours thinking about money-getting. The majority of them, I gather, think about it penetratingly and to good effect. I doubt there were many men at this reunion who earn less than $70,000 a year and an ample number earn a great deal more. Physicians and dentists and lawyers, accountants and executives and men who run their own businesses—these are the jobs of the brothers, some two hundred and fifty of whom were at this reunion.

When I walked into the reception room I felt as if I had walked onto a crowded movie set. Much vigorous gab, smoke, clinking of ice cubes, raucous laughter. Although the reunion was on a Saturday night, wives weren't invited. It was all men, and easily the most noticeable man in the room was a contemporary of mine, a man in an air force uniform, a bird colonel with much, in the service phrase, fruit salad upon his chest. Men greeted other men they hadn't seen in twenty or more years, often with startled surprise quickly easing into bonhomous talk of the old days. Some had come from Florida, one from Los Angeles. Everyone seemed quite pleased to check in with one another after long absences. Many others had stayed in close touch over the years.

Physical changes were of course the first thing one noticed. These were not men who took on the usual modern hirsute appurtenances: beards, cavalry mustaches, muttonchops, and the rest. But lots of hair had turned gray (my own included); lots more was missing in action. Some tricky hairdos had emerged, many of these designed to cover up baldness, and I

thought I spotted a few toupees. A good deal of weight had
been redistributed—some men had put on twenty or thirty
pounds, but others seemed to have taken off twenty or thirty
pounds—but total tonnage seemed about the same. A few of
them looked much better as men than they had as boys, time
having rounded off the rough angularity of their faces. In some
the same old boyish face shone out from under what William
James, in describing his colleague Josiah Royce, once called
"an indecent exposure of forehead." When I was a freshman
in this fraternity some of the seniors seemed men of great
physical maturity to me; now we were all contemporaries and
fellow members in a new and much larger fraternity—the
middle-aged.

In an uncomplicated way I had not anticipated, I found
myself pleased to be among them. Not that the few phonies
and creeps did not still seem to me phony and creepy, but they
seemed to matter less, if at all—I waved at them from a distance
or exchanged a few words of heartfelt falsity. One fellow
whom I remember as quite dull now seemed newly aggressive.
Had he had assertiveness training? If so, it had worked wonders, turning a once-dull boy into a man who was still dull but
now pushy. The institution—the fraternity, that is—mattered
even less. What did matter was the fact that we were together
a quarter of a century and more ago, and had survived, and
shared common—and comic—memories, and it all felt rather
good.

Not that everyone had survived intact. One fellow with
whom I pledged had had, a few years out of school, a nervous
breakdown from which he had never quite recovered. Another
fellow's wife had had a stroke. Yet another fellow, in the class
before mine, a great fop as I remembered him, had had business
and marital disasters, and was now driving a cab (in Brooks
Brothers shirts? I wondered). None of these men were in

attendance; reunions are notoriously uncomfortable events for people with failure or troubles to report. But for the most part there was not much to report in the way of obvious failures or troubles. At one point after dinner everyone who had been married was asked to stand, and everyone did; anyone who had been married more than once was asked to remain standing, and out of a room of roughly two hundred fifty, fifteen or sixteen of us kept our feet; two men, it turned out, had married thrice. This was a very stable group. Whatever its quotient of personal disappointment or general unhappiness, very few had come to real grief. A business bankruptcy appeared to mark the outer limits of their conception of a disaster.

To be a mite less than modest I must report that one of the most interesting people I met that evening was myself—or, more precisely, the self I was between eighteen and nineteen years old. I seem nearly to have forgotten him. Throughout the night I was reminded of funny lines I had got off, of madcap things I had done, most of which I had forgotten. For example, a fraternity brother named Roger Lewis had been able to postpone a difficult accounting examination, one that had many others in the fraternity quite terrified, by getting a local doctor to agree to check him into the university hospital for observation. Before going in he made everyone miserable with his boisterous bragging about his cleverness in evading the exam. So, once he had checked into the hospital, it seems that I telephoned, impersonating his doctor, and instructed the nurse on duty that I wanted young Mr. Lewis cleaned out by enema and sent over to my office for X rays. I scarcely recall having done this, but I was immensely pleased to take credit for it.

My guess is that I was the only bookish man in the room, though I was occasionally surprised to hear someone say he had read something I had written in a magazine. A fellow I sat near at dinner wanted to know what kind of novels I wrote.

At first I thought he mistook me for a novelist but then it became clear that he misunderstood the word *novel* to be synonymous with the word *book*. Can there be a more mistaken assumption than that which holds that because a man or woman has been to a university he or she has acquired an interest in reading?

I mentioned bookishness at all only because, for better *and* worse, it can set one apart in a crowd, even a crowd whose members have been college educated. On this particular evening I discovered I did not wish to be set apart but rather to join in the communal good feeling in the room. In my thinking about this evening I had overlooked a very obvious point: insofar as this old fraternity could be said to have stood for anything, I disliked what it stood for; but I did like a great many of the boys (now men) who had been a part of it. This, doubtless, was the work of "Time, which," as Proust says, "causes us to forget our antipathies and our disdains and even the reasons which once explained their existence." When the hour came to leave, I found myself lingering, not wanting yet to depart. In the lobby someone said that another such reunion was to be held in ten years, though, he said, he doubted it would be as successful as this one. In the parking lot some of us spoke of getting together, meeting in a restaurant, say, for an evening of talk, five, perhaps six months from now. It would be very nice, everyone agreed. I agreed, too, although I am confident it will never happen.

Our grammar-school reunion, which took place three weeks later, was a much smaller affair. It met in a banquet room at a not very exclusive country club in a suburb northwest of the city. Of a class of thirty-nine kids, twenty middle-aged adults showed up. Some members of the class could not be located, a few others couldn't care less, one woman lived in Australia, and another had years before committed suicide.

Unlike the fraternity reunion, where I was in regular touch with no one, at this one two of my closest friends were in attendance. We had in fact been talking about it for weeks before, and we drove out to it together, the three of us in one car, speculating on what time might have done to these people whom we last knew as children.

Husbands and wives were invited, but at least half of us arrived de-spoused. Thirty or so people were in the room. I felt less of an air of prosperity here than at the fraternity reunion. One or two classmates who had been born into the working class had, it appeared, remained there. One man had become a high school science teacher, another was a social worker—jobs that none of the fraternity brothers would ever, even for a moment, have considered. In the foyer I ran into the first of my old classmates. His skin was unwrinkled, his smile was unchanged, his hair was intact and combed in exactly the same way he had combed it thirty-odd years ago. He was in every way the same, except he had grown much wider, as if someone had inflated him, or fooled with his horizontal knob. I felt, in fact, as if I were looking at him in a fun-house mirror. This entire evening, as it turned out, had something of a fun-house quality—which is to say, it was noisy, everything in it appeared slightly distorted, it wasn't very much fun.

I don't know quite what I expected, but one of the things I was most struck with was how little, in thirty-odd years, everyone seemed to have changed. The boy of thirteen who could never quite look anyone in the eye was now a man heading toward fifty who still could not quite look anyone in the eye. The tall shy girl to whom I never seemed able to find anything to say was now a tall shy woman to whom I was still unable to find anything to say. The boy whose shirt was always sticking out of his pants now was a man whose shirt was sticking out of his vest. The girl I remember as always a bit overactive was now a woman, with more eye shadow than a raccoon, who could not stop talking.

Speaking with a girl who over the years had turned into a gracious, handsome woman, I asked about her brother, who was a few years older than we were. "It's sweet of you to ask," she said. "Fred's had a stroke." I later learned that someone else in the room had had quadruple bypass heart surgery. (Don't they ever do a simple single bypass?) The boy with whom I first snuck off to smoke cigarettes was a widower. Strokes, heart surgery, dead wives—Oh God, I thought, has it come to be that time already?

We stood around with drinks in our hands, cocktail-party style, mingling and chatting. A buffet with Mexican food had been set up—a taco bar, it was called. Then we were asked to take seats at tables scattered around the room for such program as there was to be. This had mostly to do with reporting the results of a questionnaire that had been sent out to each of us months before. These results were read by one of the three chief organizers of the reunion, a man who as a boy had been one of our class leaders. He looked much the same, though he made much ado about his personal gains (a potbelly) and losses (some hair). Statistically, we turned out to be a fairly average, fairly boring group: great longevity of marriages, two-point-something-average children. One of us—a woman who now lived in Florida and didn't attend—was said to have married four times. Another of us was about to become a grandmother. There was much laughter about who was voted sexiest, most likely to succeed, best adjusted, and so forth. Then a serious moment: two of our classmates were mentioned for contributions to society. One was a doctor who specialized in contagious diseases, the other was an accountant who had worked for Jewish charities. After noting this our master of ceremonies said, in a throwback phrase that nearly broke my heart, "Nice going, guys."

Why—I ask for the second time in this essay—this sadness? Perhaps because this reunion was yet another piece of evidence for the death of youth, and the death of youth, as Montaigne says, is "in essence and in truth a harder death than the complete death of a languishing life or the death of old age." Especially is this so when that youth has been a happy one, for happiness not only cannot be recaptured, it can scarcely be described, let alone analyzed. Unhappiness, on the other hand, analyzes beautifully. Perhaps this is why so many intellectuals are drawn to it. Sadness, too, implies a criticism of the world. Happiness is an expression of joy in it. And for those of us born lucky—without physical or mental infirmity and to parents who loved us—happiness was never so uncomplicatedly, so lyrically expressed as in youth. Many people write or become psychoanalyzed in order to bury the ghosts of their childhood. I wish, as best I can, to revive the ghosts of mine: to set free that pudgy child in a uniform of the Royal Canadian Mounted Police, that young boy shooting baskets in the rain, that adolescent reading Willard Motley's *Knock on Any Door* while lying on his side on a sunny day in a public park, that youth returning home at three in the morning after a night of talk and laughter with his friends. It is very important to me that I not let those fellows die.

Has the Future a Future?

THE FUTURE worries me a little, and when it's not worrying me a little, it bores me quite a lot. After all, I (we) know how I (we) shall end. Still, curiosity about what will occur between now and then does from time to time raise its impish head. I read the tags that come with my fortune cookies as raptly as the next fellow. "Your enterprise," a recent one of mine read, "will bring great profit." This is comforting, but all the same I should prefer to see some dates and figures. Cookie prophecy notwithstanding, I foresee no great reversal of fortune in my case, unless it be dramatically downward and outward. Can this relative lack of interest in the future reflect the fact that, yes, I rather like my life as it is now, and, no, I cannot see the future doing anything but altering that life for the worse?

Do we think most about the future when we are unhappy with the present? I am inclined to think we do. While being beaten by life, most of us—except those who happen to be true masochists—tend to think between lashes how sweet things will be once the beating stops. The future, for those who dream longingly of it, is always that time when the beating will have stopped. Perhaps I have not taken enough blows from life, for dwelling on the future has never been my idea of a very good time. Not, I hasten to add, that I live completely in the present. As I grow older, I seem to spend more and more time in the past, running home movies in my mind of old friends, fine times, and, as I now like to imagine them, uncomplicated and sunny days. Only rarely does my mind lurch into the future where I can be found as the subject of charming slides. *Click:* there I am on the White House lawn receiving a medal for distinguished service to literature. *Click:* and there, that elegantly turned out white-haired gentleman, strolling along a white-sand beach, that's me. *Click:* there I am again, in the toy department, buying a doll for the extremely well-mannered child (my beautiful granddaughter, of course) who is holding my hand.

Yet these little slide-show glimpses into the shiny future do not long detain me. Reality obtrudes. The possible reverses of these daydreams—daymares, might they be called?—pop up all too readily. Instead of receiving a medal, I receive a letter from a publisher rejecting a manuscript and making clear, despite perfunctory attempts at politeness, that I am professionally a back number whose scribblings are no longer wanted. Instead of maundering down a foreign beach, I see myself, in rumpled pajamas and robe, tottering down a hospital corridor doing what I think of as the prostate shuffle. And instead of that bright well-behaved granddaughter holding my hand, I see the knuckles of my hand white with suppressed rage at a grandchild brought up in a spirit of complete permissiveness crying for designer jeans. Here, I feel, I have seen the future, and it's terrible.

Joubert said that "the charm we are most sensible to is the charm of the future, and not the charm of the past." But Joubert wrote at the end of the eighteenth century and into the early nineteenth century; since then optimism, for most of us, has shifted from the future to the past. The past seems rosy, the future gray. The present, to keep this in Technicolor, seems for many people to be black. I do not know how many share this general outlook, but I was recently interested to read, in an essay by Edward Shils entitled "The Intellectuals and the Future," that these views have something of a tradition. In this tradition the present, as Professor Shils puts it, "is not the best of times but the worst of times," and the future is "even more the worst of times, a season of darkness, a winter of despair." So there you have them, the present and the future, the worst of times and the even more worst of times.

It has not always been thus, and indeed a loss of belief in the future implies no less than a loss of belief in progress. Even socialists, Marxists, and revolutionaries seem to have lost their belief in the future; the old shibboleths come rolling off their lips, but it is as if they cannot keep the scales from dropping from their eyes. Most Saturday mornings, outside my neighborhood bank, young Trotskyists hawk their sect's newspaper to passersby. I don't like to pass the lads without a word of encouragement. The last time I banked of a Saturday morning, I said to one of them, "The revolution is coming, my boy, it's coming." "Whaddaya," he replied, "a wise guy?"

"While the twentieth century is far from barren of faith in progress," Robert Nisbet writes in his *History of the Idea of Progress*, "there is nevertheless good reason for supposing that when the identity of our century is eventually fixed by historians, not faith but abandonment of faith in the idea of progress will be one of the major attributes." This sounds to me persuasive. Certainly it jibes with everything currently in the intellectual atmosphere. Among novelists, statesmen, social scientists, and columnists the consensus seems to be that we are headed for that sad, bad destination, "the dogs." As Valéry once put it, "The future isn't what it used to be." Or, to reverse a charmingly klutzy tautology made famous by the sportscaster

Curt Gowdy, who used to say of young athletes that "their whole future is ahead of them"—where else, after all, could it be?—our future, alas, appears to be behind us.

Or is it appearance merely?

One has, I think, to allow not only for the distorting perspective of the age but also for the equally distorting perspective of one's own age. Henry James somewhere speaks of "the futurity of youth," by which he meant that it is in the nature of the young to be future-minded: to have a head full of plans and a heart full of hope. It is partly because of their sense of futurity that it is splendid to be around the young; it is partly because of their sense of futurity, too, that one can't stand to be around them for too long. One listens to the young prattle on about their tomorrows, and it is difficult to repress a knowing smile or to expunge the condescension from one's voice. The knowing smile, the condescension are there because the young only rarely know what life likes to do to plans. Another of the things they do not know, though all but the permanently immature among them will discover it, is that paradise does not lie in the future but in the past, "since the true paradises are the paradises we have lost." The usual prize of ten guineas for the name of the writer who said that.

Proust said it, and about such matters the little porcelain psychologist, as one of the ladies from the Faubourg Saint-Germain called him, was seldom wrong. About paradises lost, Marcel Proust knew more even than John Milton, and one of the things Proust knew was the propensity in all of us to suffuse our past with soft colors and sweet harmonies. When I was in the army—I spent two full years of peacetime in the scenic states of Missouri, Texas, and Arkansas—I lay abed at night vowing that one thing I would never do was look back on this experience, as many people told me I one day would, as interesting, valuable, and extremely funny. Twenty-odd years later I now look back on the experience of having been in the army as interesting, valuable, and extremely funny. Another broken vow.

Now I do not wish to claim—nor have I ever been accused of possessing—superior perspective, but as I grow older the past seems better and better. Why? Is it, in my case, part of the regular disillusionment of middle age with the future? How naturally a conservatism of temperament seems to set in! Ought it to be fought against, when even the most radical-minded seem to feel it? In *Misia,* Arthur Gold and Robert Fizdale, the biographers of Misia Sert, note about Misia and Sergei Diaghilev that in their fifties these two connoisseurs and devotees of the new in art underwent a flagging of energy, a nagging suspicion "that life had been more beautiful, that art had been greater." The problem, though, was not altogether one of age; the artists of Misia Sert and Diaghilev's earlier years —among them Mallarmé, Stravinsky, Proust, Renoir, and Toulouse-Lautrec—*were* better than those who followed. Is it not possible that one's own earlier years were, similarly, better? Or is it instead only that they seem better because one was then young?

"No wise man," said Swift, "ever wished to be younger." That may be true, but even if it is, it doesn't mean that many of us do not wish to have the conditions, if not the actual fact, of our youth restored. I want to smell burning leaves in autumn again; I want shrimps and clams and oysters to be inexpensive again; I want again to be able to return home late at night without thinking about the danger of being mugged. "Ah," someone playing the progressivist's advocate might chime in here, "I suppose you also want pollution again; cheap labor again; heedlessness for civil liberties and general intolerance to prevail again."

Nope, *M. Avocat,* I would reply, I wish none of these

things. You see the years of my youth, the 1950s, as an age of stifling conformity; I see them as a time when intellectual considerations were still taken seriously. You see them as a time when the experimental spirit was held in check; I see them as the last time in the United States when the ideal was not to remain in a perpetual state of youthfulness but to become an adult. You, friend, see progress as worth the price; I often don't even see it as progress. Our differences are fundamental, possibly irreconcilable, and since this is my essay, not yours, I have a good mind to tell you to scram, which I shall do presently, but I need you for a moment longer to accuse me of nostalgia.

Well, I am not sure whether I am a practitioner or a victim of nostalgia. Nor am I altogether certain that this hunger for the past I sometimes feel is exactly nostalgia. Nostalgia has been called the rust of memory, and Robert Nisbet has said that its effect "is to divest us of the sense of history and to make of the past a cornucopia of idle anodynes and feeble pleasures." I prefer to think of myself less as nostalgic than as yearning for tradition, and it is tradition that I see as the victim of our own day's unslakable thirst for the young and the new. "The very function of tradition," Nisbet writes, "is to bind past, present and future into one, to stimulate hope in and desire to work toward the future through commemoration of the past and its extension into the present." This seems to me wise; it also seems to me to go a long way toward explaining why the future can so often appear dreary, the present dim.

As Gertrude Stein once said of the city of Oakland that there was "no there there," so of our own day it too often seems as if there is no now now. In saying this I realize I am far from speaking for everyone. People there are, and great is their number, who find a great deal of now now and who, looking to the future, expect to find plenty of then then. Yet another of the divisions of humankind is that between people

who greet the future with open arms and people who refuse
even to answer the bell for it. Of the latter camp was Charles
Lamb, of whom his friend William Hazlitt wrote: "Mr. Lamb
has a distaste to new faces, to new books, to new buildings, to
new customs. . . . He evades the present, he mocks the future.
His affections revert to, and settle on the past, but then, even
this must have something personal and local in it to interest
him deeply and thoroughly." Compare with this Mr. Lincoln
Steffens, who saw the future and thought (incorrectly, as we
now know) that it worked.

If infatuation with change be the key, I am more like
Charles Lamb than not. I tend, decidedly, to resist change;
worse, I am afraid, I greet news of innovations malfunctioning
with barely suppressed glee. When I learn that the computers
are "down," or that someone's Betamax has gone on the fritz,
a little mariachi band begins to play in my heart. I have not yet
advanced to the position on change of a dear friend, who of
himself says, "I never eat in a restaurant I haven't eaten in
before, I never read a book I haven't read before, and I try
never to write or say anything I haven't already written or said
before." Still, wherever possible, I try to go against the flow.
I live in an older building, write with a fountain pen, sleep in
pajamas. If there were more people like me, I recognize, we
might still be on horseback. Or, I hear some future-minded
heckler cry out, without indoor plumbing.

Don't get me wrong: opposed though I may be to change,
I adore convenience. I also accept the possibility of progress,
though I think one does well to be selective about it. (I should
not, for example, go so far as a mortician in my city who has
named his establishment the Progressive Funeral Home.)
Progress, in my view, has not been as undiluted as many of its
adherents like to think. It has been indisputable in medicine but
highly disputable in education; clear in technology but murky

in ethics. Yet even here agreement is likely to be far from universal. Beyond anesthesiology, some might contend, less medicine is better medicine; and others might argue quite the reverse of education, maintaining that, though the quality of education may have slipped, having so many more people going to school longer constitutes real progress. Complex stuff, all this, and not made simpler by the knowledge that scarcely any progress nowadays comes unaccompanied by unexpected drawbacks: one step forward, three steps back. Perhaps the only uncontested progress in my lifetime has been in the manufacture of tennis shoes.

When it comes to thinking about the future, the Reverend Sydney Smith's advice for avoiding depression may make good sense: "Short views of human life—not further than dinner or tea." Sydney Smith also advised slightly cold showers and good blazing fires. I would add the advice never to read the futurologists, those men and women whose job it is to predict the future on the basis of the present. You can usually count on them for bad news; you can also usually count on them to be wrong. Thus one such report, "The Global 2000 Report," issued in July 1980, spoke bleakly of our using up the earth's resources, leveling forests, eroding soil, overcrowding cities, wasting fuels. Chock-full of intimation of bad new days ahead, the report had us going downhill, down the drain, down the tubes. Then, not even two years later, a number of critics have come forth to dispute separate portions of "The Global 2000 Report." Economic output and food production are now expected to exceed population growth; gloomy energy prognostications have been discovered to be off by 30 percent; deforestation turns out to be proceeding at half the rate claimed in the report. Now, dependably, the pendulum has swung the other way, and a man named Julian Simon, professor of business and economics at the University of Illinois, insists that things have never looked better. Everything, in his view, is looking up, up, indefinitely up. Who knows the truth? The futurologists remind me of Sydney Smith's cold showers and good blazing fires; it might be the best idea first to soak all futurological reports in the former and then to burn them in the latter.

Am I alone, I wonder, in never having lost a moment's sleep over the rate of deforestation or the world's population growth? In the end, I must say, it is not food production or energy consumption that much affects my view of the future. Maybe it ought to—but it doesn't. True, hearing one piece of global bad news after another does not exactly bring forth a glow in one's complexion. Still, I have yet to toss and turn over soil erosion, or to wake screaming that something must be done about replenishing marine life. Maybe I ought to—but I haven't.

It is not, I suspect, the approaching ice age or the draining of the seas that depresses most of us; it is the little things. I do not wish to air my dirty linen in public, but may I talk a bit about my shirt problem? They seem, my shirts, in a fairly short time to have gone in price from roughly five dollars to roughly thirty dollars each. But that is not what has me down. What troubles me more is getting them properly laundered. To do so has become costly—one dollar a shirt—and even at that price they are not very carefully done. Shirts come back with buttons missing, a sleeve unironed, a deep crease running across the front. Meanwhile strong detergents—do the laundries use a dollop of nitroglycerin, I wonder?—help to shorten the life of shirts. The last time I had my shirts done well was when a Chinese man and woman, working out of the back of their shop, did them. Since this couple's retirement, the larger the laundry I have sent my shirts to, the worse they have come back. This is not a catastrophe; I am not planning to put in for a disaster loan to get my shirts laundered. It's only a bit depressing, and what is most depressing about it is the fact, all too clear, that nobody either knows or cares enough to launder a shirt. It doesn't seem likely to get better. Can I look forward to a future in which I shall wear plastic shirts, or, simpler still, paper shirts that, like the new diapers, are disposable?

What is depressing about this, too, is the signals it gives off. One of these is that there is less competence in the world. The world has always been filled with less than gratifying jobs, and laundering shirts is doubtless among them. But somehow these jobs got done. They get done no longer, or at any rate no longer with the competence required for daily living. Competence itself seems almost to have disappeared. So pervasive has incompetence become that one begins to believe in a conspiracy theory: the bunglers are out to get us. High and low, bungling exists everywhere—the button missing from the cuff, the helicopter breaking down in the desert, the book bristling with typographical errors—so that any show of competence, any concern for efficiency, leaves one stupified. The other day, for example, General Electric's service department promised to send a repairman out to fix an appliance, saying that he would arrive sometime before noon. When he arrived at eleven o'clock on the appointed morning, I felt he must have been an impostor.

On a recent visit to the Barclay Hotel in New York—single room: $110—I was met by a very decent young man at the reception desk, who, with the aid of a small computer terminal, sent me to a dark room next to an elevator and overlooking an air shaft. I returned to the reception desk, suitcase in hand, to ask: "Sir, when you punched the keys of that machine, did the board light up with the message, 'Give this guy a terrible room?'" "I don't understand, sir," he said, genuinely perplexed. I explained; he apologized; he tapped the keys of his machine again, and I was sent off to my new room. It had good light but two broken beds, upon one of which sat a broken dresser. Was I expecting too much for a mere $110 a night? Did rooms with beds in good repair begin at $150? I called down to the desk to ask if this were in fact the case. More apologies, and a promise that a bellman would be up in five minutes to take me to yet another room. And, lo, only forty minutes later, just before the large vein in my neck was about to burst, there he was. If the Barclay needs me, I am available for testimonials.

I don't think this story is so shocking. What is shocking, though, is that it isn't shocking. My guess is that nearly everyone has a story like it—a tale of being overcharged and underserved. I stress overcharged because I don't think money is at the heart of the competence problem. Every time the post office raises its rates, the quality of its service slips a notch further. Patience for details has departed; tolerance for the tough job has diminished. Surgeons sew up patients and neglect to remove an instrument. A university press misspells the author's name on his book's title page. If such foul-ups go on at fairly high levels, why shouldn't they be quite as frequent lower down—indeed, rather more frequent. I don't have a handy explanation for why there seems to be less competence at every level of life. People, plainly, have ceased to give a damn —or at least enough people have done so to encourage a feeling of hopelessness in the general population.

Having produced this litany of complaints, I am aware that —in my thirty-odd-dollar shirts and from my one-hundred-odd-dollars-a-night hotel rooms—I am not a strong candidate for pity. Trotting out these complaints (ravings?), I feel rather like a middle-aged fogey, or, if you prefer, a young curmudgeon. Bemoaning the loss of better days, after all, is almost standard practice. Doing so myself I feel like the lumpish man

in the Jack Ziegler cartoon who is standing before the railroad
schedule board that reads:

ARRIVALS		DEPARTURES	
Pestilence	4:02	Good Taste	3:32
Famine	4:15	Sleigh Rides	3:49
Martial Law	4:21	All-Beef Burgers	4:25
Triple Locks	5:00	Happiness	5:11
Unemployment	5:20	Security	5:15
Inflation	5:32	Friendly Loan Companies	5:58
Shorter Summers	5:43	Warm Blankets	6:10
Longer Zip Codes	5:46	Hardwood Floors	6:15
Plastic Silverware	6:01	Homemade Ice Cream	6:31

In the Ziegler cartoon both lists, arrivals and departures,
trail off, the further items becoming indecipherable. But each
of us could add his own, *ad* nearly *infinitum.*

Triple Locks is on Ziegler's arrivals list and Security is
found under departures, and rightly so. Crime—its increase
and, by now, pervasiveness—has done as much as anything
over the past thirty years to foul the future. I grew up neither
in the country nor in the suburbs, and ours was never one of
those families that went to bed with its front and back doors
unlocked, though I knew people who did not bother to lock
their doors. Anyone who does so today ought rightly to be
suspected of either an insurance scam or a suicide attempt. Fear
of crime can, I suppose, be overdone; yet, under current conditions, paranoia seems to me the better part of valor. News that
X has been mugged or Y's daughter has been raped is greeted
nowadays with sadness but with no real shock. We wince, and
put Mozart on the stereo. Murder can still get a rise out of the
moral imagination, but of almost anything less we tend to say,
"Well, that's the way we live now—that's the way it is." What
we perhaps do not say is that it is probably the way we shall

live for the foreseeable future. It is nearly unbearable to think
about, and thus few of us bear to think about it. But it hovers
in the dark, a mugger in the alley of our mind.

If the mugger in our mind represents the fear of violence
and early death, modern life has added yet another fear to the
arsenal of human horrors—that of living too long. I bring this
up with some trepidation, for I myself, despite all my grum-
bling, rather like it here and am counting on semi-retirement
at age ninety-six. Still, if a paradigm case of progress as a mixed
blessing were wanted, none could be more stellar than the
increase in the human life span. Most of us are grateful at the
prospect of more years to live yet fearful of the prospect of
spending them ill or alone or gaga. Modern life has supplied
much of what, in the movies of the 1930s, used to be called
"additional dialogue." One bit of such dialogue is a conversation in which husbands and wives must discuss whether, in a
comatose state, they wish to live lashed to life-supporting ma-
chines. Do we, in the hideous current phrase, want them "to
pull the plug"? Short of that, though, most of us are cheered
at hearing reports of a man in his nineties "playing with a full
deck," or a woman in her late eighties who has "retained all
her marbles." Decks of cards? Marbles? The metaphors of old
age do make it seem rather like game time. Perhaps each of us
ought to assemble his own toy box now. I shouldn't mind it
being said of me, "Ah, that Epstein, one hundred and two, and
he's still got every Tinkertoy he started out with." Except by
then there may be no one alive who ever heard of Tinkertoys.

Am I suffering future shock? Not having read the popular
sociology book of that title, I am perhaps in no position to
know. When I do think about the future, though, it does not
so much shock as dismay me. I feel disappointed in it; I feel a
sense of perturbation about it. I had hoped it would be better
than it looks as if it is going to be. It isn't really what I had in
mind. Much that I read of late—the novels of Saul Bellow and

of Robert Stone, the memoirs of William Barrett, the travel writing of V. S. Naipaul—speaks to a great yet inchoate spiritual longing. I know what they are talking about. I understand this yearning. I cannot, however, accept spirituality in so inchoate a form; nor do I expect to have it made clearer to me. Perhaps I am a spiritually shallow person. I have only to enter a house of worship to experience a fierce longing—for a cigarette.

What is to be done? Keep, as the bumper stickers advise, on truckin'? Leonard Woolf, in the fifth volume of his autobiography, at age eighty-eight, looked back over fifty-seven years of political work he had done and concluded that "I must have in a long life ground through between one hundred and fifty thousand and two hundred thousand hours of perfectly useless work." But, Woolf writes:

As I have said before, all through my life I have always believed and, I think, acted on the belief that there are two levels or grades of importance. *Sub specie aeternitatis,* in the eye of God or rather of the universe, nothing human is of the slightest importance; but in one's own personal life, in terms of humanity and human history and human society, certain things are of immense importance: human relations, happiness, truth, beauty or art, justice and mercy. That is why in his private and personal life a wise man would never take arms against a sea of troubles; he would suffer the slings and arrows of outrageous fortune, saying to himself: "These things are momentarily of terrible importance and yet tomorrow and externally of no importance." And in a wider context, though all that I tried to do politically was completely futile and ineffective and unimportant, for me personally it was right and important that I should do it, even though at the back of my mind I was well aware that it was ineffective and unimportant. To say this is to say that I agree with what Montaigne, the first civilized modern man, says somewhere: "It is not the arrival, it is the journey which matters."

If Montaigne and Leonard Woolf, two good men of very good sense, are correct in believing that it is the journey not the arrival that matters, it may well be that it behooves the rest of us not to ask too often or too insistently, "Is this trip necessary?" No refund is offered on the ticket in any case. Besides, along the way one is accompanied by family and friends, the pleasures of art and intellect, many minor delights, and sufficient ignorance—one's own and the world's—to keep one busy for the entire trip.

Obviously, one cannot live without planning for the future. But beyond planning of a fundamental kind—insurance, savings, a cemetery plot—the future, it may well be, does not repay too much thinking about. Thinking too much about the future resembles thinking too much about breathing—the result is to make one feel very uncomfortable. Best to glory in what was finest in the past, to concentrate on the present, and to allow the future to fend for itself. On the subject of the future, we would all do well to emulate the magazine *Next,* a journal billing itself as *The Magazine of the Future;* that worthy journal, it turns out, has recently suspended publication.